SEX, DRUGS, & PILOT SEASON:
CONFESSIONS OF A CASTING DIRECTOR

SEX, DRUGS, & PILOT SEASON:
CONFESSIONS OF A CASTING DIRECTOR

BY JOEL THURM

BearManor Media

2023

TABLE OF CONTENTS

PROLOGUE

DAVID HASSELHOFF: BLAME ME

Go ahead, blame me. I take full responsibility for the eye and ear damage you may have suffered while watching David Hasselhoff in all his junk TV glory. It was I who paved the way for David's best years as the dimpled curly-haired hunky star of *The Young and the Restless*, *Knight Rider,* and *Baywatch*. I had nothing to do with getting his judging post on *America's Got Talent* a few years ago, however. I feel for the guy because his is a classic case of build-'em-up-then-tear-'em-down. David was, and for all I know still is, a very sweet man; though only modestly talented, he was blessed with looks, luck, and me. All joking aside, I was blessed with him, too, and with so many other fledgling actors I helped push up the ladder. It was one of the joys of my profession, and even if the shows themselves weren't always classy, it felt good to help create entertainment that brought fun to millions of people worldwide.

In the early 1970s I was a member of the CBS Casting Department, which was headed by an extraordinary woman, Ethel Winant. Ethel was network TV's first female vice president in a creative, non-business area. There were six of us, and we did the casting for some great, or at least very popular, TV series, movies, miniseries, pilots, and soaps. Sometimes they were both popular *and* great. In 1973 Ethel and her department had just cast a new daytime soap opera, *The Young and the Restless,* which was almost immediately successful and has been on the air for about forty years. (Note: I had nothing to do with the soap's original casting or daytime TV.)

About a year into the show, I joined her department. One day as I sat in my tiny, very non-private glass cubicle at CBS Television City, I received a phone call from personal manager Joyce Selznick, a legend in her own mind and a force of nature. Joyce had come to Hollywood with a famous last name: that of David O. Selznick, the MGM executive who produced *Gone with the Wind*. Joyce traded on the Selznick name, though in reality she was either a very, very, very distant relative or as many believed, not a relative at all. At the same time, Joyce was one of the few "out" people working in TV. She was a big butch dyke, though one frequently clothed in Chanel. Joyce was tall and built like a refrigerator; she often sported a DA haircut that would have put any cast member of *Grease* to shame. To her credit, she didn't change herself to fit the image of what she should be to society or the business. More importantly, Joyce was very good at her job. She was a great salesman, ahem, salesperson. I can sound authoritative even if I'm spouting bullshit, but Joyce was better at it that than I ever was. Whether she was right or wrong, you had to be impressed by her delivery.

That day back in 1975, Joyce called and in her baritone voice asked me to meet a new client. "He's a straight (as if that would have made any difference) six-foot-two, gorgeous hunk. Kid, I'm tellin' ya, there's no one like him around now – an old-fashioned movie star. You'll love him." I said sure – hey, that was my job to meet new actors for all kinds of shows. Later that afternoon, David came in. Joyce was right. He was, I suppose, gorgeous – although a bit too pretty for my personal taste – tall, dimpled, and very polite. If he could walk, talk, and chew gum at the same time he could be very successful. Coincidentally, we were replacing a young leading man on *The Young and the Restless*.

Never having watched an entire episode of this soap, I knew little about the character, "Snapper Foster," a medical student from a working-class family. But then I did something I'd seen in an old movie. Right in front of David, I picked up the phone and called my friend John Conboy, the show's executive producer. "John," I said, "I have your next Snapper sitting in front of me right now. Wanna meet him?" He said, "If you think he's right, sure!" Still not having a clue if he was "right," I sent him to meet Conboy figuring, hey, a soap is a soap is a soap – how wrong could I be? Making that phone call in front of David was major showboating on my part. Honestly, it was my first taste of having a bit of power and letting someone else know it, and I liked the feeling. To this day young leading men on soap operas are very similar to each other but a lot more ethnically and racially diverse. I had no idea if David could act but he definitely had the rest. Of course, he got the role. Quickly he became one of daytime TV's most popular leading men. Score one for me.

Years later, in 1981, with a few more credits under my belt, such as casting the pilots of *Taxi, The Love Boat, Fantasy Island,* and the movies *Grease, The Rocky Horror Picture Show,* and *Airplane!,* I found myself replacing Ethel Winant, who'd also moved on, as vice president of Talent and Casting at NBC. I arrived at NBC when the network's ratings were at their lowest. The one bright spot was that my new boss, Brandon Tartikoff, was not only the most capable person ever to have that job in television, but also a wonderful human being. He had the ability to make you want to be on his side. For me, a non-athletic boy from Brooklyn who was always chosen last for any sport, it was a wonderful feeling to be wanted on the team of a handsome, talented, charismatic, jock-type guy. In a very unusual corporate situation,

I reported directly to him with no bureaucratic layers between us. He was there for me and I was there to watch his back.

In 1982 I was handed the script for a new pilot called *Knight Rider*, written by Glen A. Larson, one of Universal Television's most successful writer-producers, now called "show runners." Glen was a tall, imposing man with terrible taste in clothing, tending toward bad polyester. It wasn't that he couldn't afford better, for his writing credits included *Magnum P.I., The Fall Guy*, and *Battlestar Galactica*. Glen was known for his macho, guy-oriented writing. *Knight Rider* had a great concept: Handsome leading man solves crimes, international intrigues, and other crises with the help of a big, black talking car named KITT – one that did everything but give him a blow job on his way to saving the day and the damsel. Because of the show's "high concept," a star was not needed. The folks at Universal had chosen Nick Mancuso, an unknown but talented

New York actor in the Al Pacino mold. Nick had had a recent big success Off-Broadway and was considered a great "get" for a pilot because he had turned down many TV opportunities in hopes of breaking into movies. Even today, the more you say "no," the more you are wanted.

At that time you either worked in movies or television; the twain did not meet like they do today. Since his film career was not happening (and to satisfy his early-acquired habit of eating, I suppose) he needed a job – badly. Glen and the Universal executives showed us a few screen tests, and they were positively beaming when they got to Nick's. We at NBC, and most of all my boss, Brandon Tartikoff, were underwhelmed. All of Universal's good actors were indeed good, but somehow what they did wasn't working – most likely because they *were* good actors and treated the words like they did Ibsen or Mamet. But there was no way to *act* the lines of *Knight Rider*. You just had to say the words and not think. After the Universal folks left, Brandon asked me what I thought of David Hasselhoff for the role. He said that he had met him on a plane coming back to L.A. from New York and liked him, finding him open and charming, which he is. He also noticed how heads turned when Hasselhoff walked through the airport. I said that I honestly did not know but let me think.

By now David had left *The Young and the Restless* and was looking for a job in prime time. Brandon had a great sense of what the TV audience loved, and he knew how popular David was with the audience that we flew over between the coasts. Translated: Midwestern women loved him, and he didn't threaten their beer-bellied husbands. Pretty as he was, they imagined themselves to be him at the car's steering wheel. It also didn't hurt that David also had a big following as a pop singer in Germany, where *The Young and the Restless* was a big hit. No elitist snob, Brandon loved television, both quality and cheese. He knew that *Knight Rider* could only work if the cheese factor was celebrated, not ignored. Brandon was not perfect, however. One of his flaws was that he avoided conflicts with studio execs and creative people at all costs. Rather than take on the Universal Army and tell them that their choice for the role was dead in the water, he made that responsibility mine. After all, that's one of the things I got paid to do. After impugning David's abilities and denouncing him as a horrible soap actor, the Universal contingent agreed to meet him. This led to a screen test and, for all I know, a proctologic exam as well, and they still did not want him. Next step was a meeting in my office with Glen, Brandon, various NBC execs, and the Universal brass. I became David's biggest advocate. I was positively

Obama-esque in my oratorical extolling of him. They remained unimpressed.

Finally I got inspired *and* foul-mouthed, which is still my default mode. I announced, "What the fuck do you think will happen if this show becomes a hit when Nick Mancuso realizes he is not the fucking star of his own fucking show and that the fucking car and Bill Daniels' voice [Bill had the voice role of the talking car] are the real stars? He's going to think about his artistic sellout and be miserable, and him being miserable will make *you* miserable, and he will want to go home early or come in late and change the lines to 'better,' more socially conscious ones, and since he really does not want to be there, when he renegotiates his deal, you'll be in deep shit because he will already have made enough money to let him go back to being happy Off-Broadway, and you'll have to sell off the fucking back lot to keep him. You hire David, and he will be happy as a pig in shit to be a prime-time star, and he will be there to promote the show when it plays in fucking Albania and not complain for as long as the fucking show is on the air." Or I said most of that. In any event, it worked; he got the part. This was one of my finer *Norma Rae* moments. Score two for me.

Now for the trifecta. It was 1986 and *Knight Rider,* which had premiered four years earlier, was fading fast. Ratings had dropped steadily as the costly show became a bit shopworn. Universal had more than enough episodes for syndication (which is when a show goes off a network's schedule and begins to appear at different times and on different stations all over the country or the world), and thanks to KITT, the talking car, Brandon's populist taste, my foul mouth, and Mr. Hasselhoff's chin dimple, David was now a bona fide TV star with a burgeoning international fan base. Unfortunately, he had no film career, and no one was rushing at him with new series offers, either. His German singing career was going fine, however. Other things had changed as well. David's manager, Joyce Selznick, had died. Her former assistant, Jan McCormick, had taken over the management company and seemed to have held on to most of the clients, including David. If Joyce at six feet and 200 pounds was the linebacker of the team, Jan, at five-three and weighing barely a hundred pounds dripping wet, was the very sweet water boy. Jan was not only Joyce's work partner, but her life partner as well. Having bonded with them both thanks to David's success, we had become very friendly.

Enter Grant Tinker, who had been Brandon Tartikoff's boss as chairman of the board at NBC; Brandon was merely president. He also had been my boss when I cast *The Bob Newhart Show*. Grant had left NBC to form a new venture called GTG Productions, a partnership with Gannett Industries, owner of many of the largest independent newspapers across America, as well as most of our lovely highway billboards. Like the rest of the world, Gannett wanted to be in showbiz, and what better way to do it than hire one of the classiest, silver-foxiest, WASPiest, most successful men in the business. Earlier, Grant had partnered with his then-wife, Mary Tyler Moore, to form MTM Productions, the company whose logo at the end of each series episode was the little kitten that mewed in imitation of the MGM lion. Most if not all of MTM's shows were both commercial and artistic successes: *The Mary Tyler Moore Show, The Bob Newhart Show, Rhoda, Hill Street Blues, St. Elsewhere, The White Shadow, NYPD Blue, L.A. Law,* and more. MTM also started the careers of many great television writers including Academy Award winner James L. Brooks (*Terms of Endearment*), Ed. Weinberger, Stan Daniels and Dave

Davis (*Taxi*), Glen and Les Charles (*Cheers*), and Gwyneth's dad, Bruce Paltrow (*The White Shadow*).

With all that class, Grant's first foray into TV production at Gannett was with a script written by Michael Burk, Gregg J. Bonam, and Douglas Schwartz. Its title was *Baywatch*. These misguided individuals truly thought that they had written a version of *Hill Street Blues* at the beach; indeed, that's the shorthand they used to pitch and describe it. I'm guessing that though they wrote the script, they never read it.

Fortunately, Grant had hired a very talented man to supervise casting and work in development for his new company. Peter Golden was to become executive vice president of Talent and Casting at CBS for more than twenty-one years. Earlier in his career he was one of the casting directors who worked for me at NBC. We had a terrific department in those days – so good that at one point in 2000, the heads of casting for CBS, NBC, and Fox were all former members of my department. Peter, unlike me, had the ability to know when to keep his mouth shut; he also knew when to push his bosses in the direction they should take for their own good.

He sent over his list of possible choices for the leading role. Included were the likes of Sam Shepard, Jon Voight, Kris Kristofferson, Harrison Ford, all the way up to Laurence Olivier and Peter O'Toole – really. I asked Peter if he had been drinking when he made this list. He said no; the producers were insisting on that caliber of actor. I asked Peter to add Hasselhoff's name to the others. Yes, David Hasselhoff and Laurence Olivier on the same list. Peter had also thought of the idea, but being the smart and tactful person he is, he knew that his producers would hate it. I said something like, "Tough shit. I'll call Jan McCormick and let her know that we (NBC) are interested in David for this role in the running with Olivier and others. You just keep him alive until all those stars pass." Which is exactly what happened. Every single actor on Peter's list declined the part – some nicely and some with, "Are you fucking kidding?" And so it came to pass that the entire male star and semi-star population of New York, Hollywood, and London passed on the project. Leading men (like Hugh Jackman) were not yet imported from Australia.

It was now only a few weeks from production, and the producers were getting a severe reality check. They finally relented and asked Peter to set up an audition for David. Peter called Jan, who said David would not audition, but out of respect and deference for Grant Tinker, would meet with the writer/producers. Peter sent the script, and guess what? David read it and even he said no way and cancelled the meeting. Can you imagine the mental state of those writers now?

Peter then called Jan and begged for David to meet with Grant, *mano a mano*. Jan being no dummy, realized that it would be very impolitic for David to refuse. David and Grant met and I cannot imagine an odder couple. The names Grant Tinker and David Hasselhoff did not belong in the same sentence. Everything David represented as an actor (but not personally) was what Grant had despised when he was at MTM. However, times had changed, and Grant, I, guess, had a come-to-Jesus moment and substantially lowered his standards. Whatever transpired in that room is known only to Grant, David, and their accountants, but David came out of that room having agreed to do the part. What's more, he also signed on as an executive producer. He was on his way to untold riches. But the story is not yet over.

The series aired on NBC, and Brandon's worries were justified. *Baywatch* received bad reviews and low ratings in the

United States and was cancelled after one season. But my friends at NBC and Gannett were not minding the overseas financial store. Remember David's German appeal? *Baywatch* was doing very well in the international marketplace. This story gets even weirder with the entrance of Sherwood Schwartz, a beloved former top television producer and eminence grisé. He was the man who had given TV two long-running shows, *Gilligan's Island* and *The Brady Bunch*.

Sherwood was also uncle to two of Baywatch's creators, Douglas Schwartz and Michael Berk, who were first cousins. After the NBC failure, Sherwood gave some superb advice to his nephews. Having had a huge amount of experience with first-run syndication, he urged them to go to Grant Tinker and try to buy back the syndication rights to the show. Sure enough, Grant allowed the cousins to option the world-wide rights to the cancelled *Baywatch* for … $10! If they succeeded in setting up the deal, Grant and Gannet would receive $5,000 per episode, a very low figure even for that time. I guess you know what happened next.

In 1990, *Baywatch* began airing all over the world. But it wasn't until a couple years into the run that a former *Playboy* playmate named Pamela Anderson joined the cast. Hasselhoff originally opposed her hiring, arguing that *Baywatch* was a family show. However, he did agree to meet her and was overwhelmed by her "charisma." Later on, when a sex tape of her with her husband Tommy Lee found its way onto the internet, many stations and distributors wanted her fired.

But when the ratings came in, some had increased by double digits. Those who called for her removal did an abrupt never mind. *Baywatch* lasted in syndication for ten years. It was a huge hit in more than 140 countries, with an estimated viewing audience of 1.1 billion viewers weekly, and is the longest running show never to receive a single Emmy nomination.

David Hasselhoff has had the last laugh and made enough "fuck you" money to outlive any subsequent tabloid scandals – notably the one in which his high school aged daughter taped him while drunk eating a cheeseburger off the floor. Whoever put him on the panel of *America's Got Talent* in 2006 was brilliant. David was a perfect fit. Like I said: Blame me.

INTRODUCTION

I didn't set out to become a Casting Director, but even at seven, when my mother took me to see *Samson and Delilah* – the 1949 Cecil B. DeMille's biblical movie epic – I had strong opinions about who should be playing whom. As a second grader at the Yeshiva of Eastern Parkway in Brooklyn, I spent much of my time reading violent Old Testament stories. "Samson's real name is Shimshon", I whispered to my mother, "and Delilah should have been pronounced Duh-lee-law". Annoyed audience glances came our way. My mother giggled and sushed me me. I did, however, approve of the casting of hunky, bare-chested Victor Mature as Samson, the first adult man I had ever seen who was completely hairless from the neck down (at least tohis waist) and the exotically gorgeous Hedy Lamarr as Delilah. I paid special attention to the aristocratic yet snarky and menacing Brit George Sanders, who played the almighty Saran of Gaza. Later on I saw him in all sorts of other films – *Ivanhoe*, *All About Eve*, *Call Me Madam*. I learned that he could go from costume to costume and role to role while somehow remaining the same.

From then on, I saw every film that came to the neighborhood movie house. Victor Mature seemed so well-suited to playing a half-naked gladiator or slave in films set in ancient Rome or Egypt that I couldn't accept him in street clothes. But I quickly learned that the force of some actors' personalities transcended any part they might play. The last star billed in the *Ivanhoe* trailer was announced unforgettably: "… and Elizabeth Taylor as Rebecca, the Jewess." Whatever I saw her do for the rest of her career, she was always Elizabeth Taylor. Then there were all the supporting players who were first-call choices if you needed a certain type. The smart, funny sidekick or best friend: Thelma Ritter or Eve Arden. The cartoon-like, rich guys: Charles Coburn and Lucille Ball's banker, Gale Gordon.

We were the last family on the block to get a TV set, but once we did, I stayed glued to it whenever I wasn't in school or at the movies. Watching that small, flickering black-and-white box, which reduced everyone to living-room size, I learned more about the magic that can happen when the right performer gets the right part. Out of those thousands of hours of viewing eventually came my career as a casting director. Working at CBS in the mid-1970s, I cast *The Bob Newhart Show*, which *TV Guide* would one day rank among the greatest series of all time. I'm not sure I agree with that, but, hey, I didn't argue. As head of Talent at Spelling-Goldberg, a hugely successful TV production company, I cast *Starsky & Hutch*, *The Rookies*, *Family*, a few episodes of *Charlie's Angels*, and pilots for *Fantasy Island* and *The Love Boat*, all of which, in one way or another, defined the '70s and earned cult followings that last to this day.

While at Spelling-Goldberg, I produced and cast *The Boy in the Plastic Bubble*, a TV movie that starred John Travolta, whom I had known since he was 17; he had just debuted as Vinnie Barbarino in the hit high-school sitcom *Welcome Back, Kotter*, but had yet to make *Grease* or *Saturday Night Fever*, the films that would bring him superstardom.

Next, Paramount TV hired me as vice president of TV Talent & Casting. One of my projects there was *Taxi*, which won eighteen Emmy Awards over five seasons and launched six great careers: those of Judd Hirsch, Danny DeVito, Marilu Henner, Tony Danza, Christopher Lloyd, and Andy Kaufman. Paramount gave me the job of casting *Grease* and *Airplane!* two movies destined to outlive us all. The same is true of *The Rocky Horror Picture Show*, whose screen and initial U.S. stage versions I also cast. Its fabled midnight screenings are still a rite of passage for American teenagers.

In 1980 I landed at NBC, where I became vice president of Talent and Casting for a decade. Today I look at the list of some of our hit shows in those years: *Cheers, Miami Vice, The Golden Girls, Seinfeld, L.A. Law, CHiPS, The Cosby Show, A Different World, The Facts of Life, Hill Street Blues, Diff'rent Strokes, Family Ties, Remington Steele, Night Court, Matlock, Knight Rider, The A-Team*, etc., and I know my work helped define the ethos of a generation.

There is a joke that everyone in Hollywood has two jobs – their own and casting. But no one outside the business (and many inside as well) has any real concept about what casting is and what a casting director does. Therefore, here is Joel Thurm's Casting 101.

101.1. The first part of casting is to know actors. I don't mean personally, but through going to the movies, watching TV, and going to see plays and musicals in theaters both large and small. Of course, watching and going has to include *remembering* or keeping records of both the good and not so good performances.

101.2. Reading the script. I read the script twice. The first time to get a feeling about the whole project. Is the writer, director, or other creative folk known or unknown? Is it a pilot for a series or an episode of one? If it is a series, is it a classy, award-winning one or just an ordinary time filler? If it is a movie, is it being directed by Steven Spielberg and written by Aaron Sorkin or by much lesser knowns or complete unknowns? Of course, the budget sets certain parameters. The bigger the budget and the classier the project, the easier it is to cast prominent actors. Then, as I read the script for the second time, I write my ideas on paper, making a separate column for every important role, and start writing actors names down. At this point, a bit of common sense needs to be applied. One does not write down the names Tom Cruise or Meryl Streep for an episode of *NCIS Los Angeles*. However, if the TV series is award-winning, a movie script is sensational, or the project is being directed and/or written by someone big stars might want to work with, you write those names down, too. The best example of this was when Jane Fonda agreed to do an episode of *Mork & Mindy* because it was her kids' favorite show. Unfortunately, at the last minute she had to drop out, but she was replaced with another movie star, Raquel Welch.

101.3. The next step is to meet with any or all of the following to make sure all of us are on the same conceptual page: producer, director, studio and/or network executives. This will delete many of my ideas and add new ones from those above. If we all agree on actors for various roles, cash offers are made and negotiated. Backup choices are then agreed upon should our first choices decline.

101.4. Next, a few pages detailing what the project is, who are the involved creative folk, and what roles are available are distributed to agents and managers via Gary Marsh's Breakdown Services" – a free service to casting directors that gets out our information quickly and accurately. An experienced casting director will know which agents and managers represent enough good actors to warrant being given a full script in addition to those several pages. That's when the real work begins, with the arrival of tons of U.S. mail or e-mailed suggestions and photos. These days thanks to cell phone cameras, computers and tablets, actors often record themselves and submit their own auditions. During this time my phone also begins to ring and ring with verbal suggestions, too. When I started out, I would return every call. I quickly learned which of those calls were from smart and creative agents and which were the opposite.

101.5. Of course, not all our actor choices accept the offers, and then begins the process of auditioning actors not known to the show runners nor often to me, either. For those actors I do not know, appointments are set up and those actors read portions of the script with me in my office. This is called a "pre-read." What these actors read for me are generally called "sides". These are a few pages from the script often provided without context. I always made sure when I used sides there was adequate information about the character and the project. I might give the actor a suggestion about how to change something in reading. A good actor will be able to make adjustments to the reading; a not-so-good one won't.

After this process, "callbacks" are set up, for the writer and/or the director. Those being called back usually get full scripts. In television the writer is usually the most important one in the room, and in movies it is the director. Finally, after callbacks, those actors who have made it thus far are invited back to read again or sometimes to be put on tape for whoever is financing the project – meaning the head of a TV network or the head of a motion picture studio. Often groups of actors we like are read in smaller groups to see if there is any chemistry between them. These so-called final auditions are when a casting director can help enormously or not. For example, if an actor comes in and does a poor reading, it is my job to inform those making the decisions that this actor does not audition well, but his or her performances are great. The converse also can also happen, when I know that a particular actor does great auditions but will never get any better.

101.6. Sometimes all goes well and we – the network or studio and all the creatives – agree. But about half the time no agreement is reached and then we go to actual screen tests either on film, which is expensive, or tape, which costs nothing. Unfortunately, actors look very different on tape versus film, and it's again my job to point this out. Ultimately when these tests are viewed, the studio or network almost always has the last word about who gets cast because they are financing the project. The only time this does not happen is when one of the creatives is a true big star in their field; like a Ryan Murphy or a Steven Spielberg. Then they become the 800 lb. gorilla in the room and usually get what they want. At NBC my job was to represent the network's choices and somehow bring all the different opinions together. With a lot of give-and-take and gentle or often not so gentle persuasion, *finally* all eventually come to an agreement and the actor is chosen.

Almost every question I've fielded about my work has involved a wink-wink allusion to that most notorious practice, the casting couch. I had an enormous couch in my office, but it was never used for that purpose. I was a #MeToo advocate decades before that hashtag was invented. But God knows I witnessed plenty of that behavior, as you'll learn later in this book. Also, please do not call me and my fellow casting directors "casting agents"; there is no such thing. The reason you do not see the phrase "Casting Director - Joel Thurm" on a movie or TV screen is because the

Directors Guild's contract with all production companies and networks prohibits the use of the word "director" in that title. Therefore, you'll see on screen "Casting by Joel Thurm." Then again, the same guild that uses its enormous influence *not* to honor casting directors but is OK with an Oscar for hair stylists. Fortunately change seems to be in the wind regarding a Casting Oscar and the use of the term Casting Director. If you stream shows made in the UK, the phrase Casting Director is already in use.

Most everyone will agree that casting the right actor is about ninety percent of the success of a movie, but, hey, (hands raised) just sayin'. Also just sayin' that I recently watched the *Friends* reunion show. There was a long sequence in which the producers talked about the difficulty of casting the right actors, but not one mention of Ellie Kanner nor Barbara Miller, who cast the pilot. I guess they forgot their names, but I'll bet they remember cashing their checks

It never occurred to me to write a book about my experiences until 2008, when I was having dinner with actor Joaquin Phoenix and his mother, Heart, at Joaquin's home. Heart was my first assistant at NBC; one of only two assistants I had over a 10-year period. She and I began talking and laughing about our time together. Joaquin, who was eight years when I'd first worked with his mother, was transfixed. Finally, he said, "You got to write this stuff down!" – and so I went home and did just that. While now almost a cliché, it dawned on me that, as in the song from *Hamilton*, "The Room Where It Happens," I'd been in rooms where show business history had happened. I was one of a group of people who made decisions that affected the future of countless actors, TV productions, a few iconic films, and Broadway shows that became big hits and cultural touchstones. We worked hard, though not always successfully so, to break down walls like racial diversity, and to make it possible for the cream to rise to the top.

As far as I know, there has never been a book about show business written from the point of view of a casting director. Casting is not an exact science; it all comes down to personal taste (or lack thereof), tact (or lack thereof), and most of all the ability to help writers and directors fulfill their creative desires without shooting themselves in their feet. As you will read, there were often a dozen or more people making decisions. No doubt some will disagree with my interpretations on why a certain star or show worked or didn't. Please remember these are *my* opinions and feel free accept them or not. But be sure to carefully read the last chapter of this book, **NBC Series Notes.** It is there thatI discuss and dissect every pilot that made it on to NBC's primetime schedule between 1980 and 1990. Hopefully you will find what I write informative and funny but at least interesting.

CHAPTER 1

KOSHER MILK

I spent much of my childhood on a dairy farm in Brooklyn, just two blocks from what is now called the No. 3 subway train. Yes, when I was born on September 16, 1942, in Brooklyn, that section of the borough known as East New York still had farms. My grandfather, Abraham Balsam, whom we called Papa, was a tall, solid Orthodox Jew with a handsome, flat Slavic face. He bought the farm after emigrating from Poland. My mother, father, and I lived a few blocks away in a tiny two-bedroom apartment. But while my father was away in World War II, my mother and I spent most days on the farm. We shared it with the inhabitants of the long, narrow, red-brick barn: fifty-six smelly, bony Holstein cows in neck shackles. Papa sold their milk and manure.

This native city boy became intimately familiar with the little shed where fresh milk was collected in twenty-five-gallon cans and instantly chilled in an ice-water bath. The cans were then brought to a bottler and sold as kosher milk. A rabbi had to certify that the cows did not eat pigs and that the milk was pure. Then he got paid for his services, waved his magic wand, and the kosher quart now cost two or three cents more than the gentile kind. My grandfather and great Uncle Nathan, who had a similar farm in Queens and who had emigrated with him, had a virtual monopoly on kosher milk in Brooklyn and Queens.

On the property, about the size of a third of a city block, was a wooden barn for hay bales and feed, which, while playing with matches, I managed to set on fire and then put it out more than once. On the property there were several sheds, one of which was used by my grandfather as his work/repair shop. In there he taught me how to use a hammer and saw and most of his other tools. I came to believe that he used this shed as his man cave to get away from it all. He also made his own Eastern European potato soup on a small cast iron potbellied stove. There were also two detached buildings for living. One was the "Farmhouse," a small, two-story building with three tiny bedrooms and one bathroom, which I thought was a palace compared to our apartment. It was there that my grandparents raised their four daughters. There was also the "Bunkhouse" for the two or three workmen my grandfather recruited regularly from the squalid and ungentrified Bowery in Manhattan. Most of the workers were virtual winos; my grandfather paid them in both cash and whisky. I was forbidden to go near there, and for once I obeyed, probably because it smelled worse than the cow barn.

One of his daughters was my mother, Florence, a beautiful woman with a naturally tan complexion, dark eyes, high cheekbones, and mounds of jet-black hair. She was the oldest daughter and the first to marry, which she did in order to get out of the house. Her own mother had died when she and her sister, my Aunt Rozy, were about eight and seven. They had little supervision for years, and when they were in their teens, my grandfather married an attractive, diminutive brunette who would never be seen in public without perfect hair and makeup. Until I was about fifteen, I never knew Jeanette Balsam was really my step-grandmother. Things like that were not discussed – why, I still don't know. But we adored each other, and when I ran away from our apartment, which I did regularly, it was always to her and the farm.

She truly loved her new husband, not only for himself but because he had "rescued" her and her two young daughters, my Aunts Gloria and Anita, from an impoverished widowhood. *The Brady Bunch* it wasn't, because my mother and her sister were pissed about this new mother who tried to set limits and came with two very cute little girls. At fifteen, Mom acted out by smoking, cutting school, staying out late, and running with a loose crowd, not unlike the character Rizzo from *Grease*. After going with lots of guys, my mother finally married the first man who treated her well and acted like a gentleman: my father, and then Nathan Bernard Thurm, called Bernie. Then WWII broke out. My father was drafted and served as an Army MP, guarding German POWs in of all places, Camp McCoy in Wisconsin. Both before and after the war, he worked for his father, George Thurm whom we called Grandpa and who owned a grocery/dairy store in the Brownsville section of Brooklyn. My grandmother was called Nani. This area was a largely Jewish and Italian neighborhood that was rapidly becoming Black and Puerto Rican. Unfortunately, my grandfather refused to change his store merchandise to accommodate the new populace, and it eventually went out of business.

Needing a job, my father became a taxi driver. Over time he turned into a very bitter man who took it out on his children, just like his father had done to him. He was psychologically blackmailed to work in the store under Grandpa's threat to force Nani, who was frail and half-blind, to work there in his stead. Dutifully he quit school, where he was studying accounting. This ruined his life. Interestingly, both my sister and my brother became accountants and I have no doubt that my father would have made a good one as well. I am so thankful that I did not get that gene. Like Papa, Grandpa was very Orthodox and a pillar of the community, but the resemblance ended there. Papa was liked by all, Grandpa by none. Sometime after Grandpa died, during our one and only adult heart-to-heart talk, Nani told me about her arranged marriage and its difficulties. When I asked her how she could stand him and the marriage in general, she shrugged her shoulders and said flatly, "You make the best of it." How sad.

Soon after my father came home from the war, I acquired a younger brother, Freddy. My parents were Orthodox-light, meaning that my mother kept a kosher house but we loved eating BLTs at the corner diner and lobster and fried shrimp at "real" restaurants. We only went to Shul on the High Holidays and did not obey Sabbath rules. I did not wear a Yarmulke or Kippah, as the little skullcaps are called now. I could not wait to start school, but Papa insisted I go to the Yeshiva of Eastern Parkway, about five miles away, rather than the local public school – and he paid for it. Why anyone thought I would fit in at that school escapes me. I hated it. I managed to get through the first year, which was first grade, but the next year I began acting out. I would exit the school bus by crowd-surfing like a rock star. I deliberately drank milk with my salami sandwich, a big kosher no-no, and during the obligatory prayer sessions I read comic books inserted into the prayer books. One day near the end of the school year, I did something that got me sent yet again to the principal's office. There were two principals: one for the Hebrew religious part of the school and another for the regular classes. The Hebrew principal was a gentle giant with a huge black beard and bald head, which was almost always covered per Torah orders. He would have fit right in today's Bushwick or Williamsburg. But the other principal, to whom I'd been sent, was a mean motherfucker who believed in corporal punishment. He began by pinching my cheeks as hard as he could; he then began to twist them, and that hurt a lot. I thrashed around as much as I could, and finally landed a kick right in his balls. He let go of me immediately. Then the school let go of me immediately, too. I was kicked out – literally and thankfully.

Although I hated it, the education I got there must have been pretty good, because at my new school, P.S. 213, I was skipped ahead by two grades. Now I was the second shortest and youngest boy in the fourth grade. Being smaller and younger did not help at fitting in. Academically I did well, but I was always getting into trouble for fooling around in class. My mother was called to school every other week, which as I found out as an adult, had gotten every boy excited. My best friend at the time and the only one shorter than I, Howard Topoff, told me a few years ago that all the boys could not wait for my mother's bi-weekly appearances. Unlike most of the other mothers, mine was a hottie. I was not a sissy and was never bullied, but I was always chosen last for team sports. When it comes to using eyes and balls and hands at the same time, I have zero coordination.

What I was good at was breaking rules, being funny, and accepting dares – like walking out onto the fourth-floor ledge at Jr. High School 149. The school was about half a mile from my house, in a not-great neighborhood. From an almost all-White school I'd moved to a racially mixed and much tougher place. It was there that I met my protectress, Denise Jefferson. She was a tall black girl who could beat the shit out of most anyone, male or female. For some reason she took a liking to me, so no one fucked with me. Ours was my first in a lifetime of relationships with powerful and so-called "difficult" black women, such as Nell Carter and Pearl Bailey.

On I went to Samuel J. Tilden High School, where I ran unsuccessfully for student body president with the slogan, "DON'T BE A WORM, VOTE FOR THURM." I guess I should have used "Make Tilden Great Again." That loss I took in stride but there was one moment during my senior year that was much worse. The photographer who took our senior class photos arrived to show us the results and sell as many copies as he could. Of course, there was to be an extra charge for retouching the images. It was there that I found out he was using my face, loaded with acne, and copy of the same photo with a complexion as clear as Jennifer Anniston's. I was devastated. The whole senior class would have seen them. Where was the Joel Thurm of later years who would have gone ballistic and torn up those pics and screamed obscenities? Instead, I meekly said that I would appreciate it if he did not use them as samples. I have no idea if he listened to me.

I was growing up fast and rapidly parting ways with my father, whose violence had become unbearable. If my brother and I did something "bad," he would come into our bedroom, take off his belt, and swing wildly at us. When I was fourteen, I came home late from a night out. He responded by coming after me with a wooden hanger as an opener and throwing a night table at me as a closer. We did not speak for the next five years. He certainly would not have approved that during high school, I began to realize I was *not* attracted to the opposite sex. I went on dates with a cheerleader, a twirler, and a chubby girl named Pepe for whom I even bought a "going steady" gold ankle bracelet, which was embarrassingly too small to fit around her ankle. I belonged to a national Jewish high school fraternity, Sigma Alpha Ro. We rented the basement of an apartment building in the neighborhood where we lined the walls with old sofas, a record player, and other furniture, and invited girls to come and dance and make out and drink beer and 7&7, a horrible tasting drink made with whiskey and 7-Up. I never got a charge out of making out and getting to second base. Bare tit did nothing for me, but I went along with all this because I was supposed to.

What did work for me was the indoor St. George Hotel swimming pool, an art deco masterpiece in the basement of a once luxury hotel in Brooklyn Heights. When I was twelve, my parents believed swimming, which I loved, would be good for me and it was – but in a different way than they thought. Getting there was also easy since the hotel had its own indoor subway stop, so New York winter weather wasn't a problem. The pool area, open to the paying public, was two stories high, with a pink mirrored ceiling. At one end of the mosaic-tiled pool was a balcony that overhung it by about four feet. From the balcony came a waterfall that cascaded into the pool, creating a water curtain you could swim through. Unfortunately, I was forced to go there with my same-aged, no-fun first cousin Stevie. He was boring, super-obedient, not terribly bright, and had no sense of humor or mischief. Wherever we were forced to go together, I usually ditched him and looked for adventure elsewhere. In this case it was the men's locker room. I remember it as a huge, gleaming, white-tiled space with a line of shower stalls on one wall with no shower curtains. It had a steam room with white-tiled benches. You had to be over sixteen to go in there, but what was another broken rule to this twelve-year-old? Fortunately, I was wearing a bathing suit, because the sight of all those naked men was visibly exciting me. I quickly learned the code. At first a foot would "accidentally" touch mine – and if I did not move away, it came back and stayed there. Then touching began at other body locations. Today, of course, this would be considered sexual battery on a minor, but I welcomed the ability to express my sexuality and never thought that I or the men there might be doing something wrong or illegal. In fact, I am almost sure that the first guy I had this kind of contact with was the neighborhood cop whose beat was near my father's store.

During all my school years from about age eleven or so onward, when other kids were playing sports after school, I was at home listening to the radio station that played musical theater albums. When that show was over, I switched to watching TV until summoned to eat supper with my mother, brother, and later on, in her highchair, my baby sister Fran. My father ate separately when he came home from work. If for some reason my father did join us there was always a no-talking rule. On Saturdays I was always at our local movie house on New Lots Avenue, the Biltmore. Twenty-five cents got me into the morning kiddie show: serials, cartoons, then usually a black-and white Western. I remember all the *Flash Gordon* serial episodes with the best villain ever, Ming the Merciless, and of course Dale and the Mole People. There was also the former Olympic swimmer, Johnnie Weissmuller, as Tarzan– yum! After the kiddie show was over, I hid in the bathroom until the grownup film began. Not only did my mother approve of my movie going, but I was given two sandwiches to eat – one for lunch and the other for supper – and money to buy one Coke. I never had popcorn in a movie theater until I was an adult – too expensive, I was told. Early in my childhood, as you can see, I was an avid consumer of show-business product. Like my whole generation, I grew up watching *Ozzie and Harriet* and *Father Knows Best* and wishing my family were like that. Early on Saturday mornings, I rarely missed an installment of the half-hour TV film series *Bomba, the Jungle Boy,* played by a half-naked kid actor named Johnny Sheffield; *Bomba* began my fascination with Africa, India, and loincloths. I loved *Sky King,* which starred handsome Kirby Grant as an Arizona pilot. Then there was Peter Graves in *Fury,* "The story of a horse ... and a boy who loves him." The boy's rancher dad was played by Graves. I wanted to be his son so badly. Years later, when I was asked to cast the movie *Airplane!,* Peter was my first and only suggestion to play the pilot who asks a little boy in the cockpit: "You ever seen a grown man naked?" It was my personal in-joke in a movie full of them. I wanted to be that boy.

When I wasn't at the movies or glued to the TV, I was licking the lids of Borden's ice cream Dixie cups. I couldn't wait to see the pictures of movie stars that were printed on them. Also, if you saved twenty-five of the lids and paid twenty-five cents, you got a bleacher seat ticket to see the Brooklyn Dodgers at their now torn-down ballpark, Ebbets Field. By the time I started casting, I knew all those stars and their movies and even saw a few baseball games, too. At home I devoured every page of the *Playbills* my parents brought home whenever they went to see a Broadway show, once or twice a year at most. When I was eight, I saw *my* first show, the musical *Guys and Dolls,* which my father took me to see in place of my mother, who had to stay home that night with my very sick brother. We watched from the last row of the balcony. Little did I know then that I would someday work with Abe Burrows, the man who wrote and directed that show, and become friends with his son, the highly successful TV director Jimmy Burrows. My most vivid memory of that experience was the musical number "A Bushel and a Peck," sung by Vivian Blaine and the chorines, dressed as farm girls because during the song, they stripped down to small daisy flower pasties on their boobs and larger ones below.

When it became time to choose a college, out of state or places like NYU or Columbia were out of the question because of our family finances. However, I received a letter from the New York State Board of Regents telling me I had won a NY State scholarship. My mother, ever-the-wise woman she was, said that it had to be a mistake. She was right. A couple of days later we got a call telling us that the scholarship was for another Joel L. Thurm who went to a different high school. This was no surprise in that while I had test scores off the charts, I barely broke a C average. So instead of being admitted to the nearest City University of New York, Brooklyn College, which was 20 minutes from home, I had to go to Hunter College's Bronx campus which was 1:45 minutes away by subway and bus. It seems they had a "special program" for underachievers. There were some advantages to attending a school so far away. First, I never had to open a book at home. All my reading and homework was done on the subway. Second, traveling from Brooklyn through all of Manhattan to the upper reaches of the Bronx brought me into contact with the "The City" on a daily basis with all it had to offer: museums, theater, foreign films, and of course the men who lived there. Not until my senior year of high school did, I see a couple more shows. On the same Wednesday in June of '59, I cut school to see a matinee of *Gypsy* with Ethel Merman at the Broadway Theater, had a $4.95 Tad's Steaks dinner, then rushed to *West Side Story* at the Winter Garden. No wonder I fell in love with musicals and theater. I also immediately fell in love with the actor who played Tony, Larry Kert, whose voice I had been listening to for a while. I knew all the lyrics to every song in the show but the only one I could sing was my favorite, "America". Future fact - almost any woman who plays that part wins an award,

At Hunter, I took pre-med courses because that was what nice Jewish boys were supposed to do. Becoming a doctor was first on my parents' wish list for their boys, followed closely by law, dentistry, accounting, and last, teaching. For women, however, the whole point was not to work but marry one of the first three on that list. I wasn't sure what I wanted but I did know it had to be a different life than that of my family. I had heard of the notorious bohemian area of Manhattan called Greenwich Village which was filled with cafés, coffee houses and gay bars. Of course, I began hanging out there. One Friday night I wandered into a gay dance bar in Greenwich Village. A young guy came up to me and asked if I went to Hunter College. At first, I freaked out but said yes. He went there too and said he had seen me on campus. Up until then, all the men I had been with were "old", like twenty-eight to thirty. This was the first gay friend I made who was near my own age. He told me if I wanted to meet more gay guys, that many were involved in the college theater organization, called Theater Workshop, and so I joined.

It opened a whole new world to me in every way except the one that had brought me there. I didn't meet any new gay students which was no surprise, given the very big closet that existed in the late '50s and early '60s. So, I threw myself into a new avocation, acting. Most of my roles were one- or two-line parts but I didn't care; I loved learning the language and customs of the theater. Rehearsals were a relief from academic classes. I learned how to use power tools (of which my grandfather had none) and build sets. I loved the very long days and nights, during which I existed on pizza and soda. Often, I did not go home to Brooklyn.

I slept backstage on a pile of very comfortable velvet stage drapes. But most of all I loved being accepted for myself, even though I had yet to come out.

I did get cast in a play to be directed by Dr. Marvin Seiger, the department head. The play was Sean O'Casey's *Juno and the Paycock*, a working-class family drama set in Ireland in the 1930's during the "troubles". I was to come onstage at the end of the second act in my role as a "IRA Man No. 2", a member of the Irish Republican Army. I think my line, as my fellow IRA Man No. 1 and I dragged the leading man offstage was: "You're cummin' with us!" At our dress rehearsal, I had way too much time to prepare for this one-line part. I had read stage-makeup books and tried to apply what I learned. I used lots of pancake to cover my remaining acne, etched on too much eyeliner, put little white and red dots in the corner of my eyes to make them appear bigger, and added rouge to give me cheek bones. I took just as long trying to make sure my costume, a 1930s trench-coat and fedora hat, was worn correctly. With collar turned up, I tightened the belt of my trench coat over and over and pulled the brim of my hat so far down over one eye that I could barely see out of it. The time finally came for *my* scene. It went off without any mistakes. I said my line and we dragged the guy off stage. I felt great. After rehearsal Dr. Seiger began to deliver his detailed notes. When he got to the end of second act, his last note was: "And Joel, you are supposed to be an IRA man, *not* Lauren Bacall." Everyone laughed but me. I began to think that perhaps I should rethink my ambition to be an actor.

At the end of my freshman year, everyone in the theater department was abuzz about finding acting work in summer stock when the semester ended. We all combed through the theatrical trade papers – *Backstage, Show Business, Variety* – trying in vain to find acting work. However, there were many jobs available that did not involve acting and that were salaried. I applied for and got a job as box-office treasurer for a suburban summer theater about thirty miles north of Manhattan. It was the Tappan Zee Playhouse in Nyack, New York. Thus began my career in the "theatah," for the staggering sum of thirty-five dollars per week.

CHAPTER 2

SUMMER STOCK: FROM NYACK TO ROME AND BACK

Tappan Zee Playhouse was an 800-seat theater about thirty miles north of Manhattan, on the west side of the Hudson River. It was a key stop on the summer-stock circuit, a series of smallish theaters up and down the East Coast from Maine to Washington, D.C., most of which only operated in the summer. These theaters did not produce their own shows. Instead, they joined together to finance a production of a play or musical that had recently closed on Broadway and had already had its national tour. Each theater was responsible for building its own sets and finding all necessary props. The only things that traveled from theater to theater were the actors and their costumes. Summer stock shows would play six nights and two matinee performances at a theater. After a day off, which was a travel day for the cast, the show would re-open at the next place with completely new sets and props.

Generally, what you saw in stock were light comedies with faded or fading stars, current TV personalities, and sometimes still meaningful stars who could make decent bucks by starring in their signature roles, such as Angela Lansbury in *Gypsy* or Zero Mostel in *Fiddler on the Roof.* But more often it was the likes of June Allyson, Van Johnson, Ann Sothern, Morey Amsterdam, Rose Marie, Dorothy Lamour, or Ann Miller. Because of her popularity as a panelist on America's longest-running game show, *What's My Line?*, Arlene Francis could fill the Tappan Zee Playhouse for a week – even after she had accidentally helped cause two deaths: one when her car went speeding out of control, and the other when a dumbbell fell from the window of her eighth-story, luxury New York apartment. Cancel culture had not yet arrived; otherwise, she would have been out of a job. The individual theaters would fill in the minor roles or beef up the chorus of a musical. The bit parts and additional chorus members were almost always given to apprentices, without whom the theaters would not have been able to operate. Apprentices were mostly college kids like me who, in exchange for theater experience and the very remote possibility of getting an opportunity to act, worked their unpaid asses off doing most of the work that enabled these places to exist, i.e., building all the sets, shopping for or borrowing props and set dressing from the local stores, driving actors to and from the theater, etc. Apprentices served as stagehands during performances even if they had those tiny acting parts. And after the last performance of the week, they immediately switched to taking down the old set and putting up a new one overnight for the show coming in the next day. However, in most cases the apprentices did get free room and board. At Tappan Zee, they were put up in one of the decaying, huge Victorian houses (which now sell for millions) that lined the nearby streets with a small allowance for communal food.

Tappan Zee Playhouse was owned by a married couple, Bruce Becker and Honey Waldman. Appearance-wise, Bruce was to Honey roughly what Robert Redford was to Barbra Streisand in *The Way We Were*, only shorter. Bruce was always perfectly and appropriately dressed, square-jawed with mesmerizing eyes. He was very handsome, and he knew it. She was a pretty, chunky earth mother with long, straight shiny brown hair, usually held back with a simple headband and she had family money. For my thirty-five dollars a week, I worked all day inside the box office, taking people's cash, handing them their tickets, and dealing with telephone orders. There was no Ticketmaster or Telecharge, nor much use of credit cards. Beside learning how to run a box office, I was unconsciously setting the stage for my future career in casting because all calls for the production office and backstage came through my box office. This is how I became acquainted with every important agent in New York and their assistants, many of whom went on to become agents. A call would come in: "Hello, this is Ed Limato from Janet Roberts' office. Is Bruce Becker available for her?" Ed and I would talk, and we became friendly while waiting for our bosses to get on the line. Years later Ed arguably became the most important agent in Hollywood, representing the likes of Denzel Washington, Michele Pfeiffer, Richard Gere, Nicolas Cage, Steve Martin, and Mel Gibson. Summer ended, and I returned to Hunter College. I was still on my pre-med path, but I clung to my fantasy of becoming an actor. For a perennial college show, *Dark of the Moon,* I learned to play three chords on a guitar and to sing the folk song "Down in the Valley." The less said about my performance, the better. My parents, of course, did not come but my Aunt Anita and Uncle Si did. They were then and continued to be the only family members supportive of the show business work I did.

Except for doctors' visits and the occasional trip to Radio City Music Hall, my family's only use for Manhattan was to schlep in once a year on a Sunday to buy cheap underwear, socks, and school clothes for my brother and me from the pushcarts on the Lower East Side. We may as well have been living in Des Moines, Iowa, for all the use we made of Manhattan. We even called it "The City," as though it were some Oz-like place far away rather than just two bridges and a tunnel from Brooklyn. But school brought me into Manhattan daily, and I had begun my own explorations. A new world was opening to me. During my fall semester I met a guy, and I began to sleep over at his Upper East Side apartment rather than take the long ride back to Brooklyn. John Greenleaf was an "older man" of about thirty. He was slim, with curly, white-blond hair, a beaming smile, a strong Boston accent. He worked as a script reader for top Broadway producer, Kermit Bloomgarden, whose shows had included *Death of a Salesman*, *The Diary of Anne Frank*, and *The Music Man*. Knowing my interest in the theater, John took me under his wing, bringing me to shows, films, ballet, and Philharmonic concerts. Just to know someone who worked on Broadway made me feel important. When John introduced me to Tammy Grimes in her dressing room during her run as star of *The Unsinkable Molly Brown*, I was in heaven.

John lived on First Avenue in a third-floor railroad flat, a long and narrow apartment shaped like railroad car. The front door opened directly into the small kitchen. To the left was a bathroom with the only other door in the place. A window in the kitchen looked out into the airshaft. It doesn't sound too glamorous, but John had the gay gene, and that tiny apartment could have been in a magazine. The lamps were just right. The couch was covered in nice fabric, without clear plastic slip covers as we had at home. He used cloth napkins and had real antiques, very different from the "Italian/Jewish Provincial" furniture my family and all my relatives had. Very soon I met John's sophisticated friends, who included Mabel Mercer, the ladylike British doyenne of cabaret singers. I didn't get her singing style, but I was very good at keeping that to myself. Now, how to explain my not coming home after school to my mother? No worry about my father since we were still barely speaking. I invented a girlfriend; a rich one whose parents took us to fabulous places. They liked me so much, I explained, that they often invited me to stay overnight in their guest room. My mother was always asking when she could meet this girl and her parents, but I always skirted the issue.

Of course, my schoolwork was suffering. Although I had advanced placement in sciences in high school, I withdrew from a chemistry class midway through the semester because lab work was eating up too much of my theater time. I assumed that dropping that one class would not affect my overall grades. I got a rude awakening when I saw my report card at the end of the fall sophomore semester. I had received a failure in chemistry, which, when factored into my grade average, meant that I had inadvertently flunked myself out of college. It came as quite a shock to me and to my family. This didn't happen to nice Jewish boys who were going to be doctors. I had no idea what do without the anchor of school, but I quickly found one – Italy. I loved mythology and figured I could more easily learn Italian than Greek. Besides, Rome and Italian movies were all the rage at the time. Those were the days just after *La Dolce Vita*, *8½*, *Cleopatra*, Liz Taylor, and Richard Burton. I was also very fond of Italian food and *Hercules* movies. Italy seemed the place to be, so why not? Coincidentally I had begun dating a guy who worked for the Italian Line, Italy's transatlantic steamship company. Jet travel had begun to overtake ship travel and ocean liners became bargain travel. I paid for my trip by asking my mother for the cash presents she had put in a savings account for me when I was Bar Mitzvah'd. While not thrilled with my plans, she cooperated.

With $1,500 in my pocket, I was on my way. I remained there for about a year.

In January 1962, I sailed away on the oldest Italian liner then in existence at that time, the *Vulcania*. Twelve days from New York to Naples. I had a great time on the ship. On the first day aboard, I met an aspiring actor, roughly my age. As we talked, we realized we had crossed paths in New York. At lunch one day, we met a strange and slightly hostile little woman with old-fashioned bobbed black hair and faded black clothing that looked slept in. Her name was Patricia Highsmith. She had written a novel that Alfred Hitchcock turned into the movie *Strangers on a Train*. Other novels of hers would become well-received films, including *The Talented Mr. Ripley* (Matt Damon, Gwyneth Paltrow) and *Carol*, a lesbian-themed work for which Cate Blanchett earned an Oscar nomination. Highsmith pretty much drank her lunch and became more belligerent toward me with each drink. But she was charmed by Walter because he was charming. Walter also knew how to meet and mate with men who could further his career. He told me he was going to Italy to play a role in a movie to be directed the Italian director Franco Brusati. He failed to tell me he was Franco's new boy toy. After we'd docked in Naples, the very handsome, Franco drove us all the way to Rome in his brand-new, baby blue Mercedes convertible. I was impressed, and jealous.

Before leaving New York, I had learned of a small pensione on Via Sistina at the top of the Spanish Steps – one of the best locations in Rome but then still inexpensive. It cost 600 lira (one dollar) per night, baths and meals extra. The first and smartest thing I did was to buy a used Vespa, a classic Italian motor scooter. I felt like Angie Dickinson or Audrey Hepburn, who tooled around Rome on Vespas in the movies only I was driving not sitting in back. From there I enrolled in an Italian language class and as patience is not my greatest asset, when I learned enough to get by, I quit. About a month into my stay, I got a letter from John Greenleaf. He told me that a good friend of his, Lee Bim, had bought an apartment just a few blocks away from my pensione and would be arriving in a few weeks. He had told Lee about me and how he thought we should meet. Lee did call, and we had lunch. When he asked what I did, I said I was an actor. My college performances became "off-off-Broadway" work. Lee was a nice-looking man around forty with thinning hair. He had been working in the family's business when his father died. Lee took his inheritance and moved to Rome. After lunch we went back to his apartment, a fifth-floor walkup, but worth the climb: It was huge, with a sweeping view of the city. We did a lot of touristy things together with him on the back of my Vespa. Lee did not like living alone in a new city where he knew no one and spoke no Italian; he invited me to move in with him. I would get the maid's room in return for paying his housekeeper and doing the grocery shopping, etc. I took the deal.

Through various connections, he had compiled a list of people to meet in Rome and planned a cocktail party to introduce himself. One cold and rainy night a week before the party, Lee was out to dinner. It was the proverbial dark, cold, and stormy night right out of the opening of a horror movie. I was staying in to read and take a nice, long bath. A little while after I'd settled into the tub, the doorbell rang, and rang and rang and would not stop. I wrapped a bulky and unsexy towel around me and answered the door.

In front of me stood a short, middle-aged man dressed very formally in a black three-piece suit, white shirt, and black tie, with a huge, dripping umbrella in his hand. He looked like a friendlier Danny DeVito as the "Penguin" in *Batman Returns.* Clearly uncomfortable, he introduced himself as Guidarino Guidi and asked if this was Lee Bim's apartment. He was here for the party.

In my bad Italian I said, "Yes, this is Lee's apartment, but the party is exactly one week from tonight." We both laughed.

Since he looked like a drowned rat, I invited him in to dry off and have some hot tea. I went to put on jeans and a T-shirt. I returned with the tea and some brandy; he asked if I was a tourist. I said no, I was an actor who hoped to work in Italian movies. This was not unrealistic since a typical Italian movie set at that time had actors from all over the world speaking differ- ent languages. Their voices would then be dubbed for whatever country the movie was destined for. He then told me that he was Federico Fellini's personal assistant and a casting director. After a while he made a very polite pass. I figured, what the heck, do something nice for him on this awful night. There was no quid pro quo as with the casting couch; it was a mercy gift from me to him.

He came back for the party a week later. It was then that he asked if I wanted to do some work in movies– not Fellini's, how- ever. I leapt at the chance. He cast me in a party scene in *Gidget Goes to Rome*, in a crowd scene in *Zorro and the Three Muske- teers,* and as a Greek farm boy in *Samson, Hercules, and Ulysses.* Though only a glorified extra, I now had minor street cred as an actor – at least in my own mind. Guidi and I kept in touch over the years, and we met again when he was in California, and I was at NBC and promised to use him if we ever were shooting something in Italy. He was a very sweet man and we giggled at how our journeys went post Rome.

My vespa and I saw and loved every ruin and loved innumerable museums. I spent many days in Vatican City trying to see everything in their museums there and let us say St. Peter's and its Piazza San Pietro cannot be oversold – much like India's Taj Mahal. I drove the Appian Way to the beach not too easy on those ancient Roman paving stones. On many weekends I drove about 175 miles south on the shoulder of the Autostrada to Positano on the Amalfi coast to visit a guy I was dating. At that time Positano was only mildly popular with a minimum of tourists; not so today. It was there one of its two the rocky beaches (one had sun in the morning, the other in the afternoon) that I once again found Patricia Highsmith. As on the ship she still looked like she just got out of bed and seemed a bit drunk. But this his time she was a little nicer to me. It was only many years later that I read her novel "The Talented Mr. Ripley" which was set in Positano. The wonderful 1999 movie with the same name was filmed there with it's incredible cast.

A few months later I met an American ex-pat, Peter Schneck. Beyond sex we also had a great emotional connection and I moved into his apartment. His place was a top floor sky-lighted studio right out of *La Boheme*. While staying there, he taught me to drive using a stick shift on his ancient Volkswagen. He did this by having me drive round and round and round The Coliseum. He also took me to the completely open and unguarded Coliseum at night. Rome , being a very conservative city with The Vatican exerting enormous influence at that time, had no gay bars. Guys met on certain streets, in certain movie theaters and in of all places, the Coliseum at night. Doing the deed there was quite a fantasy fulfilled. Peter was estranged from his homophobic Greenwich, Connecticut parents. He was studying architecture and planning to leave Rome in a few months to spend the summer perfecting his command of Italian at the Universitá per Stranieri in Perugia, which, loosely translated, means the University for Foreigners. Perugia is the largest city in Umbria with a huge student population often noted for its loose and varied sexuality. It came as no surprise to me that in 2007, an American student, Amanda Knox was accused of murder with sexual components. She was initially found guilty of but four years later in 2011, was acquitted. I followed Peter driving north on my Vespa, stopping for a few days in Florence, which back then was without the now-impossible hordes of tourists. I moved into his tiny dorm room and audited classes with him. Our romance continued between continents for many years thereafter. A few more years of school and apprenticeships, Peter was hired by Prince Karim Aga Kahn and became one of Italy's premier architects and was one of those hired to develop what was to become one of the most expensive resorts in the world and a billionaire's playground: Porto Cervo on the Costa Smeralda on the island of Sardinia.

After leaving him in Perugia, I continued driving north, stopping wherever I felt like it, including overnight in Verona, where in an ancient Roman amphitheater, I saw a production of the opera *Aida,* complete with elephants, camels, horses, and what looked like thousands of extras. I continued to Genoa, where having run out of money, I shipped the Vespa back to Brooklyn. Off I went by train and ferry to London, where a plane ticket waited for me, courtesy of my parents. I had made a deal with them to live at home and, with their financial support, return to school and get my teacher's license. This time, though, it wasn't pre-med. I changed my major to speech and theater, took two minors in education and psychology. This made my mother very happy, because in her mind a teacher would never be out of work. With a groan, I headed back to Hunter College, though this time at night school, in order to earn grades good enough to allow me to return to day school. Hunter at that time had two campuses. The one I'd gone to earlier in the Bronx was co-ed, and the one downtown on Park Avenue in Manhattan was virtually an all-girls campus, with 8,000 girls and forty-six boys. I was able to finagle my way into the downtown campus because there, in addition to getting much more classroom attention, I was also to get paid to build sets for all the school's productions. This being the early '60s, women were never considered for that work. Thus, the school became 8,000 girls, forty-six boys, and me.

Dr. Roberts, the professor in charge of the theater department, did not use women to play the male roles. I thought this a big mistake, but one that would benefit me to get roles in school productions. Unfortunately for me, working Off- and off-off Broadway union actors were hired for the male roles. That's how I met Michael Warren Powell, tall, dark, and handsome with cleft chin and a slight Midwestern drawl. He and I started to date, and through him a whole new world opened for me. Michael had moved to New York from Chicago with his best friend, future Pulitzer Prize-winning playwright Lanford Wilson. Both were heavily involved in the burgeoning off-off-Broadway theater scene in Greenwich Village. One night Michael took me down to the Caffe Cino, a coffeehouse/theater owned by a wonderfully demented Sicilian, Joe Cino. Anyone who had a script and wanted to put on a play was welcome. No one got paid but a hat was passed for donations after the performance. When the houses were full during the run of a hit play, there could be a nice bit of change in that hat; but that was the exception rather than the rule.

Joe, a former dancer, was a short, cute teddy bear and loved being the sponsor of so much creativity. He was the host, waiter, janitor, and primary barista. Moreover, Joe was devilishly sexual, and part of the rite of passage for all gay (and some not-so-gay) newbies was to be blown by him behind the bar. Joe was in a long-term relationship with Jon Torrey, a tall, thin, blond electrician-handyman. They were both volatile and nuts and had many fights, some of them quite violent, but always got back together until 1967, when Jon accidentally electrocuted himself and Joe took his own life by hacking himself to death with a kitchen knife.

But while it lasted, Caffe Cino and La Mama ETC were fertile launching pads for a new wave of daring, cutting-edge playwrights: Sam Shepard, Tom Eyen, Robert Patrick, John Guare, and Lanford Wilson. The first play I remember seeing there was *The Madness of Lady Bright*, written by Wilson. Michael and Lance, as his friends called him, shared a furnished apartment in a run-down apartment building on Broadway and 101st Street, then not the gentrified area it is now. Their neighbor was playwright Robert Patrick, a fixture on the same scene and, in time, a force in the emergence of gay off-off-Broadway theater. Lance and Michael had no source of income except for rare, part-time office work and whatever was dropped into the hat at the Cino.

Many times, their electricity was turned off, so an extension cord was run out the window and into Patrick's apartment. When things got so bad that they couldn't pay the rent, I, who had inherited my grandmother's 1955 Buick Century, became the midnight mover as they snuck out of the building to move into another crappy one.

Around this time, Bruce Becker left Honey Waldman for a younger, very attractive woman who was more connected to showbiz. An acrimonious divorce followed. When they divvied up their property, Bruce got the Tappan Zee Playhouse. Honey got custody of me, as well as a property they had bought a few years earlier: a cast-iron bank building at Bowery and Bond Streets in lower Manhattan. She and Bruce had planned to turn it into a ninety-nine-seat Off-Broadway theater; now she had the time to do it. In 1963, the now-fabled Bouwerie Lane Theatre opened at 330 Bowery. Honey was one of the first impresarios to gentrify that seedy area. The Bouwerie Lane's first production was *The Immoralist*, a daring play for its time, based on a novel by André Gide that concerned a gay archeologist who marries a woman in an effort to squelch his true urges. It starred Frank Langella in one of his first leading roles. The theater's biggest hit was a "transfer" from the Cino of the small musical *Dames at Sea*, starring then-fifteen-year-old Bernadette Peters. Needing help, Honey asked me to work finishing construction of the theater, and I did just about every job possible for her, from cleaning the toilets to running the box office to becoming the house manager. I finally earned my Actor's Equity card by stage-managing an awful play she produced. I was poor, but in the Manhattan of the 1960s, who needed money? Apartments were available everywhere for a song. Many were dumps, with peeling paint, no hot water, flimsy front doors, and fire escapes that invited break-ins. But all that mattered to me was fleeing the family house in Brooklyn and living in New York.

An apprentice I'd known at the Tappan Zee Playhouse, Bob Olson, invited me to share an apartment he'd just found, a fifth-floor walkup on First Avenue, a few blocks from Hunter. Half the rent and expenses were about $70. It supposedly had two rooms, but we never found the second one. On one wall, starting in a corner, was a kitchen sink, followed by a bathtub, followed by the oldest, three-burner, cast-iron range I had ever seen, and finally a half-sized refrigerator right next to the front door. The bathroom was closet-sized, with a toilet and a skylight – no sink. Somehow, we made it work. Bob had a real bed, and I bought a sofa bed, which, when opened, was less than a foot from the bathtub. Bob, who worked for a fabric-design company, definitely had the gay gene, and he made the place quite livable. In order to pay even that little, I had a part time job at a seafood restaurant a couple blocks away called Oscar's Salt of the Sea. I was a cashier/host and I saved money by eating one meal from the menu – anything but lobster was allowed and every now and then an edible take home gift from the kitchen. The restaurant was on the first floor of an older but clean apartment building two of whose tenants were Elliot Gould and then wife, Barbra Streisand. She had all her packages from Bergdorf-Goodman, Bonwit Teller, etc. delivered to the restaurant.

When she came in to pick up the packages, there was no small talk, but always a thank you.

I don't know how I ever managed to get my college degree – instead of four years, it took six – but I did, in January of 1965. I got my K-to-12 teacher's license as I'd promised my parents and became the worst substitute teacher in modern history. I could never manage to follow the absent teacher's lesson plans; instead, I brought arts-and-crafts supplies and taught the kids how to make trees from rolled-up newspapers, Hawaiian leis from crepe paper and thread, and other simple craft projects. I put a permanent end to my teaching career when I became assistant to the press agent at the Mineola Theatre on Long Island. This 1927 movie house had become a home for regional stage productions. One of them being *West Side Story*, with future Oscar winner Christopher Walken. Chris played Riff, leader of the Jets, one of two opposing street gangs. During the original Broadway production, Jerome Robbins, the show's director, and choreographer had encouraged the actors who played the Jets and the Sharks to hate their onstage rivals, thus making the onstage drama more realistic. That tradition had lived on in future productions, including the one in Mineola. During one of the fight scenes, Chris found himself bleeding from an actual knife wound. Pro that he is, he went on with the show.

Through my old boyfriend John Greenleaf, I made some extra spending money babysitting for the most sophisticated and gorgeous woman I'd ever met: his pal Cam Walter, the very beautiful, blond wife of New York's premiere cocktail pianist, Cy Walter. A high-class party girl, Cam was a regular at New York's swankiest clubs, which she dropped in on once the three kids had been put to bed under my watchful eye. Cam drank Chartreuse, the pricey French liqueur, and introduced me to Black Russians and all sorts of things that were alien to Brooklyn, such as amyl nitrite, also known as poppers. I'd found my own Auntie Mame. I met many of Cam's friends, two of whom, Yetta Cohen and John Whyte, owned a restaurant/hotel/night club complex right on a tiny marina on Fire Island called The Boatel. Entry-level show business jobs never pay enough and being an assistant publicist at Mineola Theater was no exception. Knowing I was always short of money, Yetta asked if I would like to work there on weekends, and of course I said yes. Fire Island is a thirty-one-mile-long sand bar off the south coast of Long Island; at its widest point it measures no more than two city blocks. On it are seventeen communities, each with its own personality. Two almost adjacent ones were Cherry Grove and Fire Island Pines (aka the Pines), both of which were gay. Cherry Grove catered then and still does now to a more racially diverse and less financially well-off crowd. In the mid-'60s, if you said you were going to Cherry Grove, it automatically meant you were gay. If you said you were going to the more expensive and chic Fire Island Pines, one could kinda stay in the closet because there were a fair number of straight women and their spouses there, as well as lipstick lesbians who could pass. The Pines was also a celebrity magnet, with beachfront houses owned by boldface names both straight (Henry Fonda, Mel Brooks, David Frost and fiancée Diahann Carroll) and gay (Calvin Klein, Jerry Herman). Liza Minnelli hung out there before she was to become a lot more than Judy Garland's daughter. Thanks to Yetta, John, and Cam, I had my own summer of love by bartending at their Blue Whale Bar on Friday and Saturday nights and waiting tables for Sunday breakfast and dinner. I found myself amid swarms of beautiful and attainable men. I was also the service bartender at a new phenomenon called Tea Dance, an excuse to drink on Sunday afternoons and dance on a large outdoor deck by the dock. I made a lot of money and banged my brains out, staying awake by gobbling Dexamyl, a popular amphetamine "diet" drug, of the time, aka speed. The cash I made paid for most of that year's expenses.

Back in Manhattan in September, I commenced another year of working part time for Honey at the Bouwerie Lane, stage-managing here and there, and any other itinerant theater work I could dredge up. By the summer of 1966, I was newly installed at the Northland Playhouse, a summer-stock theater in Southfield, Michigan, in suburban Detroit. I had been hired as assistant to the theater owner. He was seldom there, which meant I was responsible for most day-to-day operations. I had to deal with silent-film icon Gloria Swanson, legendary star of *Sunset Boulevard*, former mistress of Joseph Kennedy, and a true horror. Her film career long kaput, Swanson was working with a hack named Harold J. Kennedy, a self-styled producer, director, and playwright. He wrote horrible plays for her, which he then directed horribly, including a real stinker, she was doing there, *The Inkwell*. Now, it's one thing to be awful to people who are making big salaries, but it's another to curse at and abuse the unpaid apprentices. Swanson still expected the perks she had known as a big movie star; but this was summer stock. One Saturday night, because I could sew, I joined the apprentice stage crew staying up all night reupholstering a couch because it wasn't the *exact* shade of white that she demanded. Swanson went out of her way to terrorize everyone, but the apprentices found ways to get even. If she was trying to take a nap or chill in her dressing room, that's when the set-building noise got really loud. Harold J. Kennedy was an asshole too, and you never get good service by being mean and talking down to people. After the play closed and he and Swanson were packing up to leave, Kennedy came into my office to get directions to the airport. At the time, Detroit had two. I deliberately sent him to the wrong airport so they would miss their flight at the other one and would be forced to ride the bus with the hoi polloi cast to the next theater. Happily, among the actors to play Northland that summer were two talented and lovable actresses, then-sixteen-year-old Georgia Engel and Marcia Lewis. Later I would help boost them both up the ladder by replacement-casting them on Broadway in *Hello, Dolly!*, Georgia as" Minnie Fay", Marcia as "Ernestina." Georgia was later boosted a bit further into real stardom when I got her the role of Georgette on TV on *The Mary Tyler Moore Show*. Marcia became a Broadway star, too, and was nominated for a Tony for her role of "Big Mama" in *Chicago*. Sadly, both these marvelous women have passed away. On one of my last Saturday nights (or I should say very early Sunday mornings) at Northland, while the apprentice crew was changing the sets and lights, I was in the office at three a.m., and realized that I'd been much more than a hired lackey. All summer long, I'd been acquiring the skills necessary to produce – at least in summer stock.

After Northland back in New York at the Cino, I met the Tony Award-winning producer of Edward Albee's *Who's Afraid of Virginia Woolf* and *The Boys in the Band,* Richard Barr. Richard was a smart, funny, and terrific guy. We dated for about six months. Richard was about 6' tall and had bright red hair everywhere on his body except on his head. He looked like a friendly orang-utan. I was not physically attracted to him, but he was fun and great company to hang with. I also knew that if I was dating him, something good might come of it. Don't call me a slut. I considered this "sexual networking" and it worked, because through Richard I met Michael Kasdan, who was Barr's general manager. One day Michael called and told me that Westbury Music Fair, located about 32 miles from Manhattan on Long Island, was the granddaddy of all East Coast regional stock theaters, was looking for an assistant manager. I applied and got the job. Westbury is a 3,000-seat theater-in-the round that exists to this day as the

"Theater at Westbury." It has played host to practically every pop star, famous comedian, rock band, and touring musical in the business. During my year there, the hit attractions included Italian crooner and mob favorite Jimmy Roselli (a guaranteed sellout for two weeks at a time); Bill Cosby, in one of his earliest solo shows; and Richard Chamberlain, then TV's handsome *Dr. Kildare*, in *West Side Story*. I flirted with him, but he was in the closet and ignored me completely.

However, I had many happy nights with the actor who played Bernardo. Luckily, we had a place to meet; one of the job's requirements was that I live in a trailer in back of the theater.

I was looking forward to meeting Judy Garland, who was scheduled for a six-night engagement. She was playing a long string of concert dates in order to pay off a whopping IRS debt. Every show sold out almost immediately. The day of her opening at Westbury, she and her husband and manager, Sid

Luft, showed up during a rainstorm four hours earlier than expected. The stage door was locked and unattended, and they had to walk a long way around to the front. By the time they made it inside the lobby, they were dripping wet. I rushed out to greet them, full of apologies. Sid was very nice and understanding but Judy was pissed. I led them to the star dressing room, which was in fact a luxurious suite of rooms, and offered them tea and whatever else they wanted. It seems my cure for being rained on was always a cup of tea. Four hours later, the tech rehearsal was set to begin. I felt so bad about them getting soaked that I bought Judy a huge bouquet of roses. I knocked on her door and asked if I could come in. Judy opened the door. I handed her the flowers and offered one more apology. She grumbled something, took the roses, turned around – and unceremoniously dumped them in the wastebasket. I don't think she knew I saw this, but I was devastated for a while. A couple of hours later, and right on time, Judy, who was notorious for keeping audiences waiting, sometimes for hours, got a ten-minute standing ovation as she walked down to the stage, before saying a word or singing a note. I no longer was devastated and felt so lucky to just be there. She was in terrific form that night and every night except one, when she had no voice whatsoever. But she couldn't cancel; she needed the money. That voiceless night, she walked out, told the audience she could barely sing, but would do her best and she did. Everyone was on her side, and the standing ovation was even longer than the one on opening night. I was in tears, like much of the audience.

Not yet a star but a frequent visitor to the theater was Barbara Walters, then a reporter on *The Today Show*. Her husband, Lee Guber, was one of the owners of Westbury Music Fair. Unlike Lee, Barbara ignored all the little people, including me, the lowly assistant manager. When my boss Brian Avnet, who was only one year older than I, moved to California, Lee and his partners promoted me to full manager status. My job was to oversee the opening of, and then to run, their newest venue in Absecon, New Jersey, near Atlantic City. It was a summer theater called Smithville Music Fair. An un-air-conditioned, circus-like tent, it was many steps down from the year-round, hard-topped Westbury. We opened with a budget production of *Ilya, Darling*, the stage musical version of *Never on Sunday*, the film that had won an Oscar for its Greek star, Melina Mercouri. Unfortunately, our terribly miscast leading lady was the still beautiful 1950s MGM movie star dancer, Cyd Charisse, who had never been known for her singing or acting. By now she was more of a nostalgia figure than a star. We wound up giving away half the tickets.

If Cyd could hardly draw flies, we had no shortage of other insects. Smithville Music Fair was built adjacent to New Jersey wetlands. Swarms of nasty mosquitoes invaded the tent every night. I watched in distress as the entire audience slapped and scratched at bare arms and legs. In an attempt to combat this, we rolled down the tent's side flaps at about six p.m. every night and sprayed the entire space with industrial-strength Raid, which killed every living thing inside the tent. But as soon as we raised the flaps to usher in the audience, a whole new crop of mosquitos flew in to replace their fallen brethren, and the slapping and scratching began again. The venue deservedly closed a year or so later. I did not last a full season. Before the end of that summer, I was working for the biggest and most important theater producer at that time and arguably of all time, David Merrick.

CHAPTER 3

DAVID MERRICK: WORKING FOR THE ABOMINABLE SHOWMAN

In 1967, when I lucked into a job with David Merrick, then the most powerful theater producer in the country, Broadway was much more important in American pop culture than it is today with, of course, the exception of *Hamilton*. Its economy was also locally driven and not almost totally dependent on tourists as it is now. Straight plays had a chance to succeed without television or movie stars as leads. There were daily newspaper columns devoted to theater. *The Ed Sullivan Show*, a TV variety show that almost everyone in the country watched on Sunday nights, was the most important platform for introducing new talent such as Elvis Presley and the Beatles to American audiences. Also on his show were scenes from new musicals, thus drawing people from all over the country to Broadway. This in a way mirrors what Tony Awards TV specials do now. Many of the biggest pop tunes of the era came from those musicals. Singers, even the biggest of them like Frank Sinatra, would rush to record the songs before a show opened, so you entered the theater knowing some or all the music and lyrics. In those days New York theater was controlled by a handful of exceptionally powerful men: Broadway producers David Merrick and Alexander Cohen and theater owners the Shuberts and the Nederlanders. They were like the early movie moguls, autocratic and beholden to no one. They were stars, with individual visions and quirks. Backed by their loyal investors, they produced shows alone, not by committee or corporation. Off-Broadway there was Joseph Papp and his New York Shakespeare Festival. Recently I saw a musical that listed twenty-seven "producers" above the title of the show. Those people listed were really investors with great billing. But in the 1960s, the line "David Merrick Presents" meant exactly what it said. His investors were not called producers and were limited to about a dozen privileged people who invested in almost every one of his shows. If you didn't invest in one, you might not be invited back to invest in the next one. Merrick's reputation, which he helped stoke, was that of a mean, avaricious show-business titan. He loved saying, "It is not enough that I should succeed, others should fail." Merrick came from modest means in the Midwest and moved to New York to reinvent himself. By the time he died in 2000, he had racked up eleven Tony Awards and a producing resumé that included *Gypsy, Hello, Dolly!, Oliver, The Roar of the Greasepaint – The Smell of the Crowd, Irma la Douce, I Do! I Do!, Promises, Promises*, and *42nd Street*.

As a twenty-one-year-old who was obsessed with Broadway and dreamed of finding a way in, I saw Merrick as a god. Michael Kasden, whom I met through Richard Barr and who had recommended me for my job at Westbury, again came through. He called and told me that Jack Schlissel, Merrick's general manager, needed a new assistant. Referred by Michael, I called, and an interview was set up. See, my Sexual Networking did work.

Off I went to David Merrick Productions on the top floor of the St. James Theater building on West 44th Street. I stepped out of the elevator, and walking across a shabby, old linoleum floor I realized that no expense had been wasted or even spent on décor. I passed a very small, wooden love seat (the only furniture in the reception area) and approached the front desk which was sealed off by a plate of dirty glass; it had a window that slid sideways so the receptionist could talk to visitors. Almost any decent piece of furniture on the premises had come from the scenery of Merrick shows that had closed.

I was pointed toward Jack's office. There he was at his desk, a decent looking, slightly overweight, middle-aged guy in a drab plaid jacket and tie. As the second most powerful man on Broadway, he was frequently hated and feared. But he liked me and my resumé, and after a brief discussion, I walked out with a job. But as a friend once told me, "God does not give with both hands." In this case He had gifted me with the job opportunity I was waiting for and, simultaneously, with a draft notice. I was to report to the Army induction center at Fort Dix, N.J., in two weeks with a change of clothes and personal toiletries. Not only was I morally opposed to the Vietnam War, I had no intention of letting that job with Merrick be snatched away from me. I knew what to do. For once being gay was going to be an asset. I made an appointment with a psychiatrist. We spent that first hour talking, and by the end of it she had no doubt that I really was a fag. She gave me a letter stating that I was gay and under her treatment. Letter in hand, I showed up at the draft board. I was taken into an interview room for some questioning. In a few minutes I was turned down by the U.S. Army, but soon would be accepted warmly by the "Abominable Showman", as theater critic Howard Kissel called him in his same titled 2000 Merrick biography. It was an ideal entryway into the highest level of commercial theater production in New York. By day I was Jack's office slave; by night I became company manager of arguably he biggest smash on Broadway: *Hello, Dolly!*, then in its fourth season and starring the incomparable black singer Pearl Bailey, then known mostly for her night club work. I had to do the payroll, deal with the cast and crew, handle all the day-to-day problems, and make sure box-office receipts and ticket stubs were tallied accurately after each performance. One part of my job description was left out until the day I started work. All the office assistants had to learn to operate the switchboard, and we're talking about a device straight out of Lily Tomlin's "Ernestine" sketches on "Laugh In". Our normal operator, Sylvia Schwartz, was a vivacious widow from the Bronx. Simultaneously she worked the board and dealt with house-seat requests for all Merrick shows on Broadway and the road. She had the fastest hands in town and could talk to three people about house seats while fielding calls for the whole office. Hard as Sylvia tried to teach me, and boy, she tried, I was a complete failure. But she had to go to lunch or pee and eventually no one else was around and I had to step to the challenge. For the first few minutes I was fine. Then three or four calls came in at one time, and I lost it. Out of despair and frustration I yanked out all the cords, disconnecting the entire office, blocking all incoming calls as well as one from Merrick himself. Thereafter I was banned from this duty. There was a God or Goddess.

I didn't know it at the time, but Jack was a deeply closeted gay man. Several times a day he would pound on the intercom buzzer and snap, "Get in here," scaring the shit out of me. One morning I was summoned inside for a stern lecture. He said, "Look, I know where you were last night, and you shouldn't be there." I had gone to a gay cocktail bar in the Broadway district, where people sat around a piano bar singing show tunes. Perfectly fitting for an employee of David Merrick, right? Jack didn't think so. "When you work here you live in a fishbowl. Everyone knows everything you do. So, watch yourself." I didn't say anything; I was flabbergasted. How did he know this? Like Merrick, did Jack have spies all over town, too? I listened to his command, but I didn't change a thing. Eventually, Jack quit Merrick and opened his own general management firm. By then I had moved to Los Angeles. I was back in New York for the holidays and went to a party at the apartment of Richard Barr, the Broadway producer I had once dated. There was Jack, looking better than I had ever seen him, sitting in a chair with an adorable younger guy on his lap. Coming out had made him a much happier man. But it made me kind of sad that Jack could not be himself all those years with Merrick, whom I later realized was more than a bit homophobic. "Faggot" and "cocksucker" were two of his favorite words. I should have had a clue.

But Jack at his toughest was no match for Merrick's secretary, Helen Nickerson, an attractive, "well-born" woman from San Francisco society stock, in her fifties. She controlled all access to him and ran his very complicated life. An example of this complication was that Merrick owned two apartments in the Ritz Tower building. One was for he and his latest wife, Etan Aronson, and their baby daughter, Margueritte. The other was for his six-year-old and developmentally challenged older daughter, Cecilia, and her nanny from his second marriage to Jeanne Gibson. Helen was more like Cecilia's mother than her real one. According to Helen, Merrick rarely visited her at home and the only time I saw the little girl was when the nanny brought her to the office a couple of times. Helen wielded a veneer of class and taste along with very proper social skills, and she made people think that Merrick possessed those qualities, which he definitely did not. Helen resembled Cerberus in manner if not in looks; she had the foulest mouth ever. I had never heard a woman use the words "fuck" and "cunt" before. Helen sized me up for a couple of weeks and gave me a few "tests," and luckily, I passed. We became great friends.

Her boss, of course, was the star. For the first few weeks Merrick would whisk by my desk and say nothing to me except, "Is Jack in?" His demeanor was intimidating. He was always dressed better than you. I never saw him in anything less than black or gray or muted pinstriped suits and custom-made shirts. He wore that uniform everywhere, even poolside at the Beverly Hills Hotel. His mustache was dyed jet-black to match his toupee, and his office looked just as tacky: red velvet sofa and chairs, red carpeting, red flocked wallpaper and heavy red drapery. It looked like the interior of a heart. Clearly, he didn't have innate class; it was pretend class. Merrick aspired to be a tall, handsome WASP instead of a shortish, balding Jew from St. Louis. He had not wanted to be who he was, so he transformed himself. He changed his last name, Margulois, before he ever became famous. He always had theatrical ambitions and married the first of his five wives, Lenore Beck, who had inherited family money. He used Lenore's wealth to invest in a Broadway comedy of 1949 called *Clutterbuck*. No one remembers it, but five years later he produced his first Broadway hit, *Fanny*. If it sounds like he was a scoundrel and fortune hunter, only the former was true. According to Helen, Merrick continued to be on good terms with Lenore after they divorced in 1963. Part of my job was preparing royalty checks for our investors, and Lenore received not inconsiderable money from Merrick's hit shows on a regular basis. Lenore and Helen talked often, and Helen, who would badmouth anyone who crossed her or Merrick, only said nice things about the first Mrs. Merrick. Five years after *Fanny* came *Gypsy*, which Merrick had conceived. It made him an above-the-title Broadway star.

Of course, he was a brilliant businessman, and he flew back and forth between New York and London, working out deals to transfer shows both ways across the Atlantic. Merrick earned much acclaim for having founded the David Merrick Arts Foundation; a not-for-profit organization created ostensibly to nurture "experimental" theater on Broadway. In truth, it was a way for him to avoid paying taxes as he workshopped plays whose box-office potential was in question. If successful, those shows could be switched to profit-making status, or if another show of his was tanking he could switch it to his Arts Foundation and keep it going and get a tax loss, too. Merrick was very loyal to certain people, such as his head stagehands, and used them over and over. The person at the top of his loyalty list was Charles Blackwell. He was a tall and imposing black man with a mild but commanding manner. He had one of the most important jobs in the entire company as production stage manager for all new Merrick musicals. I met Charlie during the run of *Promises, Promises,* the hit Burt Bacharach/Hal David musical. He taught me all about casting for the theater and helped me understand how to evaluate musical performers as they auditioned. He was always there to help me, even when I was casting musicals in California. Merrick and he met when Charlie was a dancer in *Fanny.* For some reason Merrick took a liking to him and from then on sought out his counsel and advice on a whole world of show and non-show business matters. Perhaps on Charlie's advice, Merrick did something totally out of character, which I never knew about until I read Howard Kissel's book. In 1957, Merrick was producing a new musical, *Jamaica,* which was to star Lena Horne and Ricardo Montalbán. According to Kissel there had been rumblings about integrating the all-white stagehands union. There were no black union stagehands on Broadway at that time. For some reason, and it was not because of Lena Horne who at that time stayed far away from racial issues. Merrick demanded from the union that the backstage crew consist of at least five black stagehands, or he would continue the show's out of town tryout forever and not come into New York. Knowing Merrick could and would do something like this, the union caved, and backstage Broadway was integrated at least for a short time.

Unfortunately, Merrick was such a control freak that he planted spies in every company to give him the dirt – especially dirt on actors, who as a class, he hated. He was blatant about it: "Fuck 'em, fuck 'em." Sometimes he was purposely vindictive, as when he produced a comedy called *Four on a Garden*, directed by Abe Burrows. It wasn't very funny, but at least it starred Carol Channing and Barry Nelson, a charming and funny successful Broadway actor. At least, Barry was the costar when it opened out of town. The play wasn't working, so Merrick decided to fire Barry, who had a run-of-the-play contract, and hire one of the fathers of TV comedy, Sid Caesar. But he refused to pay off Barry, which under union rules he was required to do. "Fuck him," he said. "Let it go to arbitration." He knew that if it went to arbitration, he would lose, and Actor's Equity would demand he pay up. But Merrick did things like this just to stir up shit. His logic was, maybe we'll luck out and he'll get another theater job, in which case Merrick would not have had to pay the full amount. Nelson eventually got all his back salary. When a bill from a costume maker for twenty grand would cross Merrick's desk, his response would almost always be a snarled, "I'm not paying this! It's outrageous!" Three or four months later, after endless futile calls, Merrick via my boss Jack would offer ten.

They'd eventually settle for some drastically lower amount than the work was worth. Years later, when Merrick's star had fallen and he was trying to stage a personal comeback with the musical of *42nd Street,* all the old vendors he'd cheated demanded payment up front. Karma can be a bitch. His reputation as a monster was well-earned. But he fumed rather than exploded; he turned red a lot and could be utterly charming if he had to. He also had a wicked sense of humor. I knew he liked me, and he showed it in funny ways. This being the sixties, my contribution to the changing times was to wear jeans or chinos, a sport jacket, and a tie, rather than a suit to work. When the mild shock of this wore off , I took the next step and walked in one day with red, white, and blue patent leather shoes with three-inch platform heels, black jeans, a white shirt, black tie, and as a sport jacket, a blue and red U.S. Marine dress uniform jacket with large brass buttons. As I walked into the office that day, Merrick was stepping out of his. He stopped in his tracks, took a step back, and said, "No matter what anyone says, you wear that." To this day I have no idea if it was a compliment or a dis.

One thing is for sure: He changed my life by bringing Pearl Bailey into it. Pearl was then the star of *Hello, Dolly!* – the show's fifth star on Broadway in the role originated by Carol Channing. In 1967, a year of deep racial strife and rising social consciousness, Merrick had made a brilliant move by producing an all-black touring company of *Dolly!* It starred Pearl as the widowed matchmaker Dolly Levi, and another legend, the great Cotton Club star and singing bandleader Cab Calloway, as Horace Vandergelder, the moneyed grouch she wants to marry. Originally this was strictly a road-show company, but audiences including President Lyndon Johnson adored it. Pearl dragged Johnson onto the stage one night, and he took bows with her and the cast when it played in Washington, D.C. Pearl had never been better as a performer, and Merrick made the most of it. Betty Grable, the 1940s movie star and pin-up fantasy for millions of American servicemen, was then playing Dolly Levi on Broadway. Merrick announced to her that Pearl's company was going to move to Broadway, and he was exiling her and the rest of the cast to the road. If she wanted to keep working, she had little choice. Betty went out and Pearl and company came in with relatively little fanfare. Overnight the show went from all-white to all-black and opened on Broadway on November 12, 1967. It was one of the smartest moves Merrick ever made. Predictably, Pearl was a smash. The show's continued success delayed 20th Century Fox's release of the Barbra Streisand film version, because contractually it could not premiere until the Broadway run had ended. With Pearl selling out at the St. James Theater, the show could seemingly run forever, while Betty Grable's national tour did very well, too. Merrick had already made two million dollars by selling the screen rights to Fox, and now he bargained with them and got an additional $1.85 million to allow Fox to open the movie in 1969.

For now, Pearl was the toast of Broadway. Very few black female performers of her day had reached the top rung of show business, but Pearl had climbed her way there. Unlike the most famous black star of them all, Lena Horne, who was fair-skinned, svelte, and a raving beauty, Pearl resembled Queen Latifah; she was darker-skinned, with a solid build, and was usually cast as the best buddy to the star. She had gotten her start in the late thirties by singing in small black clubs in Pennsylvania's coal-mining towns. The audiences were fairly raucous. In addition to singing, one of her talents was an ability to pick up tips without using her hands. That's right: Think low.

Pearl developed a great improvisational comic persona by trying to tame rude patrons. She also became known for her way with double entendre songs. Although she appeared in several movies, she was much better known as a recording star and top-rank night club performer. Then came *Dolly!* It got her on the oversize covers of *Life* and *Look,* two of the most popular magazines of the day. Unlike some other Dollys, notably the blandest and most boring of them all, Ginger Rogers, Pearl did a lot that wasn't in the script. She used her personality. Her hands were always in motion; she added little flourishes – "That's right, honey!" – that were pure Pearl. If she forgot a line, she would turn to the audience and say, "We've gotta stop this because I just forgot where I was." People loved her. But in her acting of the serious parts of the role, she was perfect. Her less attractive qualities offstage: interfering, managing, bossy, were perfect for Dolly. In my mind Pearl is still the "best" Dolly of all the Broadway Dollys, including Bette Midler in producer Scott Rudin's pre-covid production. For me, Bette was incredible and the most accurate casting of all. But Pearl wins the Dolly contest for me because she was a more fun and went off on audience loving unscripted riffs, while, surprisingly, Bette, who was known for her outrageous stage personality was more disciplined and constrained. Scott, by the way, is the only producer who approaches Merrick in terms of style and taste; and Merrick would be very jealous of Scott's success in movies and television. Unfortunately, when word of Scott's treatment of his office staff made headlines, he was "cancelled." Hopefully his cancellation will be brief. I don't mean to defend his ways. However, he was responsible for some of the best, award-winning, and most daring Broadway shows and provided thousands of jobs in the theater, from stars to stagehands to ushers. I firmly believe that show business is not a democracy and if you can't stand the heat, get out of the kitchen or the office. I cannot tell you how many times Jack, seeing a typo or mistake in a contract or letter, would crumble it up and throw it in my face. Of course, this wasn't pleasant, but I learned.

After the final curtain came down, Pearl would then return to the stage. She would introduce Cab, who sang his classic "Minnie the Moocher" song and then go home. Then she did fifteen minutes of her nightclub act including two or three songs. You got your money's worth out of Pearl – and nobody was enjoying it more than she. Sometimes she got carried away and would not stop singing to the point where the show crossed into expensive overtime. The crew was overjoyed, but Merrick wasn't. He ordered the stage managers to call out a warning to Pearl, and if she ignored it, they were instructed to get her off stage, whatever it took. Once, I saw the stage manager walk onstage as Pearl was still going strong. He pointed at his wristwatch with faux anger. Pearl made a joke out of it. "Oh! Mr. Merrick, that cheapskate, doesn't want to pay overtime, so I gotta go!" And she left to another standing ovation. For all that, Pearl was a star fucker. The producer was always "Mr. Merrick." She thought he was God. Pearl was also very deferential to Cab Calloway, who was there for the paycheck. He did his job, stayed out of Pearl's way, and did not get involved in any backstage drama. Pearl was a Republican and very tight with President Nixon, who gave her the title of America's "Ambassador of Love." She was close to the Reagans as well. But Lyndon Johnson was a Democrat, and she loved him too. For the lesser lights in the cast, you had better stay

on Pearl's good side. A big drama queen, she could turn accidental or imagined slights into major wars. Many of those on her shit
list felt that life was too short and did not renew their contracts
or gave notice and left. But if an offending person kissed her ring
and offered a good enough apology for the supposed misdeeds, a
pardon was granted.

Keeping Pearl smiling was crucial. At that time, Zsa Zsa Gabor
was starring in a Merrick comedy, *Forty Carats*, directed by Abe
(*Guys & Dolls, How to Succeed in Business*) Burrows. Abe's son
Jimmy Burrows was the stage manager. Most people in the Merrick office thought very little of Jimmy and that he was there only
because of nepotism. Boy, were they proven wrong when just
a couple of years later after he moved to California, he became
the most successful director of half-hour comedy in history. His
shows included: *Cheers, Taxi,* and *Will & Grace.* But at that time,
part of our jobs were "to keep the black cunt (Pearl]) and the
white cunt (Zsa Zsa]) happy." What the two ladies never knew
was that "Mr. Merrick" couldn't have cared less about them. They
only represented money to him. He was not in awe of stars at all,
except in terms of how much they could do for him. I dealt with
Pearl while Jimmy had Zsa Zsa. I definitely got the better gig.
On my first night on the job, Jack took me backstage before curtain to introduce me as the new company manager. Pearl could
not have been more gracious and invited me to join her after the
show for late supper at Sardi's restaurant, at that time *the* place to
be seen after a show. I would wait with a glass of white wine in
her tiny but luxurious dressing room while she finished changing
out of her costume and into something appropriate. Then as we
were leaving, she would grab a small fist full of Soma pills (a mild
muscle relaxer), offer some to me, and we were on our way a few

doors down to the restaurant bit high. This became our ritual. We sat side-by-side in one of the more prominent banquettes as A-list celebs from Henry Fonda to Henry Kissinger came to our table to pay respects to her. I was introduced as Joel Thurm from "The Merrick Office." I knew they couldn't have cared less who I was, and I easily and quickly adapted to being celebrity adjacent. This was big-league time for the Brooklyn farm boy who had wanted more than anything to get out of Brooklyn and be somebody. Then the limo provided by the show would arrive to take Pearl to her place on the Upper East Side and then me to my apartment in Greenwich Village. On one memorable occasion, she made the trip downtown to my place. I was home with amoebic dysentery, sick as a dog. The doorbell rang. Somehow, I dragged myself down the hall and opened the door. In front of me was Pearl, wearing a sable coat over a trim pants suit. She was accompanied by her assistant, Dodi, a younger, put upon-looking woman. "How ya feelin', darlin'?" purred Pearl as she gave me an overwhelming hug. She had come to nurse me back to health and to make my apartment a bit less squalid. In her satchel were cleaning supplies and everything needed for a big pot of chicken soup. I went back to my street-found overstuffed chair and drifted back to sleep. A few hours later I woke up to find them gone, a spotless apartment, and the soup still warm on the stove.

Jack was not so happy with me. He really wanted his assistant to be a hard-assed mini-him, and I could not be that guy. Jack would cut off his nose to spite his face to get his way. One day he called me into his office and said, "Look. I can't stand working with you anymore, so you have a choice: Start working with Biff in production and reopen our casting department as our casting director with a fifty-dollar-a-week raise – or get fired." Samuel

"Biff" Liff was Merrick's executive in charge of production, third in the organization after Merrick and Jack. When I replied that I did not know anything about casting, Jack countered that I did, but didn't know I did. It seems that during our morning ritual I'd proven myself. I usually came to work about a half hour early, having picked up bagels and coffee; this was pre Mr.Coffee or Keurigs in offices. We talked about what show or movie I had seen the night before. I guess he remembered these discussions and my opinions of the actors in our shows and my suggestions for their replacements when those actors contracts expired. I said yes to the "offer," and without any prior experience, I found myself in arguably the most important casting job in New York theater. One of my first casting assignments did not work out exactly as planned. Along with *Hello, Dolly!* one of our hit Broadway shows was *Forty Carats*, a light comedy about a romance between a fortyish woman and a twenty-year-old man. Julie Harris had won a Tony for her performance, but she left when her year-long contract was up. To replace her, I suggested a movie star from the golden age of MGM musicals who was now not doing much of anything, June Allyson. Merrick liked the idea, and she was hired. During rehearsals, several us noticed that she was often thirsty, and that her husband was always nearby with a glass of water. You can probably guess that it was not water in that glass, but vodka. No one said anything because rehearsals went well, her performance and ticket sales were excellent, and once we opened, the audiences liked her. This lasted about a month. Then her husband began calling in to report that June was "sick." She began to miss more and more performances, to the point where her understudy, Iva Withers, was on stage more than she. It became obvious we had to make a change. We spoke to her agents, and it was agreed that she would leave the show "for health reasons" as soon as we found a replacement.

At this point, *Forty Carats* would be on to its third leading lady. The likelihood of a big star taking the role was very slim. I called a manager who had been bugging me for months about using his client, Zsa Zsa Gabor. I asked if she were available, and she was. Merrick gave his approval, but wanted to run it by the show's playwright, Jay Presson Allen. "How would you feel about prostituting the show to get a few more months run?" Merrick asked. Zsa Zsa, of course, was more camp than prestige. She was the best-known member of a trio of Hungarian sisters (Eva and Magda were the others) who were a sixties version of the Kardashians, famous for being famous. Both Zsa Zsa and Eva had had minor film careers, but Zsa Zsa was the most notorious because of her serial marriages to wealthy men. Eva, on the other hand, turned out to be a very talented comedienne and spent six seasons starring on the sitcom *Green Acres*. Zsa Zsa's husbands included Conrad Hilton, the hotel mogul, and the movie star George Sanders (*All About Eve*). Zsa Zsa, beautiful, blond, dripping in jewels, and reasonably funny, due largely to her thick Hungarian accent made numerous appearances on *The Tonight Show*. The show's then host, Johnny Carson, had a field day interviewing her.

Jay Presson Allen, a very classy woman and a much sought-after writer for movies and theater, thought over Merrick's query with a pensive look on her face. Finally, she said that if he thought Zsa Zsa would sell tickets, then go ahead and give her the part. Zsa Zsa showed up for rehearsals about fifty pounds heavier than anyone had seen her before. One of her requests was that she had to wear her own wardrobe in the play. No dummy she; remember the nine rich husbands? She brought in what must have been every item in her closet and had the wardrobe department let out all her clothes, each of which she wore once or twice on stage, then took home. In the end, everybody won. Zsa Zsa had a lead role on Broadway and free alterations for her entire wardrobe, and Merrick had a costume expense tax deduction. But best of all, the show stayed open another six months.

I too was in Merrick's good graces. I had cast a new original play, a psychological thriller called *Child's Play*. It was the surprise hit of the year and won five Tonys, including best actor for Ken Howard (*The White Shadow* and later president of SAG) and best featured actor for Fritz Weaver (*Marathon Man*). Both were my original and only choices. As soon as the reviews hit, there were long lines at the box office. Merrick wasn't around; he had flown off to Los Angeles to work on some movie deal. By now Merrick was just cruising along on Broadway. What he really wanted was to break into Hollywood. Nevertheless, he told Jack to thank me for the work I did on *Child's Play* - and to give me a fifty-dollar-a-week raise, unheard of in this office. I was now up to $350 per week.

Pearl was still in *Hello, Dolly!* but that was about to change. She called, said she had great news, and asked me to meet her after the show. That night in the back of her limo, with girlish glee she told me that ABC had made her an offer to host her own TV variety show: fifteen episodes on the air for mid-season next spring, no pilot. If I wanted, I could move to Los Angeles and work on her show. I asked what the job would be? "Assistant to the associate producer," she said, assuring me that it was an important job and a way to learn the television business. Although this was a very big decision, it took me little time to give her an answer, which was yes. That was the first of my many leaping-before-looking decisions. Merrick had lost his interest in producing new content for Broadway and was obsessed with becoming a major Hollywood force; in the process almost buying the film studio 20th Century Fox. He had the dough, and he should have bought Fox because his big debut as a producer was a highly publicized flop, *The Great Gatsby* starring Robert Redford and Mia Farrow. But for me there was nothing but touring productions for the next season and only one big musical on the horizon. It was a musical version of the 1959 Marilyn Monroe, Jack Lemmon, and Tony Curtis black-and-white comedy movie, *Some Like it Hot.* The book for the musical was not nearly as funny as the movie script, and I was also terrified at the thought of finding an actress for the Marilyn Monroe part. When it finally made it to Broadway, *Sugar,* as it was called, did not get good reviews. It limped along for a season and was a money loser for Mr. Merrick. Recently, I heard that Marc Shaiman and Scott Whitman, who wrote the musical *Hairspray,* are doing their musical version of *Some Like It Hot* for Broadway. They are wisely avoiding the Marilyn Monroe problem by planning to cast their Sugar with a Black actress. Brilliant! But this never would have happened back then even if I had thought of it. Diverse casting was still many years away. After the failures of *Sugar* and *The Great Gatsby,* Merrick lost his mojo and spent years in the wilderness until his next huge hit, a big splashy stage version of the movie *42nd Street.*

I was very interested in learning TV production, and since my best friend had moved to Los Angeles the year before and offered me living space at his house in Laurel Canyon, why not do it? All I would have to do was sublet my apartment, pack some clothes, and rent a car. I said yes. Shortly after that, I left for California on a high.

CHAPTER 4

CALIFORNIA, HERE I COME

After I'd accepted Pearl Bailey's offer, the move to L.A. happened quickly. It was a hard decision to make, for not only was I giving up the best theater-casting job in New York, but also a one-bedroom, rent-controlled apartment in the West Village with a working fireplace, eat-in kitchen, and unobstructed views to New Jersey. I sub-let the apartment to an old and trusted friend.

After making sure I replaced myself with an excellent casting director, Geri Windsor, whom I had known from my Tappan Zee days, I gave notice at Merrick's.

Two weeks later, on September 28, 1970, I was sitting with my best friend from New York, Mark Saegers, who had moved to California two years before. I had stayed with him on a short vacation a year before this and loved the place. Mark had been in movie theater advertising but really wanted to be a director. His father died, leaving him enough money to last a lifetime, and he moved to Laurel Canyon to follow his dream. As we shared a poolside joint and gazed into the twilight over the view, all seemed perfect. My new home was the downstairs bedroom and bath of Mark's cute little house in the hills above West Hollywood. At that time Laurel Canyon was in full flower. It was the least affluent of all the L.A. canyons, but it epitomized the then laid-back, ungentrified Southern California lifestyle. It felt like the East Village, but with hills and trees and flowers and views. Also like the East Village, it had a somewhat unsavory reputation. When I told someone, I was living there, I was asked: "But aren't you afraid of the drug dealers?" I replied, "Of course not. It makes shopping easier". That said, less fortunate were the four people found dead in a modest house a decade later Wonderland Avenue, one of the Canyon's main streets. The police said the Wonderland Murders, as they were called, were drug related. John Holmes, the porn star, aka Johnny Wadd, was tried and acquitted of participation in the murders. He and these events became the basis of two feature films: *Wonderland* and *Boogie Nights.* Our other neighbors included real and wannabe actors, musicians, filmmakers, basket weavers, and all sorts of artistic types. Laurel Canyon also was the epicenter of pop music in America from the mid-1960s through the mid-'70s. Frank Zappa, Jim Morrison, and some Doors, the Byrds, Buffalo Springfield, Jackson Browne, two of The Monkees, all the Mamas and Papas (though John and Michelle Philips decamped for the much tonier Bel Air when they got rich), Carole King, Carly Simon, Joni Mitchell (*Ladies of the Canyon,* anyone?), Crosby, Stills, Nash, and Young all lived there. The Canyon vibe was in its own way exclusive but not expensive. A car, which was virtually mandatory in Los Angeles until Uber and Lyft appeared, was unnecessary here. Everyone could hitchhike safely up and down Laurel Canyon Boulevard. Mark's house was less than five minutes from the Sunset Strip, which at that time had many music clubs and recording studios. I used to drive by Carole King's house thinking we were linked somehow because she had babysat my two cousins in Queens.

I took to Los Angeles life immediately. I bought the ultimate California car, a 1965 Mustang convertible, and began what was to become my new lifestyle. I got up early, had breakfast, went to the studio, lit up a joint on the way home from work, had dinner, and went out with friends or tried to get laid. It was now October and *The Pearl Bailey Show* would premiere on ABC in January, as a mid-season replacement. We rehearsed and taped the show at the Hollywood Palace, a few doors north of Hollywood and Vine. This big old

Spanish-revival building, a former burlesque house, had been the shooting site for many TV shows, including its namesake variety show. While none of us knew it yet, this was the end of variety shows as we knew them. *Laugh-In*, which had debuted in 1968, ushered in a newer, hipper, faster-paced form of TV variety. The vaudeville-style format, which appealed to an older, more rural demographic, was fading in popularity. *The Hollywood Palace* had already been canceled; *The Andy Williams Show* and *The Ed Sullivan Show* were next on the chopping block. Pearl's show was passé on arrival. I should have done my homework. For now, however, I was excited to be starting my first job in TV. But I was not prepared for the chill that greeted me inside the studio. As I soon found out, when the star wants someone around, in this case me, that person goes on the payroll, regardless of whether he or she is needed. There was no real job for me, and the production staff brushed me off as one of Pearl's posse. I was finally given work doing music clearances. This entailed calling those agencies or lawyers who represented the songs that we wanted to use on the show and negotiate their prices. That took no more than a few hours of the week. The only creative part of the job was to suggest other songs when the ones we wanted were too expensive or otherwise not available; often I was listened to. The rest of the time I had to try and appear busy. Since Pearl was living at home with her husband and children, she did not need me for company. Except for seeing each other at the studio, we spent no time together; no more late-night suppers at Sardi's, no laughing in the limo. I began thinking all this was a big mistake. Eventually I snapped out of it realizing it was too late to go back and that I had to make the best of this not-so-great situation.

Fortunately, there were at least a few things to do and see in what was then the sketchy and tacky heart of 1970s Hollywood. One day out of boredom I went shopping at the department store on the corner. I tried on a shaggy brown Beatles wig, looked in a mirror, liked what I saw, and walked back to the studio with the fucking thing on my head. I believe that is called shoplifting. It wasn't until the producer's secretary asked me if I was rehearsing for Halloween that I realized I still had the wig on. I was lucky I hadn't been arrested. I walked right back to the store and put it back on display.

Regardless of the shaky ground our show was on, Pearl held forth like the opinionated, headstrong woman she was. Her focus was entirely on the show and she was the boss. She involved herself in everything and got her way even if her judgment was not the best. I remember her telling the costume designer that she wanted to wear a certain dress in a particular segment. Told that it would blend in with the color of the set, Pearl wouldn't yield. She wore the dress and all you could see were her face and hands while the rest of her disappeared into the scenery. Nevertheless, there was much to be learned in this job, and I was determined to absorb all of it. I went to every rehearsal, sat in the control room during tapings on Friday nights to learn what everyone did in there. I spent Saturdays at ABC's studios to watching the all-day editing process. I made good friends with the set designer, Ray Klaussen, costume designer, Pete Menefee, and the director, Dean Whitmore. They understood my position and were very kind to me.

One aspect of Pearl's show was truly magical. I got to see and often interact with some of the greatest performers of that time and the eras before: Lucille Ball, Louis Armstrong, Tony Bennett, Perry Como, Bing Crosby, Phyllis Diller, Leontyne Price, Jimmy Durante, Ella Fitzgerald, Carmen McRae, Peggy Lee, Steve Lawrence and Eydie Gormé, Liza Minnelli, Gregory Peck, Joan Rivers, Kate Smith, the Supremes, Ike and Tina Turner, Sarah Vaughan, Ethel Waters, Andy Williams, Debbie Reynolds. Even David Merrick made an appearance. Watching them close-up was worth the whole mistaken job.

Just before the Thanksgiving break in production, Pearl asked if I wanted to go to New York with her by train. She had a major fear of flying. Never having taken a long train trip, I thought it would be great fun and a way to spend time catching up with her and restoring our former relationship. Instead, Pearl spent all her time in her compartment with her faithful assistant, Dodi, working on a book she was writing, while I read in my tiny little private compartment called a couchette. It had a large window and a very comfortable wide seat which when manipulated properly tuned into a very comfortable single bed. We did have some unexciting meals together but that was about it. The views from the observation car were wonderful but the most interesting to me was using the toilet. When I picked up the toilet cover, I could look down and see the actual train tracks going quickly by. Use your imagination to figure out where all sorts of body eliminations wound up. I guess there was no Enviornment Protection Agency at that time. Feh!! I spent Thanksgiving with my family, saw a few friends, then made some excuse to Pearl about why I could not travel back with her and flew home to L.A.

The first few shows aired to less-than-stellar ratings, and the handwriting was on the wall for cancellation. By early spring, all the shows had been taped and the numbers continued to drop. Most of the staff left for hiatus, the downtime between production cycles. But since Pearl was still coming into work and I was still being paid, I figured I would show up as well. The show's imminent demise was quite evident to all, but Pearl refused to admit defeat – at least outwardly. One day we got into some silly squabble and in the heat of our argument, she summarily fired me. I was relieved to be thrown off the sinking ship. The next day Dodi called and asked me to come into the office; Pearl wanted to see me. She greeted me warmly and handed me a little red jewelry box from Van Cleef & Arpels. Inside was some useless but expensive trinket. With no apology, she asked me to come back to work. I grew a pair on the spot and said that while I was grateful for her help and friendship, this was not a good situation, and I was not coming back. I left the box behind. It turned up the next day on my doorstep, so what the hell, I went to Beverly Hills and exchanged whatever it was for a bamboo-shaped gold ring.

On May 8, 1971, ABC aired the final episode of *The Pearl Bailey Show*. We didn't speak for years, but I'm happy to say we reunited in 1982, and I was able to repay her for being a great friend and changing my life. It was now 1982 and I was Vice President of Talent and Casting for NBC, and we were preparing a live broadcast version of Carson McCullers' 1950 play, *The Member of the Wedding*. Both on Broadway and in the film version, Ethel Waters, one of the earliest black movie stars, played the lead role of a maid who develops a very close, parental relationship with a twelve-year-old tomboy in a small Southern town in 1945. During *Hello, Dolly!* Pearl had told me that Ethel Waters was her idol, and that she yearned to someday play that part. Since NBC needed a star to anchor this production, I suggested Pearl for the role. The producers were not enthused. They brought up her by then well-known heart condition, her reputation for being difficult, and their fear that Pearl might not be up to the challenge of mastering the lines of a long play in a relatively short rehearsal time, then performing it on live TV in front of an audience with no stopping for retakes. Remember, Pearl was famous for her ad-libs, not for delivering a script as written. I was adamant however, and finally they offered her the role, pending a meeting to be held in my office.

It was time for me to demonstrate how I had grown and matured. Pearl showed up early for the meeting. She looked great, not physically changed except for an additional pound or two, and seemed to be the same person I had known and loved many years before. For several moments we just stood there, then I began to get very emotional and tear up. She grabbed me in a bear hug until my sobbing stopped and I dried my eyes and composed myself; so much for growing up and maturing. She again told me it would be her dream-come-true to do this role. Predictably, she charmed the producers when they arrived, and they gave her the job. That was when the troubles began. Two weeks into rehearsals, Pearl could never get through a scene without stopping to have a line thrown to her. The live air date was coming up very soon, and she had not improved. I went to see her after a rehearsal and told her of everyone's concerns. She paused, then offered up a story about Ethel Waters in rehearsal for the original play. It seems that Ms. Waters had the same problem with learning her lines. When confronted about it, she reassured the producer by saying: "When the fucking begins, I'll be there."

Pearl told me the same was true for her, and I believed her. I had seen many actors' adrenaline kick in and come alive the moment they faced an audience. The producer and director were not convinced. They proceeded to hire an understudy who would be in costume and standing by offstage if Pearl screwed up. Well, Pearl indeed did show up when the fucking began. Her performance was flawless. She never ad deviated from the script, nor missed a cue or a line. This made me very happy.

After *The Pearl Bailey Show* fell apart, I dropped by studios and networks in L.A., hoping to find work as a casting director. I could not get arrested. No one gave a shit that I'd been David Merrick's casting director; the excuse was always that I did not know the Los Angeles acting pool. Then, from out of the blue, I got a call from an old friend, New York producer Morton Gottlieb. He was coming to town for a meeting with James A. Doolittle, who ran the Greek Theater and the Huntington Hartford Theater in Hollywood. The Greek, which then had about 4,000 seats, was a smaller version of the Hollywood Bowl, which had 17,500. Both were open-air amphitheaters. The Huntington Hartford (now called the Montalbán) was a medium-sized legit theater that presented recent Broadway fare; the Greek booked music and comedy star attractions, usually for week-long runs. The night before he met with Doolittle, I had dinner with Morty and regaled him with Pearl Bailey stories. Knowing I was out of work, he offered to ask Doolittle if there were any positions open at the Greek or Hartford. The next day Morty called. It turned out that there was a position. The production manager for both theaters had just left, and Doolittle needed a new one. I met him and got the job.

I worked there from the winter of 1971 to the spring of 1972, but it was a mixed blessing. Doolittle and I were like oil and water. He was a disgusting man on many levels including being a liar, a cheapskate, corrupt, and had a very bad comb-over. His version of arm candy was a wife who dressed like a zaftig Russian hooker. It was widely believed that through his political connections in downtown L.A., he held the lease on the Greek for one dollar per year. The city owned the property; Doolittle's service was to provide cultural enrichment for the city. An enormous amount of money poured into the Greek, and a lot of it went indirectly into his pocket. I found this out when the head stage-hand offered to have the Greek's construction crew work on the renovations I was doing on the house I had recently and unexpectedly purchased. He told me that he and other stagehands had been doing this for Doolittle for years. Appalled at what to me was just another form of thievery, I declined the offer and told him that this practice would stop right now, and that I would look over his crew's time sheets with a fine-tooth comb. This did not endear me to him nor Doolittle. Doolittle kept things looking somewhat kosher by fulfilling his commitment of cultural enrichment for L.A. by presenting one opera for one week per season at the Greek. While I was there, it was soprano Dorothy Kirsten in *Tosca*. The sets looked like they were dragged out of some high-school basement. The rest of the theater looked pretty ragged as well; Doolittle was too stingy to pay for improvements. Music agents were wary of any deal they made with him. He'd promise one thing, but the contract would say something else. By the time the contract arrived, it was often too late for those agents to book their clients elsewhere.

There was almost always behind-the-scenes drama. We booked Ike and Tina Turner, with the superb Black comedienne Moms Mabley as the opening act. Moms' stage persona was that of a toothless old woman in a house dress and floppy hat who told very dirty and very funny jokes. The show was terrific, and the enthusiastic audiences were something rare in L.A., ethnically diverse. In one of their classic numbers, *I've Been Loving You Too Long*, Tina treated the microphone like a penis. The audience loved it, but on opening night Doolittle was hysterical over what he called "an immoral display." "What have you done?" he demanded. That meant it was my fault. "I can't have that. The city will take this theater back. I could lose the lease!" That's what he was endlessly and needlessly afraid of; he wasn't morally outraged by Tina. He insisted I make Tina take her gestures out of the number. I tried to point out how silly that would be, but he was wouldn't give. "Okay," I said, "I'll ask!" Of course, I knew what the answer would be, but I went backstage the next night and embarrassingly talked to their tour manager, Rhonda Graam, who just looked at me in disbelief. I did the same the next night with the same result. Finally, rather than change anything in the number they cut it entirely, shortening the show by almost twenty minutes. At the end the audience booed, and the following night the cut number was restored. And guess what, Doolittle didn't lose the lease. We took a chance on Liza Minnelli, who at that point was still known mainly for being Judy Garland's daughter, even though she had won a Tony and was Oscar-nominated as well. Ticket sales were not good. When she came in for her sound check she asked me how the shows were selling. "Not as well as we'd hoped," I said. "But once you're onstage with the lighting, you'll only be able to see the first section of the audience, and that will be full." Timing is everything, and shortly thereafter, when the movie *Cabaret* premiered in 1972, Liza would not be having a problem selling tickets again.

The purchase of my first home came out of necessity, not desire. Mark Saegers, my friend and host, had not gone far in his ambition to be a director. His only credit was a porn scene that he shot outdoors in an isolated part of the canyon with his new, top-of-the-line, 16 mm film camera. Because his father had left him all that money, he didn't have to work. He smoked weed all day and watched TV. That inheritance eventually changed him from a bright, energetic, funny, and life-loving person into someone I would not recognize.

I knew I had to get out of there and find my own place. Mark's friend Derek, a real-estate agent who also lived on the street, came to my rescue. "Why don't you buy that house on the corner, the yellow house that you pass every day?" I told him I'd never thought of buying a house; that was for grown-up, settled folk. Derek said buying and selling houses in California was different from New York and I could easily sell it whenever I wanted. We took a tour of it. It was a little cabin with the entrance directly on the street. It wasn't in great shape, but I have a good visual sense and I could see that it had great possibilities. I leapt once more without looking and decided to buy the house. One little problem was how to pay for it – an astoundingly low $22,500 even in 1971. The first thing I did was to call my mother and ask for a $2,500 loan towards the down payment of $5,000.00. She said I did not need a loan; she would just give me the balance of my Bar Mitzvah money. "But didn't you give me all the money when I went to Rome?" I asked. She said she hadn't, and when I asked why, she said, "Because I knew you would spend it." You had to love her logic. I solved my also unaffordable mortgage problem by taking the empty space underneath the house to build a separate one-bedroom "guest" apartment for myself while I rented out the rest of the house. My first tenant was an old school chum and now-successful Los Angeles playwright, Harvey Perr. Having no money to spend, I furnished the house with discarded pieces of sets from shows at the Huntington Hartford. They included the bed that Carol Burnett and Rock Hudson had romped on while performing the Merrick musical *I Do! I Do!* But Jimmy Doolittle every day was still an ordeal. One day he called me into his office because he was unhappy with something I'd done. The confrontation turned into an ugly "you can't fire me, I quit!" situation. Fortunately my unemployment application went unchallenged and I would be able to survive until whenever the next job came along. I also liberated all the unused Le Creuset cookware from the theater's massive kitchen as a going-away present to myself.

Speaking of Rock Hudson, he had been my teenage idol and a major crush thanks to his work in *Giant* and the movies he made with Doris Day. We kind of once almost got together. Mark Saegers, who despite his failings had great real estate smarts, had moved from the house we'd shared to a much larger one, with a huge living room capable of holding twenty-five to fifty people comfortably if standing. One night the room was full of gay men, most of who worked in "the biz." We gathered to see one of the first full-length, big-budget, gay-porn flicks, *Boys in the Sand*, soon to premiere at the local porn movie house. There was no internet then; I guess this was direct marketing to a targeted crowd to get the word-of-mouth started. Lots of liquor was poured, and I found myself standing just a few feet away from Rock Hudson. His being gay was an open Hollywood secret. I noticed that Rock kept looking over at me, and I began to do the same to him. As with most porn movies, the scenes got less and less interesting. But Hudson seemed more and more interested in me. He made a "follow me" motion with his head and I followed him up the stairs and into Mark's bathroom for some quick sex. Unfortunately, I was so anxious and nervous that my body below the waist would not cooperate. After all, he was ROCK HUDSON! Totally ashamed and embarrassed, I left the bathroom and went downstairs, where the movie was still playing, and took up a position far away from where we had been standing. I avoided being any place he could see me for the rest of the night. Years passed before I saw him again, which was in my office at NBC. We were casting a detective series, *The Devlin Connection,* which would star Hudson in what turned out to be his last series. He came to my office for meetings and auditions, and thank goodness, he did not remember me.

Following my dramatic departure from the Greek and Huntington Hartford Theaters, I began freelancing as a company manager and casting director. My former boss at Westbury Music Fair, Brian Avnet, came through for me. Brian had wisely moved to L.A. a year or so before and had the theater general manager field pretty much to himself. A general manager is hired by the producer(s) to deal with all the legal and business things. He also is the one who recommends actors and designers and negotiates their salaries, He was now general manager for two upcoming Los Angeles theatrical productions, an outdoor presentation of *Jesus Christ, Superstar* at the newly opened Universal Amphitheater, and a production of *The Who's Tommy* at the Aquarius Theater on the Sunset Strip, where *Hair* had just closed a two-and-a-half-year run. Brian handed me the *Tommy* LP and asked if I wanted to cast it. "How do you cast from an album with no script?" I asked. He answered, "I don't know. That's your job - figure it out." And I did.

I lucked out with the title role: We got Ted Neeley, one of the hottest (and sexiest) musical-theater leading men of the day. It was a modest success running for several months which was an unusual event in theater-adverse L.A. The show got excellent reviews, so much so that I called then choreographer Michael Bennett to see if he was interested in taking over the direction of the show with the hope of bringing it to New York. We had become friendly when I worked with him casting *Promises, Promises*; he was the show's Tony nominated choreographer. We flew him out, he saw the show, and liked it. But after a week or so, he turned down the offer. Just a couple of years later, he became a superstar director/choreographer with *Dreamgirls* and *A Chorus Line.* One very good thing did come about because of casting *Tommy.* An astoundingly beautiful dancer auditioned and got the role of "The Acid Queen". Her name was Annette Cardona, later to be known as "Cha Cha DiGregorio" the brunette temptress who takes John Travolta away from Olivia Newton-John during the dance at the gym in the movie of "Grease" and later starts the drag race in the concrete L.A. river bed.

When a new national company of *Jesus Christ, Superstar* was slated to open at the Universal Amphitheater as the first stop on a tour, Brian again called on me again to cast it. In the title role I again cast Ted Neeley, who looked like the Jesus of anyone's dreams. He went on to star in the film version, along with Carl Anderson, whom we used for Judas. Among our chosen chorus members was the future star of *Married ... with Children*, Katey Sagal, then eighteen and a complete unknown. Katey was a true hippie, which included unshaven legs and hairy pits. Her look worked for the director, Tom O'Horgan, whom I had first met when he was directing at the Caffe Cino and who went on to direct the original Broadway production of the smash musical *Hair*. But for budget reasons, we had to cut two men and two women from the chorus. While she had a great middle-range voice, it was not a necessary one for the show; Katey got cut. Enter her father, Boris Sagal, an important TV director. He called and offered to let me cast his next couple of projects if I put Katey back in. I explained that as much as I liked her, it was not my decision to make, but that I thought Katey was terrific and I would always look for other roles for her. Boris had a horrific accident with the spinning blades of a helicopter in 1981 while directing a TV movie for us at NBC. By this time, Katey had been one of Bette Midler's backup singing group, the Harlettes, and had played Mary Tyler Moore's best friend on a short-lived CBS series. Her agent arranged a general meeting for us, and I told her what her father had tried to do years before on *Superstar*. She got very emotional and thanked me for telling her the story. It made me feel good to be able to share something like that with her.

Before moving to L.A. I had asked all my showbiz friends to give me the names and numbers of people they knew who I could contact both for business and socially. One of those contacts was Wally Hiller, a respected talent agent with his own boutique talent agency. His clients included John Ritter (years before *Three's Company* made him a star) and Jean Stapleton, whom every family in America knew and loved as Edith Bunker on *All in the Family*. Wally was about forty-five and a classic handsome silver fox. Divorced, with four children, he had only recently come out. We began to date. He met my friends, and I met his. All of them on both sides worked in film and TV, not an unusual thing in Hollywood. That Thanksgiving he invited me to dinner with his ex-wife and their kids. In Brooklyn, a guy like me didn't have Thanksgiving dinner with his boyfriend and his boyfriend's ex-wife and their four kids. I thought this is what Hollywood is all about and decided to go with the flow. A joint or two helped the flow and we all had a great time. Wally's best gal pal was a groundbreaker in an almost all-male field. Ethel Winant was Vice President of Talent and Casting for CBS. No woman before had made it to such a high position in network television in a creative area. Having had a casting career herself in New York before moving to L.A., she was very impressed that I had been David Merrick's casting director and hinted several times that I would be a good addition to her staff at CBS. I invited Wally and Ethel to the opening night of *Superstar,* as well as producer Norman Lloyd who was considering me to cast a TV movie for PBS.

My chosen outfit for the opening: a pirate shirt that Errol Flynn had worn in one of his films and later lampooned by Jerry Seinfeld in the classic "Puffy Shirt" episode of *Seinfeld* I'd bought it at the studio clearing house sale of MGM's old props and costumes. To complement the shirt I wore beige suede, bell-bottom pants, and cowboy boots which was very much in style for the era. Brian asked me to drive his wife, Maria, to the opening night of *J.C. Superstar* at the outdoor Universal Amphitheater. Maria, only a slightly less va-va-va-voom Sofia Vergara, asked me if I wanted to do some blotter before we left for the show. For those of you who are as unfamiliar with drug slang as I was at the time, "blotter" is a small piece of thin cardboard that when licked you get a hit of LSD. Without asking what it was, I licked.

At the theater, I found myself in my puffy shirt sitting between Ethel and Wally on one side and Norman Lloyd and his wife on the other. With pending job offers on either side of me, I began tripping on acid for my very first time. Somehow, I managed to hide my condition from everyone and not embarrass myself. To my enormous relief, Ethel and Norman loved the production, particularly the casting. Because no one in her department in L.A had any New York theater experience or knew the many actors that were arriving daily from N.Y., she asked if I would like to work for her at CBS. And so, the very quality that had made me unable to get a casting job in Hollywood had turned into my greatest asset. Ethel asked me to call her at her office the next day. I jumped at the opportunity and must have called every two hours. Finally, she called back and explained that the CBS corporate wheels turned very slowly when making new hires but that I should relax. "It's going to work." And it did. P.S. I got the TV movie job for Norman Lloyd as well.

CHAPTER 5

LIVE FROM TELEVISION CITY IN HOLLYWOOD: BOB NEWHART MEETS THE *ROCKY HORROR SHOW*

Ever since I was a child, I'd heard an exciting phrase announced over and over on TV: "And now, live from Television City in Hollywood ..." Along with the famous black-and-white logo of an eye, that line was the trademark of CBS, known as the Tiffany of TV networks. Now I was working there. Wow! On my first day, I drove up to the guard at the gate. He had no parking space for me yet and told me to "take any unmarked space over there" as he gestured with his hand. After work, I returned to my car. I found a scrap of heavyweight orange paper on my windshield probably torn from a script cover, with a message written in very good cursive handwriting: "Do not ever park in this space again!" The space now had a name painted on it: CAROL BURNETT. On my very first day I had managed to piss off CBS's biggest star. Embarrassed as I was, it gave me a thrill just to walk through the front door. Walter Cronkite, "the most trusted man in America," was anchorman of the *CBS Evening News*, and our top-rated entertainment shows were lauded as high quality. On Saturday nights, people stayed home to watch *All in the Family,* followed by *M*A*S*H,* followed by *The Mary Tyler Moore Show,* followed by *The Bob Newhart Show,* followed by *The Carol Burnett Show.* Among those staying in were my friends and I. We timed our drug use to be in synch with CBS's programming. Just beer and a little weed till *Carol Burnett.* Then a quarter of a Quaalude pill at the beginning of her show then another quarter at the middle, and then the remaining half pill at the end. Then off to the happening disco at the time, PROBE. Our timing was usually perfect with all the Quaalude kicking in by then. Most of my friends ingested a few other drugs, which kept them going till dawn. I rarely made it past 2 a.m. On other nights our roster included *Gunsmoke, Hawaii Five-0, The Waltons,* and *Playhouse 90,* a live series of original dramas and comedies, many of which were later made into feature films.

I was excited to arrive at a time when CBS was changing the focus of its casting. Before Norman Lear and *All in the Family,* series TV was populated mostly with good-looking California types, perfect bodies, perfect hair, perfect teeth. But with the monumental success of *All in the Family* and its later spin-offs, *Maude, The Jeffersons,* etc., emphasis all over TV shifted to more realistic looking actors. My knowledge of the grittier New York theater crowd was just what CBS wanted. It certainly appealed to Ethel Winant. She was a genius at recognizing talent and for manipulating the network's all-male executives on both coasts – especially her boss, Fred Silverman, who was almost young enough to be her son. I saw the power that Ethel had along with the respect and admiration of the television community. It's exciting to be in such a position. Power is attractive. But Ethel's home life was a mess. She was divorced from her seldom-employed actor husband, Haim Winant. Her biggest worry was how to keep her oldest son, Bill, out of Vietnam. She spent much of her family time doting on him, while mostly ignoring his brother Scott (who weathered her neglect to become the producer-director of TV's *Thirtysomething*), and the baby boy of the family, Bruce, now a successful New York actor and voiceover artist.

Ethel lived for her career. She was as determined to bring talented women into the office as she was to put them on TV; in this sense, she was one of the industry's pioneer feminists. Her all-women department included Pam Polifroni, a blond divorcée in great shape from skiing at Mammoth Mountain every possible weekend. Pam cast numerous shows, including *Gunsmoke* and *The Waltons*, and worked on *All in the Family* during its first thirteen episodes. Once while she was on vacation, I had to cast an episode of *Gunsmoke* and it almost killed me. I knew none of the Western-type actors that Pam had at her fingertips. For Pam, working was all about making a good living for her and her teenage son, not about career-building. Then came Pam Dixon. She was about my age and whip-smart, with beautiful, long, straight brown hair. She looked like any one of Ted Bundy's victims. She drove a '63 Jaguar XKE coupe, one of the coolest and most phallic cars ever made. I had huge car-envy. She had worked for Ethel for about a year before I got there. Pam had one of the best casting gigs in Hollywood, casting the one or two weekly guest stars who were flown to Hawaii for *Hawaii 5-0*. Many actors wanted that gig because it included a second airline ticket, thus enabling husbands, wives, illicit lovers, or just friends to tag along. Also under Ethel's watchful eye, Pam cast the weekly guest actors on *The Mary Tyler Moore Show*. That series was Ethel's baby; she often said in print that it was her proudest achievement. In 1970, Ethel, during pre-production of *The Mary Tyler Moore Show,* picked up the phone and called Alan Burns, one of the two creators of the series. Up till then, CBS had been, to put it mildly, nothing but totally unhelpful to those producing the show. Although this was 1970, not 1870, the network insisted that Mary could not be a divorced woman; this being the most ridiculous of their demands.

Ethel told Alan that she loved the script and Mary herself, and offered to personally cast the show for them and run interference with the "boys" at the network. She did both jobs brilliantly. From then on, MTM Enterprises, the production company owned by Mary and her husband, Grant Tinker, paid CBS to have Ethel and her team cast all their current and future shows.

About this time, Jimmy Burrows moved to L.A. wanting to become a TV sitcom director. He already knew that the way this happened was to get a production company to allow him to observe the weekly directing process. I was casting *The Bob Newhart Show*, a three-camera show that rehearsed four days and then shot in front of a live audience on the fifth, with all three cameras running simultaneously. This process, combining theater and television, was invented by Desi Arnaz for *I Love Lucy*, and was exactly the kind of show Jimmy was looking to work on. He asked me how he could get in on this at MTM. I kind of laughed and asked him if he remembered that one of the last jobs he had before leaving New York was an assistant stage manager on David Merrick's musical version of *Breakfast at Tiffany's*, which starred Mary Tyler Moore and Richard Chamberlain and was directed by Jimmy's father, Abe Burrows. I reminded Jimmy that his job on that show was to be constantly at Mary's side getting her from scene to scene, costume change to costume change and guide her through the theater's basement to get from one side of the stage to the other. Mary liked him very much, which couldn't hurt. Her husband, Grant, being a very formal type of person, led me to suggest that Jimmy write a letter to him. He should let him know that he was now living in L.A. and would like to observe Jay Sandrich, *The Mary Tyler Moore Show*'s director, or any of the other directors working on a three-camera show.

Grant was thrilled to help, and Jimmy soon began observing Jay, the best director working in that format at that time. He was a very quick study, and soon after, Jimmy was directing episodes of all the *MTM* shows. Jimmy remembers this a little differently, but the result was the same and he went on to become *the* most successful director ever in his field.

My sole contribution to *Mary* was having Georgia Engel play the tiny guest role of anchorman "Ted Baxter's" date in a party scene. I had met Georgia many summers before, when she was sixteen and I was doing summer stock at the Northland Playhouse in Detroit. Georgia was now a working New York actress, having gotten great reviews playing a hilarious nun in a hit revival of John Guare's *The House of Blue Leaves*. One lazy day at Television City, Ethel asked me if I'd like to fill in for an unavailable Pam Dixon and read the upcoming *MTM Show* script. There was a small role as a date for Ted's. Her character name was "Georgette". Probably the only reason I thought of Georgia was the similarity of the names. Georgia Engel was at least twenty-five years younger than Ted, but her persona was such that one never knew her age. But I sensed that she and Ted would make a very good couple. I suggested her to Ethel, who asked if Georgia, now a relatively famous actress in New York, would take such a small role. Yes, I said, she would if I asked. In 1972, Georgia began five years on *Mary* as the naïve, bubble-headed but darling Georgette. In 1975, her character married Ted in one of the show's most highly rated episodes.

The third member of our team was Pat Kirkland, who was our eyes and ears in New York. She dealt mainly with soaps. Then came me, the new kid on the block in Television City. My first assignment was to cast *The Bob Newhart Show*, which was set to premiere in September 1972. *Newhart* would occupy the time slot directly after *Mary*, which almost ensured its success. Bob had long been loved as a deadpan, quietly befuddled, everyman comic, a part he played on some of the biggest selling comedy albums in history and on countless 1960s TV shows. He made his job look easy. There was none of the forced, in-your-face delivery that many funnymen have, no histrionics or pratfalls. Bob was a mild-mannered, polite man who could be anyone's favorite uncle. Past the age of eighty he became a recurring character on *The Big Bang Theory* and won his first Emmy. As a comedian, Bob gave us his side of phone calls with various crazy, neurotic, but unseen characters. He listened, occasionally nodded, or said "um," then, with impeccable timing, told his characters something obvious, true, and hysterically funny in its simplicity.

On *The Bob Newhart Show*, he played Dr. Robert Hartley, a psychologist living in Chicago married to the husky-voiced and wonderfully funny and in real life the delightfully foul-mouthed actress Suzanne Pleshette. For the first episode, I had to cast the members of Dr. Hartley's therapy group. I realized I had built up a mental storehouse of actor's names and faces, to be recalled automatically whenever I read a script. The show had a character called Lillian Bakerman, a ditzy late-middle-aged woman. For some reason I thought of Florida Friebus, who had played the mother in *The Many Loves of Dobie Gillis*, a CBS smash of the early '60s. We gave her the part. The role of Victor, a blue-collar construction worker, gave me quite a few headaches, because the actors cast kept leaving the show, requiring replacements. One of them, Mike Conrad, later became familiar as the roll-call sergeant on *Hill Street Blues*. Remember his catchphrase, "Now let's be careful out there". When he left, I replaced him with another actor who became a star on *Hill Street Blues* as well, Daniel J. Travanti as Lt. Furillo.

A few episodes later came a lost opportunity. The script introduced a possible recurring character of a beautiful stewardess who was dating Bob's neighbor Bill Daily, an airline pilot. John Crosby, an agent, suggested his brand-new client, a gorgeous Texas-born blonde. Crosby had a reputation for discovering beautiful actresses and I don't mean that in a wink, wink #MeToo manner. I met her the next day at my office. In walked the most stunning woman I had ever seen, with flawless hair, skin, teeth, and a knockout body. Her name was Farrah Fawcett. I scheduled her audition for the next day. There were about six other women, none of them in her physical class or having her charisma. The actresses' readings ranged from good to poor, with Farrah at the fair end. After the women left, we discussed what to do. The two very straight male producers decided to pass on Farrah and go with a very pretty actress who gave the best audition. I, the gay guy in the room, could not believe what had just happened. I then tried to explain star quality. I did everything short of threatening to quit if she were not hired. It didn't work. What I did not know was that the very talented actress who got the part was a former and possibly recurring girlfriend of one of the producers. She was talented and certainly pretty, but she wasn't Farrah. No one was at that time. Sometimes the part should *not* go to the best reader. It is the casting director's job to guide those who make the actual decision. In this case, they would not be guided. Had Farrah gotten the part, she undoubtedly would have been made a series regular and possibly unavailable for that series about three female private detectives that came around a few years later, *Charlie's Angels*. Coulda, woulda, shoulda. The second season of *Newhart* brought about a forced office move for me from CBS Television City, where all the top executives were, to CBS Studio Center, just over Laurel Canyon into "the valley", the San Fernando Valley, to be exact. It was like a move from Rockefeller Center in Manhattan to Queens. Studio Center was formerly Republic Studios, which had churned out B-Westerns and other potboilers in the '40s and '50s. MTM Productions rented studio space there. It made sense to be nearer to where the show was filmed and officed. It was a logical move, but still I felt kicked out of Ethel's protective nest and feared that out of sight would be out of mind.

This place had an entirely different vibe, a lazy, mañana feeling. The studio was practically a ghost town; the lot was big, but little was going on. The only regular shows shot there were *Gunsmoke, The Mary Tyler Moore Show,* and *The Bob Newhart Show.* Pam Polifroni worked there and was not thrilled to have to share a secretary /casting assistant with me after years of being totally on her own. I do admit to having been being a messy neighbor. Pam was much more experienced than I was and rarely had to meet actors before auditioning them. But I, being new to L.A., had to meet practically everyone, thereby taking up much of our shared assistant's time.

A much happier change involved the *Newhart* show's two new producers. Tom Patchett and Jay Tarses had written many great *Newhart* scripts and had been promoted to producers, now called show-runners. They were in their late thirties and looked like Mutt and Jeff. Tom was tall, trim, and good-looking in a WASP-y way; Jay was much shorter, rugby-player stocky, and Jewish-cute, with a mop of curly-brown hair. They were a perfectly matched pair until they subsequently broke up. Tom and Jay had wicked senses of humor, displayed by their choice of office décor. The room was about thirty by thirty feet. Instead of desks and couches and chairs, the place was designed to look like a huge kitchen. Remember, this was a movie studio, where feats like this can easily happen. There was a mock stove and sink, a frequently used foosball machine, and a large Formica kitchen table that they used as their desk. They said they liked to be reminded of their early days when they had to work in their family kitchens. Jay took an instant liking to me because of my casting the season before of Florida Friebus in *Newhart*. He, too, was a *Dobie Gillis* fan. I noticed that many shows used the same character actors over and over in the same type of roles. I thought how much better it would be to use new "old" faces, or just new ones that had not been seen much on TV. Patchett and Tarses were happy to let me fly actors in from New York, and because I technically worked for CBS, not MTM, I could almost always get the network to pay the costs. For many of these actors, *Newhart* was an early network TV job, if not their first. Their names include Henry Winkler, Raúl Juliá, Katherine Helmond, Ron Rifkin, Brooke Adams, Penny Marshall, Sharon Gless (her first comedy role), Teri Garr, and Veronica Hamel who went on to play the ice queen leading lady on *Hill Street Blues*. One of Bob's best friends in real life was actor/comedian Tom Poston. I'd been looking for a part for him for two years and when I found one, it turned out to be my best casting work; he and Suzanne Pleshette, both single, hit it off and married.

Ethel's boss and the head of programming at CBS was a brilliant young man named Fred Silverman. He was and still is the only person to have held that position at the three major broadcast networks. Silverman was short, doughy, and always had a rumpled, "I don't care about clothes" look. His whole life was television. He had started his career at WGN in Chicago and was hired by CBS when he was twenty-five. By 1963, when he was thirty-five, Fred had worked his way up to head of daytime programming. He turned those hours into a hugely lucrative success for CBS. By the time I arrived, he was head of all programming: morning, daytime, prime time, and late-night. Fred had turned things upside-down by getting rid of all "rural" shows: *Green Acres, Mayberry RFD, Hee Haw,* and *The Beverly Hillbillies.* Ratings-wise they were doing well and did not "deserve" to be cancelled. But Fred realized that those shows' audiences were becoming less and less desirable to advertisers. Let's not forget that network and now cable TV was and is all about the commercials; the programs are there to get you to watch the ads. Audiences were getting younger and hipper and less interested in the rural shows. Overcoming fierce objections, he replaced them with more advertiser-friendly hits, many of which became iconic: *All in the Family, The Mary Tyler Moore Show, The Bob Newhart Show, M*A*S*H, The Sonny & Cher Comedy Hour.* He was also one of the first programmers, if not *the* first, to actively mine these shows for spin-offs. *All in the Family* begat *Maude;* *Maude* spawned *Good Times; Mary* yielded *Rhoda* and *Phyllis.*

Hawaii 5-0's very popular villain, Wo Fat, scored his own detective series, *Khan!* It was my second casting assignment, and it did not go too well. Silverman was never what one would call culturally sensitive. *Khan!*, intentionally or not, was a modern version of the old black-and-white *Charlie Chan* movies, which later became known as paragons of "yellow face", casting white actors in Asian make up. The title character was a middle-aged Chinese detective whose assistant was his "number-one son." All the actors who played Charlie Chan in the movies were white men in make-up. Fred's timing could not have been worse. Following the lead of the black community, the Asian community had begun to make noise about the almost complete lack of Asians on television. My personal involvement with this phenomenon happened when doing *Starsky & Hutch,* where I had pretty much free rein to cast the smaller roles without producer approval. There were many roles whose only purpose was exposition – such as "I saw them go down the street." There was a small role described in the script as a middle-aged Jewish woman. I gave the role to a talented Chinese actress named Beulah Quo. After her day's shooting she came to my office with a rose. She showed me her character's hospital name tag, "Dr. Moskowitz", and said that had never happened before. At that time unless a character was specifically described as ethnic, it was always cast white.

I always tried to use actors of color in roles that were not specifically described as such. This was pointed out to me by a later assistant, Angela Campolla while casting a TV movie. She said that I told to her to go through the script and see where we could cast actors of color. Ironically, there were no minorities in the most successful movie I cast – *Grease!*

Charlie Chan was the Asian version of Uncle Tom. Kigh Dheigh, the actor chosen by Fred to play Khan, was a light-skinned man of British, Egyptian, and Sudanese roots. Born Kenneth Dickerson, he had specialized in playing exotic villains for years. His *Hawaii 5-0* character's race had never been an issue because of the multiracial population of Hawaii. But giving him the specific Chinese lead of a series was a different matter. Ethel had warned Fred that Mr. Dheigh was neither Chinese nor Asian and that someone might object.

Fred saw it as a non-issue and continued the series' development. As soon as the pre-show publicity for *Khan!* began, so did the shit storm. The show premiered on February 7, 1975 and was greeted with well-deserved terrible reviews. Various Asian groups pressed for an advertiser boycott. The show was cancelled after four episodes, which was almost unheard of at that time. Interestingly, Kigh Dheigh had insisted on receiving no billing, even though he was the central character. Perhaps he was prescient and foresaw all the problems that would kill the show.

I had far more fun working on a project called *The Bicentennial Minutes*. These one-minute documentary-style programs were broadcast every day in primetime from July 4, 1974, through 1976 to celebrate the forthcoming two-hundredth anniversary of the founding of our country. Each minute consisted of an on-camera celebrity narrator who introduced him or herself then recalled an event or a person who had made history on that same date during the American Revolution. When I wasn't casting a celebrity, the trick was to book a narrator who had some sort of connection to the story at hand. For example, for a Bicentennial Minute about newspapers and publishing, I managed to get Dorothy Schiff, publisher of the *New York Post*. Her minute began: "I am Dorothy Schiff. Two hundred years ago today, Benjamin Franklin began publishing the first real newspaper, to be printed on a brand-new, imported printing press. Soon after, many other newspapers began spreading revolutionary ideology throughout the colonies ..." She closed as all our narrators did: "I am Dorothy Schiff and that's the way it was." The line was homage to Walter Cronkite, CBS's immensely beloved and respected nightly news anchor, who always ended his broadcasts that way. Schiff was my second choice after Katherine Graham publisher of the *Washington Post* cancelled a few days before shooting. *The Bicentennial Minutes* were parodied by everyone from Redd Foxx to Sonny and Cher to Carol Burnett. I think Foxx's parody began: "I am Redd Foxx, and two hundred years ago today, Thomas Jefferson invented the first toilet bowl. Unfortunately, he forgot to include the plumbing necessary to make it work and pretty soon shit was all over Monticello ... I'm Redd Foxx, and that's the way it was." Ethel knew my long-term goals went beyond casting, so when she asked me to find the narrators, she explained that I would be present at the tapings, that I could make directorial suggestions and make cuts and rewrites to make the material fit the inflexible one-minute timing. The *Minutes* director was happy not to have to deal with the creative whims of the on-air talent. All this gave me a taste of what producing was like. When I met Charlton Heston ffor his *Minute* at the CBS artists' entrance, he seemed to think I was a slightly better dressed page. He handed me the keys to his Corvette and a twenty-dollar bill and asked me to "fill her up" while he went upstairs into makeup. As the OPEC/U.S. oil boycott and gasoline shortage were in full swing, filling her up promised not to be easy or quick, with long lines of cars waiting to gas up at most stations. And I was not good at using a stick shift. But while I may have irreparably damaged his gear box, miraculously I made it back just in time for him to do his *Minute*. He was surprised when the parking attendant started directing him, but he was one of the most cooperative of all our narrators.

It was Lewis J. Freedman who came me up with the idea for the *Minutes*. Freedman had built a terrific career as a public TV producer, winning many Emmys and Peabody Awards. I had done the casting for Lewis' CBS miniseries *The Lives of Benjamin Franklin*. It won twelve Emmy Awards, including Outstanding Limited Series. Each of the four two-hour episodes had a different actor playing Franklin at different ages. For the first episode with

Lloyd Bridges, I made the no-brainer suggestion of casting his son, rising actor Beau Bridges, as the younger Franklin and having him morph into his father halfway through the episode. For the younger version of his wife, I suggested to director Glenn Jordan that we fly out a new ingénue who I knew from New York. Susan Sarandon was just beginning to get some heat. This was only a short while before I cast her in *The Rocky Horror Picture Show*. For her older counterpart, I suggested a former blond bombshell from the Marilyn Monroe/Jayne Mansfield era, Sheree North. Despite her theatrical name, gorgeous looks, and bodacious body, North was a trained and excellent actress. Perhaps even more important, she had the same huge eyes as Ms. Sarandon. They were a perfect match. Ethel developed a serious crush on Lewis, who was around her age. He was a handsome man with salt-and-pepper hair and a small pot belly, and he was gay. He in turn put a full-court press on her to push *The Bicentennial Minutes* through CBS corporate, who were leery of the concept. Ethel worked her magic in knowing how to manipulate the suits. She called her old friends Paul Newman, Edward Asner, and Cloris Leachman and got them to narrate test minutes as a sort of a pilot. CBS Corporate gave the series the green light. But before they began airing and about six months into production, without telling Lewis or Ethel, they decided to change the minutes from unsponsored public service programming to a big profit center by getting Shell Oil to sponsor them. This made it much harder to get big names, because the actors were getting a token union-required payment; now, with a huge advertiser, many of them wondered why the fuck they should do this chump-change gig for Shell. I don't think they were wrong. So outraged was Dorothy Schiff that she called me directly – no secretary said, "Can you hold for Mrs. Schiff?" – and boy, did she rip me a new one. Eventually I think she believed me when I said that at the time she had taped her Minute, I had no idea there would ever be a sponsor. Lewis Freedman made out like a bandit financially while Ethel got zip, and no sex, either. I think Lewis tried to make it up to her by buying her a much-needed car to replace the ancient heap she owned. But come on, Lewis – a *used* Datsun B2-10? A small Mercedes or BMW sedan would have still been a pittance compared to the cash he earned because of her efforts. But who said life is always fair? After paying her off for her help, Lewis moved back to New York. Since he did not need her anymore, their relationship ended. The CBS portion of my con-tinuing relationship with Ethel would soon end as well. My salary was very low, and Ethel continually apologized saying that was the best she could do; she hadn't been able to get any more than that from the CBS bean-counters even though they were selling more beans than Heinz and making money hand over fist. To make up for it, she said that during down times, of which there were many, I could do outside work as long as it was not for any other TV net-work or somehow in conflict with my duties at CBS. Theater and feature film work were okay. An example of such work was defi-nitely not in conflict in any way with CBS. When my friend New York restaurant owner Joe Allen opened an L.A. location, I told him that I made a cake very similar to the wonderful chocolate fudge cake he served at his self-named restaurant in New York. He asked for a sample, and I made him a cake. He loved it and started buying cakes from me. Every day, I would get up, mix the batter, and put the cakes into my oven. Then I would do the shower and shave thing and get dressed. By that time, the cakes were ready to come out of the oven and into their pink cake boxes. I brought those boxes to the studio, and via the CBS messengers, sent them over to Joe's. No one at CBS cared and the cakes got so successful that after a few months, Joe needed more per day than the four I could fit in my oven at one time. Not being able to spend an extra hour at home and not wanting to get up an hour early, sadly my baking career came to an end. Joe got another vendor whose cake was very good, but with all due modesty, not as good as mine.

For as long as I live, I will be grateful to Ethel for letting me be part of a project that was to become iconc: *The Rocky Horror Picture Show*, then called *The Rocky Horror Show*, in its theatrical incarnation. I cast its first U.S. stage production, which was in Los Angles, not New York. I had heard about the ultimate in cult musicals from friends in London who saw it in its first performing space, a real old movie palace about to be demolished. Brian Avnet, who had hired me to cast *Tommy* and *Jesus Christ, Superstar,* came back to me with another offer: Would I cast a new musical that the record mogul Lou Adler was importing from London? I leapt at the chance. Adler had produced and developed the recording careers for the likes of Carole King, the Mamas and the Papas, and Cheech and Chong. He founded two record labels, Dunhill and Ode; under his auspices, the Mamas and the Papas recorded all their hits and Carole King made *Tapestry.* After seeing *Rocky* the year before in London, he bought every single right available in perpetuity. Actor and musician Richard O'Brien had written the book, music, and lyrics. As almost everyone now knows, *Rocky* concerns a mad transvestite scientist who creates a homoerotic Frankenstein: a blond, tanned muscle god. In that budding age of rock-and-roll androgyny, gay liberation, camp, and increasingly overt sexuality, *Rocky*'s arrival was well-timed. Rex Reed would later trash the show, declaring that it was "only for homosexuals" – this from the biggest queen in media. But history, of course, has proven him wrong. Even in its embryonic phase, the buzz of success was unmistakable. Adler planned to produce *Rocky* at the Roxy, a nightclub he owned on the Sunset Strip. It was a daring choice; At that time New York theater and press people had a serious prejudice against anything theatrical that came from L.A. But Lou's instincts hadn't failed him yet, and he was on the brink of one of his greatest triumphs.

The only actor from the British cast to come to L.A. was the star, Tim Curry. Rail-thin and rock-star handsome and sexy, Tim was extraordinary in the role. I had such a crush on him. To this day I remember his entrance from the back of the Roxy, whipping his head from side to side, as he pranced down the aisle singing "Sweet Transvestite." With each move of his head, a cloud of glitter, carefully folded into his dark, curly hair, sprayed the audience on either side of the aisle. The only theatrical entrance I can think of to match it is when Dolly Levi walks down the red staircase in *Hello, Dolly!* Since most musical-theater talent resides in New York, I called my two Manhattan casting-director friends, Linda Otto and Geri Windsor, and asked them to scour the city for me while I covered L.A. My first choice to play handsome good-boy hero Brad Majors was Broadway's Barry Bostwick, then living in Los Angeles. Barry turned it down; he had his eye on the movies and told me to remember him if a film version were ever made. Good if not famous actors were found for that and most of the other roles. Our notable catch was the still-obscure Meat Loaf, who walked into an audition and killed. On the spot, Adler offered him the dual role of brain-dead, zombie biker Eddie and science tutor Dr. Everett Scott. Three-hundred-pound Meat Loaf was nothing if not eye-catching. One night after the show I went backstage and there he was, sprawled out in a chair, pink, sweaty, arms and legs spread wide, and completely naked – an unforgettable sight. I'm just glad he was still alive, considering an onstage mishap. His character, Eddie, made his entrance out of a freestanding Coke machine, and at the first dress rehearsal, no one knew that the machine was completely sealed and airtight. He was in it for at least fifteen minutes before emerging; the door had stuck, and he was trapped. Only when he didn't jump out of it at the expected moment was the machine pried open. The gasping Meat Loaf was saved. *Rocky* ran at the Roxy for nine months, during which it became *the* show to see. Many celebrities came, including Elvis Presley. But the most important viewer was 20th Century Fox executive Gordon Stulberg. He offered to put up a million dollars and partner with Adler in producing a movie version. Among the more interesting people attached to *Rocky* then were the show's pianist, David Foster, a handsome young man who moved on to a huge career as the record producer of superstars, including Whitney Houston, Barbra Streisand, Michael Jackson, and Celine Dion, and is currently married to *American Idol*'s Katherine McPhee. On the lighting crew was the future junior senator from Minnesota, Al Franken. After I'd joined NBC, he and his writing and performing partner, Tom Davis, came in for a general interview for possible future casting. He giggled when I reminded him of where we had first met. Then they honored me with a perfectly executed performance of the old Abbott and Costello routine, "Who's on First." Possibly my biggest perk came when Lou released a cast album of the Roxy production on Ode Records. Linda Otto, Geri Windsor, and I were the first casting directors ever to receive billing on a record album. I hadn't gotten paid much for the work, but I got the credit I'd wanted.

After *Rocky* closed in L.A., casting for the movie began. It would feature almost the entire original London cast plus Meat Loaf. I was hired to cast the two American characters, Brad and his fiancée Janet. True to his word, Barry Bostwick wanted to play Brad – badly. His hoped-for film career had not taken off; instead, he was making a nice living playing leading man to star actresses like Jaclyn Smith and Lindsay Wagner in TV movies, and guest roles on series. As for Janet, I wrote only one name on my list: Susan Sarandon. In addition to being a highly skilled actress, I knew that Susan could and would go from virginal ingénue to major slut in less than thirty seconds which was essential in this role. I had met Susan and her then-husband Chris Sarandon in New York as they just starting out. Both their careers were heating up, but Susan's was white-hot. After playing the ingénue in the low-budget Peter Boyle hit film, *Joe,* she co-starred in a highly rated TV movie, *Last of the Belles,* alongside Richard Chamberlain and Blythe Danner. Chris had also scored big being nominated both a Golden Globe and an Oscar for his co-starring role in the movie *Dog Day Afternoon,* playing Al Pacino's transvestite lover. It was now time for the Sarandons to move to L.A. Susan then acquired hotshot new agents. When I called to set up an audition for *Rocky,* I was told that this project was not right for her at this time, and certainly she would not audition. As these calls were happening, Brian Avnet and I invited Susan and Chris, along with my manager friend Bob LeMond and his client Barry Bostwick, and up-and-coming director Randal Kleiser, to Laurel Canyon for dinner. I was still living in the downstairs guest apartment I had built for myself under the house. There was no dining room; it was spaghetti and meatballs on laps. At some point, Randal and Chris wanted to watch a TV movie called *The Killer Bees.*

They decamped the living room for the bedroom and the rest of us continued eating and drinking. Finally, all went home. The next day Bob called and asked if I was aware of what had gone on the night before. It seems that Susan and Barry had locked eyes and shared some very sexually charged silent moments. I did not know that Susan and Chris' marriage was not going well. Not long after, Susan left Chris, and she and Barry became an item. By now Susan knew of the *Rocky Horror* movie and was interested in playing "Janet." But she did not want to cross her new and powerful agents and felt she could not, per their instructions, audition for the role. If it were offered outright with no audition, that could be a different story. The devious Joel came out. I asked Bob to tell Barry that when he came in for his audition at the Roxy, he should bring Susan and just follow my lead. At his audition, I called Barry to the stage, where, ostensibly, he would read some scenes with me, which is the usual way readings happen. Before beginning to read, I said to Lou Adler and director Jim Sharman that since Susan was already here, wouldn't it be better if Barry read with a beautiful young woman rather than a balding male casting director in his thirties? Susan and Barry read the audition scenes brilliantly. Lou had no idea who Susan was. He asked her if she was an actress, and she laughed a bit and told him her credits. He asked her if she could sing. Not really, she confessed. Could she sing something? "I don't know any songs," she said. I suggested "Happy Birthday." She sang it in the small, pretty voice just like you hear in the movie and it appealed to Lou. He wanted her to play Janet.

Now I could call her agent and offer the role. A deal was made. Her affair with Barry fell apart soon after they had begun shooting in England. According to Bob LeMond, Susan liked to fuck upward, and Barry was merely a little-known actor. Her later relationships proved that out when she had relationships with director Louis Malle, David Bowie, and then back to actors with Sean Penn and Tim Robbins, with whom she had two children. The film opened to mostly bad reviews and quickly disappeared from movie screens. I found it vastly inferior to the stage version, and in what might be considered heresy, I thought several of the actors in the L.A. stage version were better than the original stage show Brits in the movie. By now *Rocky*, with most of the L.A. cast, opened and closed on Broadway in less than a month, despite the participation of Tim Curry and Meat Loaf.

Another character entered the *Rocky Horror* story and altered its course dramatically. A young marketing executive at Fox, Tim Deegan, had gone to Seattle to visit family. A local movie house had been showing *Rocky* at midnight screenings. Deegan saw fans lined up dressed like the characters in the film. He bought a ticket, and inside he saw mayhem break loose as fans in the film's costumes shouted lines back at the screen, pantomimed scenes, and threw props at the screen as if on cue. He convinced Fox to rerelease *Rocky* at midnight screenings throughout the U.S. They became rites of passage for many teenagers across the country. Suddenly America caught up to England and realized how much fun *Rocky* was. I no longer believe in coincidences, since a few years after the midnight screenings that made *Rocky* a fixture in pop culture, Tim Deegan began renting the very guest apartment in my house where the fateful spaghetti-and-meatball dinner had taken place. My fortunes had improved, and I could now afford to live in the larger upstairs half of the house. Even then, it was a while before Tim and I talked in depth and discovered that we had *Rocky* very much in common. In 2016, the Fox Network remade the movie as a live TV event, casting Laverne Cox, the transgendered actress from *Orange Is the New Black*, as "Dr. Frankenfurter", the Tim Curry role. I applaud Fox for trying, but unfortunately it was not good. Cox was very good when she was vogue-ing around as a super drag queen, but her line readings fell flat. It is a very difficult acting role *and* you have to sing! Tim Curry will always own that role.

Business had continued as usual in the casting department at CBS, but outside opportunities kept distracting me. In early 1975 I got a call from David Merrick's former secretary Helen Nickerson. Now his general manager, she asked me if I could help her and Merrick out by doing a day of casting in L.A. for a new Tennessee Williams play, *The Red Devil Battery Sign*. Anthony Quinn and Claire Bloom had already been signed for the leads. For a former theater student to have anything to do with a new Tennessee Williams play was a dream come true, even if it was only for a day without pay. I immediately said yes. The timing could not have been better; *Newhart* was on hiatus and all the CBS fall pilots had been cast. I reserved a large rehearsal room at Television City for a day and charged it to our department code, #7550. Ethel, both Pams, and I used this account number for everything from ordering office supplies to getting a dozen rental chairs for a Thanksgiving dinner, as Ethel did one year, and of course for sending cakes to Joe Allen's. CBS was making so much money that our use of this number was never questioned. I made a list of actors to contact to audition for the play. I had heard that a particular actor I was interested in now lived in L.A., but I could not find his agent or if he even had one. Actors' Equity gave me his home number, so I called him and set up an audition. He never mentioned having an agent. Almost immediately after he auditioned, an agent from the very powerful William Morris Agency, who happened to be the boyfriend of my co-worker Pam Dixon, called Ethel. The gist of the call was that I had seriously violated protocol by calling the actor directly rather than the agent. Further he threatened that all of William Morris would not deal with me unless some action was taken. I had no idea this was happening. The actor in question came in, read well, but did not get the role. I got back to my office and had a feeling something was up. Pam glared at me but said nothing. Ethel called me into her office for what was to be a come-to-Jesus moment. She dismissed the threat from William Morris as silly but said, "It's obvious you want to do other things, and what you want to do may not be compatible with CBS. Take your time, but you should start looking for another job." That hurt, but she wasn't wrong. While I liked what I was doing, my appetite had been whetted for more. Ethel had not given me a timetable for leaving, so I began to think of what I wanted to do next. I didn't have to think very long. Within two days I got a call from my longtime friend Linda Otto, then head of talent for Spelling-Goldberg Productions. She wanted out of casting to concentrate on producing documentaries. Linda simply said, "Do you want my job?" I told her what had happened with Ethel and Pam and Pam's William Morris boyfriend and said YES! The next day I met with Messrs. Spelling and Goldberg. A week later I was in a new job in a new office on a real movie-studio lot, 20th Century Fox, where SGP had its offices and shot its series and TV movies. *The Rookies, SWAT, Starsky & Hutch, Charlie's Angels, The Love Boat, Fantasy Island, Family*, and most importantly, the TV movie *The Boy in the Plastic Bubble* were soon to enter my life and by the way, The Tennesse Williams play opened and closed almost instantly on Broadway.

CHAPTER 6

SPELLING-GOLDBERG: COPS & ROBBERS & BIMBOS, OH MY!

At last, I had a job on a "real" movie studio lot, 20th Century Fox, where Spelling-Goldberg Productions (hereafter called SGP) had its offices and soundstages. Once inside the gate, I saw the elevated train tracks and imitation New York Street built for the critically and financially disastrous Barbra Streisand film version of *Hello, Dolly!* Those sets had been used over and over for many TV and movie shoots until the studio was sold to Rupert Murdoch and those elevated tracks disappeared as did most of the charm of the lot. I was blown away at being on a movie lot, I was directed away from the main studio toward a parking lot right off the very busy Pico Boulevard, where the casting offices were located in two double-wide trailers joined together to form four offices with one in each corner and a large open space in the middle used as a waiting room; so much for big studio glamour. The waiting room was a great place for me to meet actors whom I might not have known who were auditioning for the other casting directors. After I met my trailer mates and their assistants, it was time for lunch. I decided to go to the studio commissary. 20th Century Fox had been the studio that made three Rodgers & Hammerstein musicals: *The King and I, Carousel,* and *The Sound of Music.* Marilyn Monroe was a contract player there, and it was Fox that financed and produced the infamous Elizabeth Taylor and Richard Burton movie *Cleopatra.* I expected faded elegance at the very least. What I got was a large, virtually empty dining room with yellowed photos of old stars on the walls and a steam-table line on a par with a school cafeteria. Since there was no one else waiting in line when I paid the cashier, I asked her if the place was always this deserted; she said this was crowded for them. The only shows shooting on the huge lot were SGP ones, and they fed their casts and crews mostly from catering trucks. Moreover, excellent restaurants were nearby in Beverly Hills. Once again, I found myself on a tired, sleepy lot. I also found out that the studio was in financial turmoil and on the brink of bankruptcy; SGP's shows were keeping it open.

Aaron Spelling and Leonard Goldberg, both now deceased, were an incredible team. Len was a formal, businesslike, bearded, cultured Upper West Side New Yorker who had worked his way up through the ranks of ABC to become its head of Programming. Aaron had grown up as a self-described poor Texas Jew-boy who, by 1974, had white hair and looked like an aging leprechaun; but one who spoke with a Texas twang. A World War II correspondent, he moved to L.A. to be an actor. Instead, he wound up becoming one of the most prolific writers and producers in TV history. In 1972 he began his partnership with Len. At ABC, Len had helped introduce *The Dating Game*, *The Newlywed Game*, and the immensely popular soap opera, *Dark Shadows*. Later he moved to Screen Gems, where his projects included *The Partridge Family* and the Peabody Award-winning TV movie *Brian's Song*.

Len's office reflected Len: quiet and understated and rich. To me, he seemed to be marking time (and making tons of money) during his partnership with Aaron. He seethed with the desire to be a feature film producer, and a few years later he became a very successful one, starting with the movie versions of *Charlie's*

Angels. Aaron was the ostentatious one. His office was easily four times as big as Len's. He employed two secretaries plus a longtime personal assistant (Len had one lone secretary), and his taste in furnishings was more nouveau rich than Rothschild. He was a populist character who unabashedly loved television and had no great desire to move into the then far more prestigious area of film.

For all their differences, he and Len were an unbeatable pair. Both saw each day's dailies (the uncut raw footage shot the day before) of every episode of every series and TV movie in production. They then gave verbal notes to each individual producer. When the episode or movie was screened in a loosely edited, rough-cut form, their unique talents truly came into play. Usually, Aaron got up first, turned to face those in the screening room and gave his notes. Then Len got up and did the same. Between their notes, which were almost always excellent and right on point, they covered everything necessary to make the final product as good as it could be. But Spelling-Goldberg's specialty was meat-and-potatoes TV. At CBS, I had worked on award-winning, classy shows such as *The Mary Tyler Moore Show* and *The Bob Newhart Show*. Suddenly I found myself dealing with crowd-pleasing commercial television, something I had considered beneath me, having come from The Theatah. But I quickly adjusted my attitude and began to enjoy the work, especially when I was able to help launch the careers of wonderful new actors, including Nick Nolte, John Ritter, Amy Irving, and James Woods.

My first show was *The Rookies*, a once-highly rated cop series that was now in its fourth season and sinking in the ratings. *The Rookies* was about a team of rookie cops at the fictional Southern California Police Department. Kate Jackson (later a star of *Charlie's Angels*) played a nurse who was married to the oldest cop (Sam Melville). In an attempt to squeeze some more life out of the show before it died, SGP had proposed a spinoff about a female rookie cop. *Police Woman*, no coincidence, was already a hit on NBC. My choice for the part was Joanna Cassidy, who was destined to make a name for herself in TV and movies; in a few years she would costar in *Blade Runner* and other major movies and win a Golden Globe and three Emmy nominations. Tall, beautiful, and physically imposing, she would have made a believable policewoman.

However, I could not sell either Aaron or Len on Joanna. They favored and eventually hired for the role a pretty, petite blonde named Cheryl Stoppelmoor. Cherie Moor was her stage name in her biggest credit up to that time, as a voice-over artist on the cartoon series *Josie and the Pussycats*. Having just married the head of Fox Studios, David Ladd, Cheryl took his last name and became Cheryl Ladd. "Rookette," as we derisively called the spinoff around the office, was rejected by ABC, but Aaron and Len knew a primetime television star when they saw one. A few years later when she left the series after only one season, Ms. Ladd replaced Farrah Fawcett in the role of a private detective on SGP's biggest hit, *Charlie's Angels*.

I was learning a lot about what made the TV viewing masses happy. After *The Rookies* was cancelled, I segued to another West Coast law-enforcement series, *Starsky & Hutch*, then in the middle of its second smash season. Its stars were no lightweights. Paul Michael Glaser was a former Broadway actor with two master's degrees, while David Soul, a blond surfer-type, had once turned down an offer from the Chicago White Sox to study political science. But *Starsky & Hutch* was a shoot-em-up, action-adventure cop show replete with car chases and busty babes. The show had rotating directors and a fleet of producers. Linda Otto, my predecessor, had given me a heads-up as to which ones were good, which ones were sleazy, and which ones were harmless hacks. I made sure the sleazy ones behaved when we were casting women, and I forewarned the actresses about one particular producer. Joe Narr, the "harmless" sleazy one, mandated that every actress up for a "sexy" role, which was almost all of them, come in wearing a tight T-shirt or some other such attire. I gave advance warning to all concerned, and there was never a serious objection. Joanna Kearns (*Growing Pains*) told me that she eventually stopped coming in for auditions because she had run out of outfits. There was never a problem beyond moronic leering, and no actress was subject to further improper requests or suggestions. The classiest of the rotating directors was Fernando Lamas, the Argentine-American Latin lover star of dozens of forties and fifties films and the husband of MGM's star bathing beauty Esther Williams. I had loads of fun working with him. He was charming with all the actors, and knew he was not curing cancer but directing an episode of a flavor-of-the-month TV show. Fernando asked me to meet his son, Lorenzo Lamas, who wanted to be an actor. In a couple of years, I was able to make Fernando a proud father when I cast his son in *Grease*. Another of our guest directors was the Hungarian filmmaker Iván Nagy, later to become notorious as the live-in boyfriend of Heidi Fleiss, the latest Hollywood Madam. Nagy had drifted into television from directing independent European movies, and he brought a wonderful sense of style and panache to his *S&H* episodes. Our producers were wary of him, but Len Goldberg was his champion. What was more important was that Paul and David liked him. One script he directed had the character of a friendly neighborhood loan shark. I knew who I wanted for the role, but Ivan asked if I would be open to trusting him this one time with a New York actor who he had thought would be a much better choice for the job. I knew of the actor from his small part in the Jack Nicholson movie *One Flew Over the Cuckoo's Nest* but had never met him. Physically and age-wise he seemed right for the part. After checking him out with casting director friends in N.Y., I said sure, why not, and he flew himself out and we paid him scale. Nagy was correct; he was terrific in the part. And that is how I met Danny DeVito. A short time later, when I was casting *Taxi,* Danny was my only choice for the role of "Louie".

Only twice was my casting judgment called out by Len and Aaron. Both instances were valuable learning experiences. Typically, after the producers, directors, and I had come to a decision, I would send over head-shot photos of the actors we wanted to hire. Rarely were there any questions. My first reprimand, however, came when I hired a very good actor from New York to play the primary villain. After the first day's dailies, Len asked how I could have cast him. He went on to note that the actor was shorter than both David and Paul – and "we could not have Starsky or Hutch beating up on guys smaller than they were". I said, "But Len, he has a loaded gun pointing at them." Len said, "Never mind the gun, the optics are more important than the reality." Another script called for an over-the-hill female model who was now a crazed killer. I sent over photos of a terrific actress, Gail Strickland, then in her late thirties, with cheekbones up the kazoo. She was approved via the photo process, but after seeing the first dailies, a call came: "How could you use someone like that? Wasn't (a pre-*Charlie's Angels*) Jaclyn Smith available?" So much for over-the-hill models and my New York schooled casting realism Looking back at all the guest actors we used on *S&H*, they were an incredibly varied group. There were unknowns in some of their earliest TV appearances: Nancy McKeon, Melanie Griffith, Jeffrey Tambor, Kim Cattrall, Jeff Goldblum, Veronica Hamel, Suzanne Somers, Kristy McNichol, and Ed Begley, Jr. And there were veteran stars: José Ferrer, Joan Collins, Jean-Pierre Aumont, LaWanda Page, Audrey Meadows, Matthew "Stymie" Beard, and Joan Blondell. I also used many actors from the shows I'd cast on Broadway who had come to Hollywood seeking higher paychecks. One of them, from Pearl Bailey's *Dolly*, was a beautiful and talented biracial actress, Marki Bey. She became a semi-regular as a policewoman and implied girlfriend for Paul. In the mid-seventies, such a relationship like this was quite daring and extremely rare on network TV. I was very proud at the time for my suggesting her and Len and Aaron agreeing. It was not yet that I realized I, too, as was the rest of Hollywood was unconsciously biased.

All was going well on *Starsky & Hutch*. But gradually both Paul and David began to realize that they were in a lightweight show that had little to do with real life. They began to scoff at the writing, and both wanted to join the growing herd of actor/directors. Little could be done to make the show more socially relevant or authentic, but Aaron and Len did encourage Paul and David to direct – and each went on to direct one or more episodes per season. Both did fine jobs, and Paul would go on to direct several TV and feature films, including Arnold Schwarzenegger's *The Running Man*. *Starsky & Hutch* came to an end after four seasons. To this day I don't know why, but Paul and David had gone from being best buds to not talking to each other. In time they were filming many of their joint scenes separately, with the script supervisor reading the other actor's lines. Since there were over eighty episodes already filmed and ready for syndication and Len and Aaron had made more than enough money, they, with ABC's okay, cancelled the show. Paul recently told me his version of why the show ended. He said that both he and David were just not into doing it anymore. This made sense because doing an action series like this year after year, with often sixteen-hour shoots, can be draining not to mention killing any family life. I was saddened not so much because I would no longer be working on the series, but because all had seemed so wonderful just a few years earlier and I missed any warning signs of what was to happen.

There were many more projects to keep me busy at SGP, including the very classy new series *Family*. Mike Nichols was an executive producer along with Aaron and Len, and the writer was Jay Presson Allen, whose credits included *The Prime of Miss Jean Brodie, Marnie*, the movie version of *Cabaret*, and the Broadway comedy *Forty Carats*. She was the one who okayed "prostituting" *Forty Carats* by casting Zsa Zsa Gabor. This series starred Tony-winning Broadway actress Sada Thompson and James Broderick (Matthew's father) as a middle-class Pasadena couple with three kids, played by Meredith Baxter, Gary Frank, and Kristy McNichol. The show was an almost true-to-life, un-clichéd look at a contemporary American family of its day, albeit a family with a few bucks in the bank. Originally SGP had wanted a former movie star, the beautiful, blond Hope Lange, to play the matriarch. However, Len was able to be convinced that Sada, who was short, dark, and dumpy, would be much more real and better suited for the role. Sada, along with Gary and Kristy, went on to win Emmys for *Family*. The guest stars reflected this same high quality: Helen Hunt, Tommy Lee Jones, Ted Danson, Veronica Hamel, Michael Keaton, James Woods, Annie Potts, and Charlotte Rae.

While *Family* has quietly disappeared from our collective consciousness, two other SGP shows, both on ABC, have become iconic: *Fantasy Island* and *The Love Boat*. Though it was little more than escapist fluff, *The Love Boat* proved to be catnip for the primetime audience. Set aboard an actual cruise ship, the *Pacific Princess*, each episode told two or three light comedic/romantic stories, along with some other yarn that involved the crew. Jolly Captain Stubing presided over everything. He was played by Gavin MacLeod, with whom America had fallen in love on *The Mary Tyler Moore Show*. There, he was Murray Slaughter, a news writer at the TV station for which Mary worked as associate producer. Bald, blue-eyed, and cuddly as a teddy bear, he brought a fatherly warmth to the gentle mayhem on *The Love Boat*. Adding to this confection was the show's most famous feature: the guest stars. The list of them – you can find it on Wikipedia – is a who's-who of seventies TV and movie favorites and stars, kitsch celebs, and fondly remembered has-beens. They include: June Allyson, Frankie Avalon, Sid Caesar, Linda Blair, David Cassidy, Ernest Borgnine, Joan Blondell, Phyllis Diller, Lola Falana, Zsa Zsa Gabor, Lillian Gish, Gene Kelly, Gina Lollobrigida, Ethel Merman, Donny and Marie Osmond, Joan Rivers, Lana Turner, Charo, *and* the Village People. In the beginning it was easy to get them, since the show was a hit and many of these performers welcomed the exposure, along with the handsome paychecks. At its peak, *The Love Boat* was definitely a show to be seen on. Later, as it declined in ratings and stature and became a bit of a joke, fewer and fewer real stars wanted to do it.

There were three, two-hour TV movie length pilots. *Love Boat* pilots. I cast the third one. Fred Silverman, my former boss at CBS and now the head of ABC, was dissatisfied with the actors initially chosen as the captain and cruise director and wanted them recast. For Captain Stubing, he specifically wanted someone from the now canceled *The Mary Tyler Moore Show*. The only available actor was Gavin, so that one was easy. But the casting of cruise director Julie McCoy was a madhouse. I brought in hundreds of young women, but the part was so unspecific and underwritten that everyone with a say-so in the decision, (and there were many) had a different opinion. I had almost run out of actresses, and the first day of shooting was rapidly approaching. Unlike the two previous pilots, which were shot on real *Princess Line* cruise ships, this one was to be shot on sound stages and the former luxury liner the *Queen Mary,* which had been decommissioned and was handily parked in Long Beach, just forty-five minutes from the studio. That gave us a bit of extra time, but a decision had to be made to secure the location. Pert, all-American Lauren Tewes, with her Dorothy Hamill hair and glowing smile, was it. None of the actors playing crew members in the original pilot made it to the series!

The Love Boat was not a Spelling-Goldberg production. It was produced by Aaron Spelling Productions and the Douglas S. Cramer Company. Strain had set in between Aaron and Len, and in a few years, it would tear them apart. Nothing had gone wrong in their personal relationship; the scuttlebutt was that the fierce and unhidden animosity between their wives, Wendy Goldberg and Candy Spelling, caused the split. So intense was the women's dislike for each other that they refused to be in the same room, including industry and company functions, where the absence of one woman or the other was noticed and gossiped about. I never knew Wendy well; to me she seemed reserved and pleasant, much like Len himself. Only recently did producer /casting director Joan Barnett, who had known and dealt with Wendy, tell me that she was, in fact, tough as nails, a social climber, and not very nice to other women. Apparently, she and her nemesis had more in common than either would have cared to admit. Candy was like Aaron, ostentatious and eager for the limelight; she never hid her jewelry under a bushel. One day I had a meeting with Aaron at his home, where he was working that day. This was his "old" house, not the 123-room mansion in Holmby Hills called "The Manor" that he had built in 1988, then the largest private home in L.A. County. Aaron gave me a mini-tour, and he was positively gleeful when he showed me Candy's closets. One of them was bigger than my entire house and included one of those carousel racks suspended from the ceiling like one would find in a dry cleaner; unlimited outfits could be twirled around.

Business went on at SGP, although the handwriting was on the wall with regard to Aaron and Len parting ways. Aaron was working with his new producing partner, Douglas Cramer, whose resumé included *Star Trek*, *The Odd Couple*, *The Brady Bunch*, *Love American Style*, and *Mission: Impossible*. On *Love Boat* I also had to deal with him. Casting for Aaron had been a breeze, but Doug was no fun. He resisted using new actors he didn't have a history with, and he shot down many of my ideas. One of the plot lines of Love *Boat 3*, involved a romance between two older passengers. For the man, I suggested Phil Silvers, famous as Sgt. Bilko on *The Phil Silvers Show* in the fifties; fine, no problem there. As for the woman he meets on board, hooks up with, and in the morning who is found dead in bed with a smile on her face – really – I suggested my pal, Pearl Bailey. Aaron loved the idea. Soon, however, he called and told me despondently and a bit angrily that it couldn't happen. To this day I don't know if Doug or ABC had quashed the idea for racial reasons. Audra Lindley, later famous as the sexually frustrated housewife Mrs. Roper on *Three's Company*, got the part and played it nicely, but a great opportunity to push the color barrier on TV had been lost. In future episodes a fair number of black actors were used, but never in an interracial manner. If you were Hispanic and were named Charo, Rita Moreno, Fernando Lamas, or Ricardo Montalbán, you got work. Otherwise, good luck. As for Asians, they did not exist at sea. The pilot sold, of course, and *The Love Boat* ran for nine seasons. But Doug had been such a drag that I was relieved never to have cast anything with him but that pilot.

Fantasy Island brought further millions flooding into Spelling-Goldberg. Though filmed in Burbank and at the Los Angeles Arboretum in nearby Arcadia, it was set in a mysterious island in the South Pacific, where people, played by big-name guest stars, flew in by private plane and paid a lot of money to have their fantasies made real. Once immersed in them, they found themselves tested in ways they hadn't bargained for, making their dreams-come-true seem more like careful-what-you-wish-for. The idea for the series was a fluke. Len and Aaron were having a pitch meeting with an ABC executive, Lou Rudolph. Mr. Rudolph snickered at all their ideas. Sarcastically he suggested they come back and pitch a show about a bunch of beautiful people stranded on an island led by some sinister guy. And Len and Aaron did just that. I cast the 1977 two-hour TV movie that served as *Fantasy Island*'s pilot. There were only two series roles to fill, each requiring a magnetic personality. One was the lead character, Mr. Roarke, the handsome, mature, eerily debonair host of the island; the other was for his assistant, Tattoo. The part of Mr. Roarke cried out for an older movie star. ABC was pushing for Orson Welles, but Welles, though a genius, was equally well-known as an unreliable pain in the ass, and Aaron didn't want to deal with him. Enter the British-born James Mason, a celebrated cinematic leading man since the forties, with numerous classics (including *A Star is Born, North by Northwest, 20,000 Leagues Under the Sea,* and *Lolita*) among his credits. In those days, to go from movies to TV was a no-no for big stars. It meant several steps down in down in prestige, but oftentimes, a big step up in earnings. In Mason's case, money was not an issue. After saying yes to our offer and then no and then yes again, he finally decided he could not take the step down and passed. Before meeting with Aaron to give him, the bad news and discuss other possibilities, I talked to his secretary, Renee. "Isn't it a shame about James Mason?" she said. I agreed, adding, "I don't know what we're going to do." Renee asked if I'd thought of Ricardo Montalbán. I practically jumped up and kissed her because I then remembered seeing him all tuxedo-ed up and looking elegant and suave onstage reading passages from the works of George Bernard Shaw; and doing them very well. "No!" I said, "But that is the best fucking idea." A very proper woman, she ignored my vulgarity and smiled. Though a prolific Latin lover and suave character actor in countless films of the forties and fifties, Montalbán was never considered to be more than a B-grade actor. Now, in the 1970's he was back on the boards thanks to starring roles in two *Planet of the Apes* films. I told Aaron about Renee's idea and he loved it. After ABC approved, the deal was made in one day. Renee never got credit for this suggestion though she was richly rewarded financially by Aaron for the rest of her career.

Someone involved with *Fantasy Island* had the idea of using a little person as Mr. Roarke's sidekick. In 1973 I had cast a new musical, *Mary C. Brown and the Hollywood Sign*, in L.A. The second lead character was a little person, and director Tom O'Horgan (*Hair, Jesus Christ Superstar*) wanted Hervé Villechaize, a Paris-born midget (Hervé's preferred term). Unfortunately, after much going back and forth, Hervé passed on the role. *Mary C. Brown*, alas, died quickly in Los Angeles, but I'd never forgotten Hervé. His other parts were few but equally memorable, notably his role in a James Bond film, *The Man with the Golden Gun*. *Sesame Street* also employed him as Oscar the Grouch's legs, hanging out of a trash can. Hervé had also appeared at La Mama, the experimental off-off-Broadway theater in downtown New York. Hervé was an intellectual, but generally broke and out of work. At various times he lived in his car and in a seedy Hollywood transient hotel. That's where he was when *Fantasy Island* found him and changed his life. Though he would be able to afford much better housing, the poor man lived in constant pain due to constant compression of his internal organs, which were those of a normal sized person. A year after the *Fantasy Island* TV movie aired, the series began what turned out to be a seven-season run. It gave Montalbán the greatest success of his career and made Hervé a star. On the set Hervé was impossible, hitting on all the women and making constant demands, which included wanting the same salary as Montalbán, who was getting paid a lot more. Because he was so popular, possibly more so than Montalbán, the producers tolerated him for five seasons; then they let him go and that did not seem to affect the ratings. I supervised most of the first-season casting; for nostalgia-lovers the show, like *The Love Boat*, was a bonanza. In my time there we had Jane Powell, Sheree North, John Gavin, Leslie Nielsen, Don Knotts, Ray Bolger, Jim Backus, Anne Jeffreys, and Jane Wyatt, to name a few. Beginning with episode three, *Fantasy Island* was slotted on Saturday night at ten p.m., following *The Love Boat*. The combination helped ABC to stay number-one in the ratings for years. Between those two and *Starsky & Hutch,* and *Family,* I was responsible for the casting of four hours or one whole night's plus one hour of ABC's prime time schedule!

One of the early storylines was basically a knockoff of the Disney movie *The Parent Trap,* in which a brother and sister try to bring their divorced parents back together on the island. Aaron asked me to do him a big favor and to be honest about the results. He wanted me to meet and audition his five-year-old daughter, Victoria Spelling, known as Tori, for the role of the young girl.

Renee brought her to my office and introduced us. Tori was very quiet and shy and with me. It seemed she wanted to be anywhere but there. But even at that age she was well-prepared and knew we were supposed to read the script together. She tried very hard and wasn't bad, but nowhere near ready to handle a role as big as the one I was casting. I told this to Aaron and suggested a smaller role in one of the later episodes. That became her first TV acting job. A dozen years later, when she became a star on *Beverly Hills, 90210* produced by her father – I could look back alternatively with either satisfaction or regret by having helped push the kindergarten-aged Tori in that direction.

CHAPTER 7

JOHN TRAVOLTA - THE BOY IN THE PLASTIC BUBBLE

Nowadays, over-the-air free broadcast networks, cable, and streaming made for TV movies are often bigger, more prestigious, and better for an actor's career than the kind that play in theaters. Back in the seventies and eighties, that was far from true. With occasional exceptions, TV movies were considered lowbrow, a refuge for television actors who were not likely to graduate to movie stardom and for faded film stars who needed a job. Rarely would the agent of a viable movie actor permit his or her client to do a TV movie or series. The reasoning being, if audiences could see a star for free in their living rooms, why would they pay to see them in a movie theater? This held true until Michael J. Fox broke the mold with two *Back to the Future* feature films. He shot these movies while also doing *Family Ties* for NBC. *Family Ties* prescient and wise producer, Gary J. Goldberg, worked closely with Universal to enable crazy scheduling. That said, the made-for-TV movie was a staple of television back then, especially at Spelling-Goldberg Productions. By no means had SGP devised the genre; that credit goes to Barry Diller, who as ABC's then vice president of development created the ABC Movie of the Week in 1969. SGP provided ABC with a steady supply of TV movies, a few of which I cast. Though some of these productions masqueraded as "serious," the vast majority were merely salacious and exploitative. But the sleaze factor attracted viewers, which in turn pumped up advertising rates. Both Aaron and Len were all for that, but they disagreed sharply as to what type of TV movies they wanted to make. While both worshiped at the altar of celebrity and craved every star they could get, Len preferred to take the higher road with films that, at least superficially, had "messages" attached. I must say he scored big on several occasions. *Brian's Song*, a 1971 ABC Movie of the Week, was a breakthrough in its field. It starred James Caan (*The Godfather*) and Billy Dee Williams (*Star Wars: The Empire Strikes Back),* two Hollywood stars still at their career peaks. The movie was based on a true story about the interracial friendship between two pro football players, one dying of cancer. Millions of viewers tuned in and cried their eyes out at the end, when Brian (Caan) dies at age twenty-six. *Brian's Song* won a slew of awards and has been proclaimed as one of the best TV movies ever made.

Aaron's taste, by comparison, was commercial and crass. A lot of the films he approved made quick killings for SGP, although I dare you to remember *Love's Savage Fury* (Connie Stevens, Jennifer O'Neill, Robert Reed); *Cruise into Terror* (John Forsythe, Stella Stevens, Ray Milland); or my two favorites, *Satan's School for Girls* (Kate Jackson, Jo Van Fleet, Cheryl Ladd) and *Murder on Flight 502*, a rip-off of the highly popular *Airport* feature-film franchise. The cast of that one served up a bonanza of seventies *TV Guide* boldface names: Sonny Bono, Farrah Fawcett, Robert Stack, Polly Bergen, George Maharis, Brooke Adams, Fernando Lamas, Hugh O'Brian, Robert Stack, Ralph Bellamy, Danny Bonaduce, Walter Pidgeon, and a Tappan Zee Playhouse and Yiddish theater favorite, Molly Picon. Although it wasn't SGP's film, we owed a debt of gratitude to *Born Innocent*, the highest-rated and most scandalous TV movie of 1974. Linda Blair starred as a teenage runaway who winds up in a detention center and reform school for girls. That September, when the movie aired on NBC, all anyone in the vicinity of a TV could talk about was a scene in which a gang of mean girls rape Linda's character in the communal shower with a toilet bowl plunger handle. The publicity was golden, and although the resulting hue and cry got the scene cut from re-runs, *Born Innocent* kicked open the door for a new genre of TV movie: the pseudo-significant, teenage sexploitation drama. NBC jumped on top of the trend with *Dawn: Portrait of a Teenage Runaway* (i.e. a young hooker) and *Alexander: The Other Side of Dawn* (the male equivalent). Along came ABC and SGP with *Little Ladies of the Night*, cast by yours truly. It's a wonderfully dreadful "socially concerned" movie about an L.A. detective (David Soul) who helps save Hailey, an underage runaway hooker (Linda Purl). Lana Wood, Natalie's sister, played the lead whore in the stable of Hailey's pimp (Clifton Davis). Carolyn Jones (Morticia from *The Addams Family* and Aaron Spelling's ex-wife) was the coldhearted mother who has driven Hailey away. Dorothy Malone, the former star of *Peyton Place*, came in at the last minute to play an ex-hooker who now owns a bar. Jane Russell had said yes to the part and then got cold feet. Never mind the fact that she hadn't made any kind of movie in seven years and was currently all over the tube selling Playtex Cross Your Heart Bras for "us full-figured gals."

There was one made-for-TV movie, adored by both Aaron and Len, that changed my life. It would never have happened if not for the tenacity of Cindy Dunne, the one-woman script development department at SGP. Cindy was the daughter of Elton Rule, then the president of ABC. Nepotism certainly helped her get the job, but once in it, this very bright woman delivered. Late one Friday afternoon she came into my office, looking dejected. Her favorite script of the moment had been turned down by ABC's movie department, yet again after several rewrites. She wanted to see if I had any casting ideas that could possibly rescue it from the trash heap. The script was *The Boy in the Plastic Bubble*, written by Douglas Day Stewart, a veteran TV writer. I added it to my weekend reading pile. Weekend script reading had become a ritual for me and my best friend, talent manager Bob LeMond. We would lie on my tiny back deck in Laurel Canyon, blissfully unaware of melanoma, soaking up the California sun, doing our script reading, then we'd go out for a meal and a movie. We'd become friends in New York when he and his business partner Lois Zetter and a third talent manager and office mate, Bill Treusch, had a near-monopoly on the best up-and-coming talent. Their yet-to-be-famous clients included John Travolta, Diane Keaton, Eric Roberts, Christopher Walken, Brooke Adams, Patrick Swayze, Sissy Spacek, Treat Williams, Barry Bostwick, Jeff Conaway, Katherine Helmond, and Holland Taylor. Realizing that they had to have a presence in Los Angeles to properly service those clients, Bob moved to a small apartment in Hollywood, while Lois remained in New York. Bob was particularly worried about his most important client, John Travolta. John was in the middle of his first smash season of *Welcome Back, Kotter*, a sitcom about a racially and ethnically mixed group of Brooklyn high-school students, and the teacher (played by comic Gabe Kaplan) who uses humor and compassion to help lift them up. Gabe was supposed to be the star, but it was John who rose to the top.

I met John when he was seventeen. Bob sent him to my office at David Merrick's in hopes that I might be able to cast him in something. He was handsome, dimpled, charming, intelligent, and well-spoken; the opposite of all New Jersey cliches (think

The Sopranos) where John is from. His mother, Helen, taught drama, and dance and was closely involved in community theater. John was looking forward to trying everything: theater, TV, film, and flying airplanes. Not long after our meeting, John – with no help from me – got a small role in a touring company of *Grease,* followed by a part in the Broadway musical *Over Here,* which starred the two surviving Andrews Sisters, America's best-loved female singing trio of the '30s and '40s. Once *Kotter* exploded, John became the perfect cover boy for the teen magazines, notably *Tiger Beat,* which glorified teenybopper idols for a readership of pubescent girls. But his appeal extended to older women and to guys who wanted to be just like him. He'd been deluged with film offers, but in 1976 he was bummed out because the feature film he really wanted to do, the one that could have given him a more mature image, was not going to work out for him. *Days of Heaven* was an expansive romantic drama set in the Texas Panhandle. Its writer and director, Terrence Malick, had scored a critical smash, *Badlands,* in 1973. Terrence wanted John for *Days of Heaven,* but he could not give him a stop date, the term for a contractually stated closing date for the actor's commitment. Malick took so much time finding the exact kind of prairie grasses he wanted for the location (he had ultimately settled on western Canada) that John's narrow window of opportunity between seasons of *Kotter* had closed. Production on *Days of Heaven* would continue for months. Instead of John, Malick used Richard Gere in his first starring role. Practically all of Gere's early career happened because John had turned down or dropped out of a couple of other movies you may have heard of, *An Officer and a Gentlemen* and *American Gigolo. Bob* was desperate to pull a rabbit out of a hat and find a classy project that John could do in the now less than one-month's time before going back to *Kotter.*

After Bob told me his Travolta saga, we started on our respective reading piles. I started with *The Boy in the Plastic Bubble,* a silly-sounding title at best. It told the story of David Vetter, an real boy who was born in Houston with a nonfunctioning immune system. Prior to his birth, his parents had lost several babies immediately upon birth. Doctors told the couple that only way to keep their next born David alive, was to give him a completely sterile birth, then to put him immediately into a germ-free incubator, the plastic bubble. Unless a cure were found, David would have to live his life in protective covering, not unlike a human-sized hamster habitat, and eerily not too dissimilar from what we are doing now during the Covid-19 pandemic. The script followed the true story until the boy turned five; everything after that is fictional as David enters his teens and falls in love with his next-door neighbor. Immediately after reading *The Boy in the Plastic Bubble,* I tossed the script to Bob and said, "Here's your rabbit!" I explained that although this was just a lowly TV movie, the lead character was the polar opposite of Vinnie Barbarino, John's character on *Kotter.* Most people assumed that John *was* Vinnie because he was from New Jersey and his last name ends in a vowel. No one knew how skillfully he could act. David was modest, quiet, and complex, certainly no Vinnie Barbarino. Just as important, I knew this script could be filmed in under a month, thus enabling John to return to *Kotter* in time for the new season. Bob read the script and to my great surprise, loved it. I assured him that John's role could be completed in a very short period of time and he got into his cute BMW 2002 and delivered it to John's apartment. By Sunday night John, too, had read it and he wanted to do the movie. This was kind of amazing because very few agents or managers of a "hot" actor would give his client a script to read without a firm cash offer. This only happened because of my long standing friendship with Bob. Most things happen in this business because of relationships, and ours was solid.

First thing Monday morning, I walked into Cindy's office and gave her the news. Facetiously I asked if John were a big-enough name to get the project green-lighted. She was flabbergasted: "Are you sure? He really wants to do it? You're *sure*?" Those sentiments were echoed by Aaron and Len, who at first did not believe that Travolta would do this project. They called Michael Eisner, the senior vice president of Programming and Development at ABC. He, too, did not believe it, for John had turned down everything ABC had thrown at him. The business people at SGP and ABC made the cash offer and it became real. John received the highest salary paid to an actor up to that time for an ABC movie: $75,000., $25,000 higher than the next best, Ed Asner. Today you can often add at least another zero for a mid-level actor's salary for a streaming movie. Aaron, Len, and Cindy walked into my office the next day, all smiling broadly as they told me the good news that the deal was done. Knowing that no director had been considered and we had no time to lose, I reminded them of a rising young director, Randal Kleiser, whom SGP had employed recently at my suggestion.

Randal was thirty years old, tall, square-jawed, leading-man handsome, sun-tanned with naturally streaked blond hair, the perfect California beach boy. A couple of years earlier he had chatted me up at a party. At the time he was a grad film student at USC. My ego deflated when he told me he knew I was a casting director at CBS and asked if I would take a look at his master's-thesis script for a thirty-minute short film and help him cast it. Before I left, he handed me a copy of his script, called *Peege*. Lesson No. 1 for aspiring actors and writers in L.A.: Always keep copies of your scripts, resumés, and headshots in your car. You never know what potentially useful person you're gonna meet. I did read it – and it was a brilliant piece of work. *Peege* was based on the true story of a time when Randal went home from college to spend the holidays with his family. During the visit, he and his parents go to visit his grandmother in a nursing home. The word Alzheimer's had not yet entered the language, but clearly his grandmother has the disease. The bulk of the script has the Randal character talking to his grandmother about the happiness they shared in his younger years. The grandmother does not react at all until the very end, when for a moment she becomes lucid. Randal found investors to finance the film and he and they owned it, not USC, because USC funds and equipment were not used. The cast I lined up for the project might have helped. Barbara Rush, once a regular on TV's most popular primetime soap, *Peyton Place,* and a 1960s movie star, played the mother. I knew her from my Merrick days when I cast her in a national tour of *Forty Carats.* The father was William Schallert from *The Patty Duke Show.* For the Randal character I brought in Bruce Davison, who was riding high as the star of *Willard,* the film about a social outcast and his pet rats. *Peege* gained Randal instant acclaim. It went on to become a Christmastime staple for ten years on NBC and to gain inclusion in the National Film Registry. Right after the short film was finished, Randal was signed to direct a few episodes of various series for Universal TV. After I introduced him to Aaron and Len, they signed him to direct episodes of *The*

Rookies, Starsky & Hutch, and *Family*. Randal earned raves from the SGP stars, and even more importantly, he impressed the folks who watched the money by always finishing on time and often under budget. Not surprisingly, Aaron, Len, and Cindy all loved the idea of having him direct *Bubble*; as did John, after the two had met. I went to Cindy and asked if she realized what we had accomplished in a matter of days. We had resurrected a dead script, signed the hottest TVstar around and a happening young director. Essentially, as I pointed out, we had produced this project, and should continue to do so through its completion. Cindy agreed. With my pushy New York attitude perfectly in place, we went to Aaron and Len, and with me doing the talking, explained what we had done so far asked to be able to continue producing the film. Since Cindy and I were year-round, full-time SGP employees we did not ask for, nor expect any extra money, but we did ask for proper credit and billing as producers. We got a definite maybe.

After Travolta's deal was set, we proceeded to cast the rest of the movie. As if John were not enough, ABC insisted on having stars play his parents. We went with Diana Hyland, who had starred on Broadway with Paul Newman and Geraldine Page in Tennessee Williams' *Sweet Bird of Youth*. ABC wanted her because she had just been signed to star in a new family series, *Eight Is Enough*. To play David's father, we scored *The Brady Bunch*'s dad, Robert Reed. As Travolta's girl-next-door love interest, we hired an SGP favorite, Glynnis O'Connor. For years, though she was over 18, she continued to play teenagers all over TV. Len and Aaron nixed our choice for the minor role of a teen dying of cancer, a ward mate of John's character in the hospital. The actor was Tom Hulce, later to play Mozart in *Amadeus* and be Oscar-nominated. Their ridiculous reason was that he had a "funny eye." When we pointed out that the character was dying of cancer and who cared about his eye, they held fast.

Off we went to our two main location sites, Malibu Beach, and nearby Lake Malibu. The first beach scene called for John to take off his shirt inside the bubble. John would have been the hairiest fifteen-year-old in film history except for *The Planet of the Apes.* Someone from makeup came over with a beard trimmer and clipped off all his chest and back hair. I asked that person to sweep up the hair and put it in a baggie. I told John I was saving it because I knew it would become very valuable in years to come. Unfortunately, by the time eBay arrived, I could not find the fucking baggie! Though dependably funny and dear, John, thanks to *Kotter,* was also a huge star. Completely aware of his position, he had begun to be very guarded. He couldn't go anywhere without getting mobbed. But he loved doing this movie, and the John we saw on the set was like a kid, having a ball and very friendly to all members of the cast and crew. The only annoyance in that shoot came from Robert Reed, who turned out to be a royal pain in the ass. Understandably, *The Brady Bunch* had pumped up his ego, and Reed was used to being as important as anyone on the set. But in *Bubble,* he was neither the star nor the center of attention. The shooting schedule depended on John finishing his scenes in the seventeen days he was available. All scheduling had to be worked around this. Reed couldn't handle the demotion. He was sulky, curt, and made it all too clear that this job was just a paycheck to him.

His annoyance came to a head, literally, on a day when his curly hair had to be laboriously straightened then re-kinked twice, to show his character's changes in appearance over a course of years. Reed wound up storming into his dressing room, which, by the way, was equal in all respects to John's. I followed him and apologized, trying to explain, once again, our ridiculous schedule. He was frosty, but things got warmer when I offered him a back rub. It graduated into more serious rubbing, and the deed that should not have been done got done. I did leave him in a better mood, but Reed, who was professionally closeted, never looked me in the eye for the remaining few days of shooting and returned to being a pain in the ass. As the seventeenth day came rushing toward us, we were much more concerned about the last scene, because no one liked the ending as written. One day the prop man turned to me and said offhandedly: "Why don't you just have them get on their horses and take off into the blue?" And that is how *The Boy in the Plastic Bubble* ends. Randal liked the image so much that later, when he directed *Grease*, he closed the film by having our costars, John and Olivia Newton-John, drive off together into the blue sky.

As promised, we finished with John within his seventeen-day limit. John came back a few days later for the on-set modest wrap party. A couple of surprises turned heads there. Though then only a semi-out gay, Randal began a brief fling with Glynnis O'Connor. The bigger surprise was John and Diana. They sat together for almost the entire party, head-to-head in deep conversation, broken only when cast and crew came over to say goodbye. I called Bob LeMond the next day, and he confirmed that, yes, something was brewing between the incipient superstar and this wonderful woman eighteen years his senior. The story did not end happily. Just as *Eight Is Enough* began to air in the fall, Diana was in the hospital, fighting a losing battle with breast cancer. None of us knew that earlier that year, after having finished the series pilot, Diana had had a mastectomy, followed by chemotherapy and breast reconstruction. She and her doctors and family were hoping for the best, and all had seemingly gone well during the shooting of *Bubble*. Later I wondered if, at the wrap party, Diana had been telling John about her situation, which could have accounted for their intense conversation. Pretty soon their relationship hit the tabloids. Then he and Diana came out publicly as a couple, or rather as a family, for she had a four-year-old son from a previous marriage. The boy, Zachary, adored John, and I believe the adoration was returned. But on March 27, 1977, Diana died, reportedly in John's arms. Her son went to live with his father, and I returned to my corner of the casting trailer. My *Bubble* story has an amusing coda. Before the movie aired, it was a slow Friday, and not being able to afford a contractor, I took the day off to do some long-delayed repairs on my house. Late afternoon while relaxing in the bathtub with a glass of wine and a joint, my phone, with a twenty-five-foot cord that could reach into the bathroom, rang. A voice said, "Can you hold for Mr. Spelling?" I tried to quickly sober up as Aaron came on the line to tell me how much he and Len appreciated our work on the film and that Cindy and I would receive our well-earned producer credits. Aaron let me know he'd overruled Len who had opposed it. On Monday, Len called and told me the same story, except for his claim that it was *he* who fought Aaron to give us our producer credit. How Hollywood! Cindy and I had a huge laugh over it, but WTF, we got the credit we deserved.

The Boy in the Plastic Bubble premiered on November 12, 1976. By popular demand, ABC aired it twice more in close succession, which was almost unheard of. It was the most-viewed TV movie of the year and earned three Emmy nominations and one win for Diana, who was not alive to accept. John did the honors at the Emmys. Our writer, Douglas Day Stewart would go on to write *The Blue Lagoon* (directed by Randal) and *An Officer and a Gentleman*, which he had written for Travolta. But John didn't see himself in the role, and this became number two in Richard Gere's trifecta of Travolta-rejected roles.

Bubble did not earn John an Emmy nomination, but it brought him something more important: It showed America that he was *not* Vinnie Barbarino, and that he could act. Two years later we worked together again on *Grease*, also directed by Randal, as well as *Moment by Moment*, where John and Lily Tomlin played a very unlikely duo of May/December lovers. The movie was written and directed by Lily's partner, Jane Wagner. Although universally critically decimated, lately it has begun to be looked at today in a more favorable way. Hindsight is always 20/20.

CHAPTER 8

GREASE

It was hard to readjust to life back in the Spelling/Goldberg trailers. The success of *The Boy* in *the Plastic Bubble* had shown me I could be a good producer. After all, I had put together the package of star John Travolta, director Randal Kleiser, and an orphan script. The spring and summer of 1977, when *Starsky & Hutch* and the company's other shows were on hiatus, brought the vehicle that I hoped would carry me into a full-time producing career. None of us involved in creating the film version of *Grease* could have predicted that it would go on to become the largest-grossing movie musical in history. Olivia Newton-John and John Travolta, our stars, were huge before *Grease*, Olivia from her string of pop music hits, John from *Welcome Back, Kotter*, *The Boy in the Plastic Bubble*, and countless teen magazine covers. But by the time *Grease* went into production, the movie musical genre seemed cursed. After a last golden flowering in the 1960s, including *Gypsy*, *My Fair Lady*, *Mary Poppins*, *The Music Man*, *Bye Bye Birdie*, and the Elvis Presley and *Gidget* musicals, movie musicals had, for the most part, become box-office poison. With very few exceptions (notably *Funny Girl* and *Cabaret*), they were huge, costly flops with major though miscast stars, such as Barbra Streisand (*Hello, Dolly!*) and Clint Eastwood (*Paint Your Wagon*). In 1977, Martin Scorsese's *New York, New York*, which starred Liza Minnelli and Robert DeNiro, cost fourteen million to make and just about broke even – eventually. The next year, when *Grease* was released, there were only two other major American movie musicals, *The Wiz* and an all-star Beatles jukebox musical, *Sgt. Pepper's Lonely Hearts Club Band*. Both bombed, though *The Wiz* was later to achieve cult status.

Grease had popularity built into it. Having run from 1971 to 1980, it stands as one of Broadway's longest running shows. John and Olivia, of course, were idols. And the subject matter; rowdy, rebellious, love-struck teens of the '50s tapped into a nostalgia craze that was then at its peak. America had lived through the racial and sexual turmoil of the '60s and the financial recession of '70s; now, partly for camp value and partly through an honest yearning for the past, there was a huge nostalgia revival. It warmed audiences' hearts to recall the seemingly innocent Eisenhower years, when dads were the sole breadwinners and moms stayed home and vacuumed the carpet while wearing high heels and pearls. No wonder *Happy Days*, which celebrated that era, lasted on TV for eleven seasons.

The *Grease* movie happened because Robert Stigwood, the Australian music mogul who managed the Bee Gees, Eric Clapton, and Peter Frampton, and a showbiz phenomenon named Allan Carr partnered on producing the movie. Short, fat, unabashedly gay in ultra-closeted Hollywood, cocaine-snorting, outrageously funny and gossipy, and at times witheringly vindictive, Allan had left Chicago in 1966 and moved to L.A. to start a management company. Allan's clients would include Ann-Margret, Tony Curtis, Peter Sellers, Rosalind Russell, Dyan Cannon, Marlo Thomas, Joan Rivers, and future *A Chorus Line* composer, Marvin Hamlisch. Allan made a fortune and spent a fortune. He bought the Beverly Hills mansion that had once belonged to Ingrid Bergman and used it as the setting for many "business" parties, the tax-deductible costs of which would have bankrupted several small countries, including two successive "Rolodex" parties – one night, guests from A-L, and the next night, the M-Z crowd. The less publicized part of his parties took place in the basement of the mansion, where he built an Egyptian themed disco. That's where half-naked gorgeous and available men and some of Allan's guests danced all night, fueled by the drugs Allan provided. There in the middle of it all was Allan, the life of the party, his bulk covered in a wardrobe of vivid caftans. He was definitely an original.

Allan had seen an early production of *Grease* in Chicago and gone crazy for it. He became an even bigger fan when the show moved to Off-Broadway, then ultimately became a Broadway smash. Allan approached Stigwood to partner with him and buy the rights. At first, they were stymied because the movie rights had been sold to Ralph Bakshi, who had produced the enormously financially successful first full-length, X-rated animated film *Fritz the Cat*. Bakshi planned to also make *Grease* as an animated movie but could not get the production off the ground and his option lapsed. By then Stigwood was fully on board and loved Allan's idea to star John Travolta in the leading role. Stigwood liked the idea so much that he made his *own* deal with John to star in three movies, all to be produced by Stigwood's company. John, according to his manager, Bob LeMond, would reputedly earn a total of two million from this deal. It was a smart move for all concerned. The first of those films was *Saturday Night Fever*, which was to lift John from stardom to superstardom. It would do much the same for three other clients of Stigwood: The Bee Gees, who wrote and performed six of the many hits on the soundtrack. Stigwood felt confident enough in Allan to place him in charge of *Grease*; the film was Allan's vision, and Stigwood was busy with his vision, the doomed feature film, *Sgt. Pepper's Lonely Hearts Club Band.*

It was only because of John that *Grease* had become a reality and Paramount agreed to distribute the movie. That gave John and LeMond a lot of clout, and they knew it. Having loved working with Randal Kleiser on *The Boy in the Plastic Bubble*, John wanted him to direct *Grease*. Bob asked me my opinion, and I enthusiastically backed up that choice. Not only was Randal a terrific film technician, but he also knew how to get things done on the cheap, due to his TV experience. This was essential, considering *Grease*'s skimpy budget of six million dollars, less than two times the cost of an ordinary TV movie. By comparison, the 2016 live Fox TV version cost more than $17 million. To this day I believe that the less money you have for a project, the more it forces the creative folk to be inventive and clever. That is exactly what happened with *Grease*. The only problem was that Randal knew nothing about musicals and had barely heard of *Grease*. That's where I came in. Bob and John wanted me aboard too, thereby reuniting the whole *Bubble* team. What's more, I was a Musical Comedy Queen while Randal was barely a Lady in Waiting. I told Bob I'd love to do it, provided that after the casting process, I could stay on as a producer, with appropriate screen credit for both jobs. Bob was all for it. He knew that I knew the show inside-out, having seen it with him Off-Broadway at least a half dozen times. Two of Bob's clients, Barry Bostwick and Carole Demas, had been the original leads, and a third client, Jeff Conaway, played Danny, at one time too.

Allan approved. But when I asked him for a contract or at least a letter of agreement, he told me Paramount would take care of it. In film and television, many deals aren't put in writing until the start of production; some aren't signed until way after the project has been completed. Farrah Fawcett, for example, never had a signed contract for *Charlie's Angels*, the show that she, arguably more than her costars, Jaclyn Smith, and Kate Jackson, had made into a phenomenon. When she left after one season and was sued by Spelling/Goldberg and ABC, the lack of a signed contract became one of her defenses, and she won. I never got a contract for *Grease,* either just a verbal agreement from Allan, which proved to be worthless; but I didn't know that yet. I loved this project, and more than anything I wanted to be a part of it. However, Randal wasn't sure *he* did. Stigwood and Carr wanted him, but Randal was sure that Allan would want to micromanage everything and would make it very hard for him to do his job. He asked me to be on the set every day, and I agreed. I assured him that others, too, had his back, from the brilliant choreographer, Patricia Birch, who had done the Off-Broadway version, to our musical director, Louis St. Louis, who had conducted it. Louis wrote a new song for the movie, "Sandy"; the one Travolta sings at the drive-in just before an innuendo-laden animated sequence of a hot dog jumping into a vagina-like bun. We also rounded out the production with the best: Cinematographer Bill Butler, Production Designer Phil Jeffries, and Costume Designer Albert Wolsky, the unsung hero of the movie in my opinion. His "bad" Sandy created a fashion trend still viable today.

Without ever being pushy about it, John had strong ideas for the film. He knew that his character, "Danny Zuko", had only one song in the first act, and he asked for another. I suggested that, rather than order up a whole new song, we have John sing the lead part in "Greased Lightning," a Beach Boys-like love song to a car. In the stage musical, the character "Kenicki" now being played in the movie by Jeff Conaway, lead that song and Jeff was not thrilled to learn that the song was now John's. But Jeff was a trouper and went along with it. Show business is often not fair and is definitely not a democracy; but John in black and Jeff in dark brown leather motorcycle jackets sang and danced the song perfectly.

No matter what you may have read or seen on TV, Olivia was John's choice for the role and NO ONE else was seriously considered. I totally agreed with him and felt it was my job to make it happen not only because John wanted it but because it was THE best idea for the movie. Though she was an inspired choice, she didn't leap at the opportunity. She was on a concert tour and wouldn't be done until a few weeks before shooting. Olivia didn't consider herself an actress and was wary of acting in general and taking on a leading role in a high-profile film opposite, in her view, a "much" younger man. She was twenty-eight and Travolta, twenty-three. She really should have had no worries about that. Forty years later in her Sandy costume she looked remarkably the same up until her passing. Olivia was humiliated at how she'd come across in a British science-fiction movie that she'd made years before, *Grease* and she didn't want to make the same mistake again. She liked the role of "Sandy", and after the two met at her house she was pretty sure she wanted in. But Olivia wisely insisted on a screen test so *she* could see how she came across. This was the first and only time I know of when a potential star asks for a screen test; normally the studio or network would ask for one. Allan had serious health issues, stemming largely from his morbid obesity and he was doing way too much coke and other drugs. He'd had one of the first gastric bypass surgeries, which ultimately failed, and it was causing all sorts of problems. But Allan's physical problems were the best thing that could have happened for the movie, because they kept him in the hospital or at home in bed for most of the shoot, thus allowing our work to be done without his micromanaging. He did come to the set several times, usually to see the musical numbers. He used these occasions to bring famous guests, like Rudolf Nureyev, to watch. Allan's greatest gift was promotion and that is what he did masterfully when the the movie was released.

As for Olivia's screen test, we were blessedly on our own. I knew why Allen wasn't there, but I have never understood why his screenwriting partner, Bronte Woodard, was not there either. The scene we chose was at the drive-in, where Danny makes a move on Sandy, and she angrily rebuffs his advances. She throws his class ring at him and bolts out of the car, slamming the door, which hits him in the nuts. After the first take of the scene for the test, none of the dozen or so crew members laughed. Second and third takes, same results. I could see Randal getting very nervous, as was I. If Olivia did not like the test, I had no backup for the role. Randal then called a ten-minute break. Then I remembered something I had read about *Hello, Dolly!* The musical was based on *The Matchmaker*, a play by Thornton Wilder. During a rehearsal prior to the Broadway opening, it was clear that the adapted dialogue by Michael Stewart was not working. The director, Gower Champion, pulled out his small Samuel French published paperback edition of *The Matchmaker* and had the actors try using Wilder's original dialogue which turned out to be a big improvement. Inspired by this story, I pulled out my copy of the *Grease* play script. While Bronte and Allan had done a great job of opening the musical for the film, they misguidedly also changed most of the musical's dialogue. I showed this to Randal and suggested we use the original musical's dialogue for the test. He agreed and gave the "new" dialogue to John and Olivia. During the next take, the crew finally began laughing and the mood on the set changed completely. John and Olivia seemed delighted. When we shot the actual scene for the movie, he was hit in the nuts on the first take, his pain was real, and that take was the one used in the movie. A couple of days later, when the scene was edited and cassette copies had been sent to Olivia and John, the rest of us gathered in a screening room at Paramount to watch. By now Olivia, satisfied with her test, was on board. We watched the test; John and Olivia had great chemistry and everyone laughed except for Allan and Bronte. After all the congratulations and glad-handing, as we all walked to our cars, Allan asked if I was responsible for the dialogue switch. Thinking I had done something very good for the movie, I said innocently and gleefully, practically jumping up and down, "Yes, yes, wasn't it great?" He just glared at me, then he and Bronte walked away. I never heard a good word from him again during the entire shoot. He was pissed because it was *his* dialogue that I changed. I was now on Allan's shit list and had to figure out a way to avoid rising higher on it. This became a real concern, for as Randal and I looked through the rest of the script we realized that Bronte and Allan's dialogue for most of the scenes was not very good nor funny as the stage version. Randal and I then hatched a nefarious plot. Before the start of each day's filming the cast rehearsed dialogue for the scenes ahead. When there were identical scenes from play and movie, we gave the cast the original stage dialogue. That plus the cast's improvisation worked! Beautifully. Allan and Bronte never noticed. As Randal Kleiser noted in his book, *Grease: The Director's Notebook,* very little of the original film script's dialogue remained in the movie. The movie contains the best of the original writing by Jim Jacobs and Warren Casey, Bronte and Allan's better efforts, and lots of genuine improvisation by the cast.

My next conflict with Allan occurred when he saw my list of suggested choices for the grownup roles. This is the list that a casting director always gives to the producer, director, and the studio or network. My idea for the adult parts in the movie were all big stars from the '50s and '60s. Allan, of course, took credit for this. He was also pissed off again because for the role of the high-school principal, I had suggested a national treasure, Eve Arden, a former movie star and the droll comic actress who had enchanted America for a decade as a high-school English teacher on radio and television's *Our Miss Brooks*. Without anyone knowing it, Allan had offered the part to his friend Fannie Flagg, the Alabama-born game-show panelist and future best-selling novelist. Paramount further annoyed Allan by loving my idea and vetoing his choice. I smoothed things over by suggesting that we create another role for Fannie; she became the school nurse with a line or two. I also suggested creating another role not in the script. For me, Eve Arden needed a foil to play off all her trademark sharp lines and facial glares. I suggested that "someone like" Dodie Goodman, a fixture of late-night talk shows, with a sweet ditzy quality, would be perfect. Randal and Allan agreed, as did Paramount, and so she was cast in a role with no lines at that time. The worst casting sin that Alan almost did, again without telling anyone, was promising porn star Harry Reems (*Deep Throat*) $5,000 for the part of the athletic coach. Paramount exploded with, "Are you out of your fucking mind???" Honorably, Allan paid Reems the five grand out his own pocket and '60s TV great Sid Caeser got the role. My lists included other beloved but under-utilized bygone stars. After the Harry Reems debacle, Alan liked my ideas of using Caesar, Joan Blondell, and Frankie Avalon, as well as a faux '50s pop rock and roll group that was then on the charts and had their own syndicated TV series, Sha Na Na, to play the band at the school dance. As Kenickie, the car-crazy tough guy, among those we were considering was the handsome, up-and-coming actor Treat Williams, who had played Danny Zuko in a past company of *Grease*. Because of that, Treat, whose breakthrough role in the film version of *Hair* was still to happen, refused to audition; at least, that's what his agent said. We wound up casting the more cooperative Jeff Conaway, also a stage *Grease* alum. I had a great time during the casting process. I let my imagination run wild. As 'Tom Chisum", the school jock with whom Olivia takes up after splitting from John, I picked Steven Ford, the son of our then-president, Gerald Ford. I thought it was a good publicity stunt, but he quit shortly before shooting began and I replaced him with a son of two famous Hollywood parents, Lorenzo Lamas, whose father was my *Starsky & Hutch* director friend, Fernando Lamas, and whose mother was the glamorous '50s film star Arlene Dahl. A bonus on his family tree was Fernando's current wife and Lorenzo's stepmother, MGM swimming movie star, Esther Williams. Lorenzo told me it was she who really raised him.

As the smoking, drinking, hard-boiled Rizzo, the choice came down to two women. At that time, future Tony winner and Oscar nominee Stockard Channing was best known for having starred in between Warren Beatty and Jack Nicholson as a sanitary napkin heiress, in a comedy movie directed by Mike Nichols, *The Fortune*. The other actress, suggested by Paramount's head of movie casting, Marion Dougherty was Beverly D'Angelo, who would later become famous as co-star to Chevy Chase in *National Lampoon's Vacation* and four of its sequels; for now she was a promising but little-known film and TV actress. In order to make it a fair audition, I had a short dark wig ready for the very blond Beverly. Both girls read well, but defying all rules of casting, the job went to Stockard, who was completely "wrong" for the part. I read stories today about how she got the part because Allan Carr was her then manager. This is completely false. He did not pressure anyone to cast her. Stockard is a New York City Upper East Side WASP who clearly had never even walked past a public high school like the one in *Grease*. But there was something very special and compelling about her audition. On a movie theater screen, watch her lightly freckled face as she sings "There Are Worse Things I Could Do."

In addition to singing the song very well, she *acts* it magnificently. Many have criticized the casting of her and others who were far beyond teen age; Stockard was thirty-three at the time. But what really mattered was not their actual ages, but the fact that the cast members looked roughly the same age as each other, though the youngest was 19-year-old Dinah Manoff, who played "Marty Maraschino". Whatever it is, *Grease* is *not* a naturalistic movie nor a documentary. It is a musical fantasy set in a high school, and if you try to make it too real, it does not work. Besides, with stars like Olivia Newton-John and John Travolta, who cared about realism? Movies are all about the suspension of disbelief. Once she accepted the part, Bob LeMond told me Olivia asked for and received a similar financial deal to that of John's for her acting services. John, in turn, wanted the same deal Olivia would get for the soundtrack album – which is where both wound up making lots of money. The *Grease* album stayed on the charts for almost twenty years and at No. 1 for a year, making anyone with even a small percentage a nice piece of change. Olivia made another smart request: to have her longtime friend and record producer and songwriter, John Farrar, write her a new solo, "Hopelessly Devoted to You," and another duet for her and John, "You're the One That I Want." Both became hit singles, and they, along with "Sandy," were added to all future productions of the stage version of *Grease*.

I happened to be just outside her trailer when she first stepped out as in her skintight black pants and the new hairdo. I laughed as our costume designer, Albert Wolsky, sewed her in and out each time she had to pee. Those now iconic black pants were actual 1950s trousers he found in a thrift shop. The zipper was gone so sewing in and out was required. *Grease* showed us an Olivia no one had ever seen before, especially when she threw her cigarette to the ground and stomped it out with her very high heel and said to Zuko, "Tell me about it, stud!" To watch the filming of that moment, and to see them performing their duet, "You're the One That I Want," on a carnival funhouse set more than made up for any of the problems I had with Allan during the shoot. Well, almost. The real problem I had was that I had no official position besides being the Casting Director. I was almost always at Randal's side providing solutions to many unexpected problems. This was not the job of a casting director but that of the absent producer, Mr. Carr. For example, one of these "solutions" came the day we shot the drag race in the smelly, bacteria-filled but scenic, concrete-lined Los Angeles River. Randal was unusually running behind schedule and had to cut filming close-ups of Olivia sitting up on the banks of the "river" after the race, singing the reprise of the "Sandra Dee" song. I told him not to worry about that. We already had her in a long shot and the song would work even better as a voice-over. He did not have to film her in a close up singing. Another was when Randal came to me bummed out because our meager budget would not allow us to shoot the last scene of the movie at Six Flags Magic Mountain. I said this was great news and it would be much more appropriate (and a lot cheaper) if we rented one of those tacky little traveling carnivals that played for local churches and set it on the campus of an actual high school. There is now a plaque at the John Marshall High School football field in Hollywood that commemorates the filming. The whole concept of Danny using street fighting techniques while trying to find a sport to please Sandy was my idea. It would be immodest to go on like this but it's all there in Randal's book. It wasn't until December 2019, forty years after the movie, when we all reunited in Florida for three sold-out amphitheater sing-along concerts that John and I talked and all the above and more came out.

Grease remains the highest grossing movie musical in history. Surprise, surprise: I never got my contract and the producer credit that was so important to me. All that Allan agreed to never came to be. To put it simply, he screwed me. For all their power, there was nothing that Randal, John, nor Bob could do about it. It was a rude awakening to another of the cold realities of Hollywood. But I did get the privilege of being part of a wonderful project. I am very proud of my contributions, and of knowing that people will be laughing at and singing along to *Grease* long after I am gone. P.S. Olivia should have never doubted her acting prowess having become a "Dame Commander of the Order of the British Empire" alongside the likes of Julie Andrews, Judi Dench, Helen

Mirren, and Maggie Smith. She should be addressed as Dame Olivia, the female equivalent of being a "Sir"!

40 YEARS LATER

In early November of 2019 Randal Kleiser called and asked if I wanted to go to Florida, where he would be directing three big amphitheater sing-along showings of *Grease,* to be followed by a question-and-answer period with John and Olivia after the screening. *Grease* started the outdoor sing along phenomena at the Hollywood Bowl in July 2010. All 17,000 seats sold out. John and Olivia were asked to participate but chose not to. In their stead, Didi Conn (Frenchie) hosted the festivities, which were designed to keep the audience happy and amused while waiting until it was dark enough for the movie to start. With a nod to the midnight screenings of *The Rocky Horror Picture Show*, many of the audience, who ranged in age from seven to seventy or more, came in costume. This being Hollywood, some were incredibly clever and accurate. There were big butch, bearded guys in Pink Lady jackets, tiny little kids as Sandy, Danny, and Rizzo, and my personal favorite, groups of little girls wearing silver smocks, with toilet paper rolls sprayed with silver paint to resemble the immense silver hair rollers piled onto the heads of the Pink Ladies in the "Beauty School Dropout" number. All 17,000 audience members were given "goody" bags containing pom-poms, a comb, and a small device for blowing bubbles for use during appropriate times in the movie. Anyone could come up on the immense stage and parade their costumes, and the audience voted by applause. All this of course while the audience was eating and drinking – alcohol was not only permitted but encouraged, and of course the occasional whiff of weed. The Bowl has repeated this almost every year since then. Once in a while there was a *Sound of Music* sing-along but it was never as much fun, but way more wholesome. Seeing the movie on the Bowl's giant screen was awesome, as was hearing 17,000 voices singing with the on-screen cast. Lyrics with a few changes, such as an image of a cat instead of the word "pussy" as in "…a real pussy wagon," which John sings in the "Greased Lightning" number, appeared at the bottom of the screen in time to the music. Year after year both John and Olivia declined offers, until John thought it could be profitable, fun, and a relatively easy gig. John partnered with Live Nation Entertainment to produce three sing-alongs in 5,000 to 7,500 seat outdoor venues in three smaller Florida cities: West Palm Beach, Tampa, and Jacksonville. These were to serve as tests for a future tour across North America and eventually Europe. Live Nation operates and controls the booking of acts at most of this country's music venues, from small clubs like House of Blues to giant stadiums. They have an international presence as well; one of their subsidiaries, Ticketmaster, controls a huge percentage of concert ticket sales. Not such a shabby partner.

The next step was to get Olivia on board. This was a way for her to continue to perform in a relatively easy manner that would not be too taxing. It would also enable her to correct tabloid stories and tell audiences the truth about how she was dealing with metastic breast and have some fun at the same time. Olivia has never been shy about this and for the past several years had not been doing any concerts or club performances. Fortunately, she had been receiving the best of Western and plant-based medicines with the help of her Sam Elliot look-alike and sound-alike husband, John Easterling. At their home in California, he grows and develops tinctures and formulas made from all sorts of rare plants he obtains from South Pacific islands and Amazonia, and good old American cannabis. She was doing great. Travolta, while still receiving many starring movie offers, wanted to try something different and make some bucks at the same time. Ticket prices for these events were modestly priced from $50 to $125. There were also 150 "very special Meet and Greet" tickets available for the not-so-modest price of $1,000 per. This got the buyer early entrance to the venue, free booze at the hospitality tent, a brief moment and photo with John and Olivia, and a flimsy red and white *Grease* gym bag. This part of the gig seemed very easy for John but a bit taxing for Olivia. It was kind of like a never-ending receiving line where you had to be smiling and nice to everyone you knew you would never be seeing again. Olivia rested quietly between guests. Her face went from genuine interest and a smile to fifteen seconds of what seemed like mini-meditation before greeting the next guest(s), while John was up and down like a yoyo. I can't imagine doing this 150 times.

My immediate response to Randal's question about Florida was negative. All I could think of was my lack of official duties during the movie shoot. He responded that this time would be different, and we would have lots of fun in Florida in mid-December. His flattery will get me most any time. He reminded me of all I had done for the movie without any portfolio, and that I would be doing the same in Florida. Also, he asked if I would help him, as I did a month earlier, at a book signing in Palm Springs for his newly released book, *Grease: The Director's Notebook,* which was being sold along with all the T-shirts, hats, etc. at each venue. In Palm Springs I came up with many different "personal" things he could write while autographing the books. I was also amazed when he introduced me as *Grease's* casting director and people wanted my autograph, too. The trip now seemed like it could be fun. Also, I usually make a trip to Florida once a year, flying into Ft. Lauderdale to see friends and then driving north to Tampa and Jacksonville for family. Halfway between Tampa and Jacksonville is Gainesville, where if they are home, I also visit the Phoenix family (more on them later). I also knew if I was not having a good time at the shows, my escape valve would be to get out of town and head north. The trip turned out to be the antidote to all my previous *Grease* issues. After spending one night in Ft. Lauderdale, I drove in the pouring rain to the Coral Sky Amphitheater in West Palm Beach. It was the worst of our venues; its most obvious feature was a huge sign behind the last row of seats spelling out BEER. I met Randal at his dressing room, and as we were walking to the stage, we saw John exiting a big black SUV. He had a huge smile on his face and yelled our names, walked over, held both our hands, said how amazing it was that we were all there together looking good and healthy. John and I started tearing up, and the three of us had a five-minute, three-way hug. It had been forty-two years since *The Boy in the Plastic Bubble,* when we first worked together, and John, now sixty-seven, Randal, seventy-three, and I, seventy-seven, were indeed healthy and looking well. Olivia looking stunning at seventy-one and in great spirits, along with her manager, Mark Hartley, publicist Mike Caprio, and choreographer Randy Slovacek, arrived soon afterward. Already in their dressing rooms were the now geriatric T-Birds, Barry Pearl (sixty-nine), Michael Tucci (seventy-five), and Kelly Ward, the baby of the group at sixty-three. Not all the Pink Ladies were available, so it was just the boys.

We got together on the stage and began finalizing plans for the first show the following night, while stagehands were assembling the enormous movie "screen," which was made of two-foot by four-foot individual LED screens all ganged together. Sound guys were installing huge speakers and a ton of other equipment. I began taking pictures with my good Nikon, not my cell phone, and John, who had been photo-phobic way back had no problem with my shooting all over, including his now buzzed-bald head. I'd been hoping to do this but figured don't ask permission but apologize later. I never had to apologize. Within a few hours we planned the show:

1. Randal comes out, introduces the show and the T-Birds. They do five minutes of shtick and explain how to use the stuff in the goody bags.
2. Everyone exits; the screen comes down and the movie starts. 3. We all take the next hour and a half to eat dinner and chill.
4. As the movie finishes and the screen rises, John and Olivia walk down-stage just as Danny and Sandy fly off into the blue sky.
5. They sit down and begin about forty minutes of questions and answers with the audience. The T-Birds are scattered throughout the audience with microphones for the Q&A.
6. After the Q&A, the T-Birds would pick six guys and because of a suggestion Olivia and I made to see if girls could do it better, six girls would also to be picked to come on stage, where John would teach the choreography for "Greased Lightning."
7. After the number, the lucky audience members would exit the stage and John, Olivia, T-Birds, and Randal say goodbyes and exit. Over and out.

With tomorrow all planned, we headed to our hotels to change for the dinner Olivia was giving for all of us at the ultra-exclusive Breakers Hotel in Palm Beach. The dinner was in a private space off the main dining room. Olivia was at the head of a long rectangular table with her husband John to her left. The rest of the seating was random, and Travolta and I wound up next to each other. We spent the next few hours eating great food and in my case drinking lots of wine. We opened our hearts to one another and for the first time after knowing each other for fifty years, really connected. We realized that most of our previous communication had been processed through John's manager and my best friend, Bob LeMond. We laughed at how during pre-production of the movie, as you have read earlier, John told Bob he wanted another song for Danny in the first act of the movie. Bob then came to me, and I suggested that rather than having a new song written, John should sing the lead in "Greased Lightning." Then Bob reported back to John, who was very okay with this. John then let on that there was no way he was *not* going to lead that number.

We realized we had so much in common, beginning with our love of classic cars, like my '65 Mustang. When I told him I had put down a deposit on the yet to be produced Tesla Cyber Truck, he confessed his love of Tesla cars and that he had two of them. He swore his blood pressure has lowered by ten points by driving semi-automatically on Florida's highways. We talked about all the non-casting things I had done for the movie and he was amazed at their extent. He bragged about the talents of his beautiful daughter Ella Blue and how casting directors loved her. Eventually we separated and schmoozed with the rest of the table. Fortunately for Uber and Lyft, no one had to drive back to their hotels, and somehow, though very hung over, we got to the venue the next morning not knowing the disaster that was to happen that night. In the beginning, all went off perfectly. When John and Olivia walked out in their Danny and Sandy costumes, not only did they look fantastic, but the audience responded as if they were The Beatles. The cheers seemed to go on forever but finally subsided when John and Olivia sat down, and the Q&A began. It was nearly impossible for them to see or hear which of the T-Birds was speaking and where they located in the audience. But somehow, they got through it. There was one special moment when a woman shared with Olivia that she had inspired her in her fight with cancer. This gave Olivia the chance to tell her story and the audience rose and responded with love and support. Olivia used this time to talk about auctioning her black leather movie jacket, which sold for almost $250,000, proceeds going to the Olivia Newton John Cancer Wellness and Research Center in Melbourne; and how the buyer amazingly returned the jacket to her and it now hangs at the Wellness Center.

Then things began to go south very quickly. Randal announced from the stage that the T-Birds would now pick six guys and six girls to come on stage for their choreography lesson. The guys were picked quickly with no problems and proceeded to the stage and began their dance lessons. But when the T-Birds started picking the girls, they were surrounded in the aisles from the over-anxious would-be girl dancers. Our guys had to run for cover and self-preservation. By this time, all able and semi-able men such as myself were in the audience guarding the front of stage, which was beginning to be rushed by the way over-enthusiastic women. We were mobbed, and in the middle of a stampede headed toward the stage's two staircases on the right and left. John's assistant, Jimmy Marino, and I clawed our way through the women and to the relative safety of the stage. The stampede was happening while John and the six guys from the audience on stage were frantically finishing the dance number. Finally, it ended. John and Olivia said their good nights very quickly, then exited, and the audience went home. Disaster was narrowly avoided.

The next day I ditched the car and traveled to the Tampa venue with the Randal, the T-Birds, Olivia's husband, and Olivia's assistant and make-up artist on her incredible tour bus. An apartment as luxurious yet as small as that bus would go for mucho bucks anywhere in New York. Having learned from the night before, we regrouped before the show in Tampa and made a few changes. Gone was the "Greased Lightning" dance instruction. Also, the Q&A was to happen only from the stage with Randal and the T-Birds asking the questions and Olivia and John answering them. John asked me to scout the pre-show audience for those who had a question for the pair. Because of my casting experience, I had pretty good instincts for this. I did short interviews with those I thought interesting and got about twenty-five possible questions. Then Jimmy Marino and I narrowed them down and ran them by John. During the Q&A, most of the questions were real audience ones. But some of the more funny and outrageous ones were written by me. Example was a question for John and Olivia: "Would you guys consider a threesome?" Both John and Olivia laughed and replied, "Sorry but we are already in one," pointing at the three T-Birds. The audience howled. At last, I had a real job. The show went over very well, and our next and last night (Jacksonville) was predictably our best, having had two performances under our belts. By now, practically everyone appeared a bit worn-out, except for John who was doing his impression of the Eveready Bunny. Randal and I thought that if an easier schedule were in place – like no more three shows in a row – a longer tour could work, and we would all be spending the summer of 2020 on the road. A little speed bump called Covid-19 ended all expectations.

The *Grease* cast is an amazingly tight knit group, constantly in touch with one another thanks to Barry Pearl (Doody) acting as our switchboard. We celebrate and mourn for each other. We were all devastated by the passing of two cast members, Annette Charles aka Annette Cardona (Cha Cha), and Dennis Stewart (Crater Face) a few years ago. And in 2020, John's wife of nearly thirty years, Kelly Preston, passed away, too. John has had great success and great tragedy in his life. I hope there will be no more sorrows for him, and like the song says, for our *Grease* team, We'll Always Be Together.

THREE YEARS LATER – 2022

Driving down the hill from my house to meet friends for lunch, I got a phone call from *Taxi's* Marilu Henner. She was calling to tell me that Olivia had died, and she didn't want me to hear about it on media. I almost had an accident because I could not see through the windshield because of my tears. I managed to make it to my friends' house where I became a basket case. I explained what had happened and they asked if they could do anything for me. I said yes "alcohol" having given up weed. Several glasses later I drove home -very carefully - along Hollywood Boulevard. As I was passing Mann's Chinese Theater (the place with all the hand and footprints of movie stars) I noticed a couple of TV news trucks and a small gathered crowed. I guessed correctly they were at Olivia's star on the "Walk of Fame". I pulled over and joined all of them sharing our grief. It was kind of cheesy but cathartic as I unloaded my feelings, crying continuously from a combination of grief and tequila to a correspondent for some Australian news station. But for the next two weeks I would think of her and spontaneously tear up. I may have been a hard ass in many ways in my career, but I am a marshmallow inside.

I cannot remember any one except JFK and Princess Diana whose deaths affected so many from so many different walks of life. Everyone leads off talking about Olivia's beauty and demeanor. They should be leading off with how smart Olivia was and how beloved she was by so many. I also cannot tell you how many of my heterosexual male friends told me, how shall I put this, that when they were alone and using one of their hands on certain parts of their anatomy and out of sight of their parents or roommates, their thoughts were of Olivia. The following is an edited version of what I wrote and posted on Facebook while on hold for a zoom interview from yet another Aussie TV station. Writing and posting this was the therapy I needed. I disconnected from Zoom and went to bed.

The last time we saw one another was in Florida but we remained in contact thru e-mail and phone up until a month of wo ago. How does one begin to deal with the loss of someone as wonderful as Dame Olivia? I don't know and have been trying to figure that out all day between crying jags. My heart goes out to her husband, John Easterling , her daughter Chloe and her nephew Emerson. Watching how John cared for her during the Florida shows was a lesson in seeing true love and devotion. At Olivia's request, one of the audience questions I always prepared was about her health. Olivia, unlike most celebrities was very open about her battle with cancer. She explained to me that talking to other women about her journey was very helpful to her own. My preparation was totally unnecessary because at each show there was always a woman in the audience inquiring about her health. She always answered with the most positive encouragement imaginable. After Olivia's answer there was always an impossible amount of love going back and forth between the audience and the stage. The world will miss this woman who's interior more than matched her beautiful exterior.

CHAPTER 9

ANGIE & THE REAL *TAXI* DRIVERS OF NEW YORK

While still casting *Starsky & Hutch* and working for *SGP*, the pilot script for *Taxi* appeared on my desk, along with an offer to cast it. As I read it, I felt that old tingle. *Taxi* was not unusual in form; it was a gang workplace comedy – in this case, about a crew of Manhattan cabbies with dreams. What made *Taxi* different was the quality of the writing. It was sophisticated and funny, and the characters were very finely wrought. The pilot dealt with a driver who has a one-shot chance to meet the grown daughter he hasn't seen in years because of a divorce. The story had plenty of belly laughs and heart.

Taxi retained that formula throughout its five seasons on the air (1978-1983). The show made stars out of a half-dozen of the best comedic actors of that era, and it won eighteen Emmys. None of that kept it from struggling in the ratings – "too New York," said its critics. But I'm getting ahead of my story.

My assistant Steve Kolzak took over most of the casting chores for *Starsky & Hutch* while I concentrated on *Taxi*. The casting process kept me busy for months – an unusually long time for a pilot, which is typically wrapped up as speedily as possible. But the writers were a distinguished foursome who had a firm on-air commitment for twenty-two episodes from ABC and they were in no hurry. All of them had written and/or produced *The Mary Tyler Moore Show*. After that series ended in 1977, they left MTM Productions to accept lucrative offers at Paramount. Though all four were members of the Tribe of Israel, they called themselves the John Charles Walters Company, which sounded like a white-shoe law firm.

James L. Brooks would later win three Oscars for producing, directing, and writing *Terms of Endearment*. His film career also included *Broadcast News* and *As Good As It Gets*, two more award-winners. One of his only missteps was *I'll Do Anything* (1994), his attempt at a movie musical. Jim wrote the script, and the music came from Carole King and Prince, who I believe not only had never worked together but the two had also never met regarding this project. They just contributed songs that were to be sung by the star cast of non-singers. However, the movie script itself was excellent, and Jim assembled a great non-singing cast that included Nick Nolte, Tracey Ullman, Julie Kavner, Albert Brooks, Sir Ian McKellen, Rosie O'Donnell – and me! Did I mention that none of the former could sing and please don't tell Rosie because she thinks she can.

In the movie within the movie, I played the casting director, who brings in struggling actor Nick Nolte to audition for Albert Brooks (*Broadcast News*), playing the producer, and Sir Ian McKellen (*X Men*) playing the movie within the movie's director. I then had to read a scene with Nick as his girlfriend breaking up with him. Cardinal rule of readings and auditions: Do not start reading at the dramatic high point of a scene – ramp up to it. The script had me start purposely starting at the top and I slid down in a very funny manner. But perhaps I was a bad-luck charm, because after the movie's first screening at a suburban L.A movie house, all the music and the non-singing actors' horrible voice work were stripped from the movie and never to be heard again. *I'll Do Anything* was released as a straight comedy without music.

It remained a very good film, but with months of bad pre-release gossip and publicity, it bombed. However, you can see my scene on YouTube and judge for yourself how terrible I was. Jim did also not laugh when on my first day on the set I asked him how he could do a musical without any of its creators being gay. But I did get paid well and to this day get residual payments from The Screen Actor's Guild. Of course, the biggest of these checks was about 72 cents.

The other *Taxi* writers were David Davis, Ed. Weinberger, and Stan Daniels, all whose credits could fill the rest of this chapter. The pilot's director was James Burrows, my friend and former colleague from the David Merrick years. Jimmy had gone on to direct more than fifty episodes of MTM shows. From there he directed almost every episode of *Cheers* as well as *Will and Grace*. With a team like that, almost every actor in town wanted in on *Taxi*. The first to be cast was a rising and highly unconventional young comedian, Andy Kaufman, in the role of the Sunshine Cab Company's resident mechanic, "Latka Gravas". His character was inspired by a creation of his that had helped make him known, first in clubs, then on the *Tonight* show. It was "Foreign Man", who spoke in an unspecific Eastern European accent, told bad jokes, and did impersonations of Elvis Presley. At other times, Andy would play a record of the Mighty Mouse cartoon theme on an old-fashioned phonograph, set beside him on a little table. He would stand frozen, then animatedly lip-synch whenever the line "Here I come to save the day!" – just that one line over and over and over. It was hilarious!

Next up was the character of Sunshine Cab Co. dispatcher Louie de Palma, described in the script as round, greasy, cigar-smoking boss of the garage. Jim and Ed. advised me not to spend much time dealing with that role. All they needed, they said, was a funny-looking type who didn't even have to be a good actor, because he'd never have more than one or two lines per episode. As with Henry Winkler's Fonzie, you never know who is going to be a break-out character. I ignored what Jim and Ed. Said, and instantly thought of Danny DeVito, whom I had met while casting *Starsky & Hutch*. Danny's only meaningful credit up until then was a small part in *One Flew Over the Cuckoo's Nest*. Danny is indeed funny-looking but also sexy in an odd way. He is just under five feet, with a head that belongs on a taller body. He can switch from anger to uproarious humor in a heartbeat and can milk a joke till it's dry. Obviously, he's also a superb actor. I brought in Danny and a second actor for comparison to the audition. The other candidate read first. He was fine. Then Danny walked in threw the script on the desk and demanded, "Who wrote this shit?" The part was instantly his. However, several of his famous friends, including Jack Nicholson, with whom he had done *Cuckoo's Nest*, told him not to take the job, that a TV series was a dead end for an actor. He proved them so wrong.

In the script was the part of a 40ish, washed-up, Irish boxer with cauliflower ears who drives a cab. A former ABC executive, Stuart Sheslow suggested we should look at a guy they had seen for a series the previous season, Tony Danza. Tony was a handsome and lovable guy from Brooklyn who had, in fact, been a professional boxer. We brought him in to read and he charmed everyone. The role was revised for a younger actor; his character, "Tony Banta", now Italian, remained dimwitted but not washed-up; an excellent move because, like the rest of the ensemble, he had hopes and aspirations. Tony and I also had another connection. A few months into *Taxi*'s airing on TV, he asked me if I had lived on East 95th St. in Brooklyn. It turns out his uncle had seen my name in the credits, and he was our garbage man. Brooklyn ties run deep.

Another character was "Elaine O'Connor Nardo", a single mother of two kids who dreams of being a beautician, but who makes ends meet by driving a taxi. There are many stories around as to the origin of that character. This is the one that I was was told. The part was written for Nell Carter, a performer who would later play a crucial role in my life, and I in hers. The four *Taxi* writers had written a made-for-TV, "urban" (code for Black) musical version of *Cinderella*, called *Cindy* which had aired just before this time. Nell played one of the stepsisters, and she was wonderful. But Nell became unavailable for *Taxi* because she got the break that made her a star: a role in the Broadway musical *Ain't Misbehavin'*. Her performance helped the show win a Tony as well as one for herself too. The writers told me that if *Taxi* succeeded, they'd write another character for Nell when she was free. That never happened for her or any black actor. We saw many other actresses – none were black – and the one who clicked was the very white Marilu Henner. She had done mostly theater and had created the role of "Marty" in the original Chicago production of *Grease*. For me, Marilu, in addition to having great comic timing could be one of the guys. She could take it and give it back right back. She was beautiful enough to be lusted after and tough enough for the guys to accept her and, more important, to treat her as an equal not a sex object. None of the other women who I brought in came close. Yet the Fab Four *Taxi* writers took their sweet time; they just couldn't decide. Finally, I told the guys that Marilu had another firm offer, and if we didn't cast her that day, we would lose her and we had no viable backup. I knew she was not going to take that offer but I used the story and it worked. They told me to make the offer.

Alex Reiger, the one character in *Taxi* who was resigned to his cab-driving fate, following a string of crashed hopes. Alex was everyone's father; he could solve *your* problems, if not his own. Experienced actors kept turning the role down. Was it because of the tinge of loser that Alex had? Or was it the fact that his part as written didn't have a lot of laughs? I never figured it out. We even got a no from Cliff Gorman, who had created the role of the swishiest party guest in *The Boys in the Band* and who later won a Tony for playing Lenny Bruce on Broadway and in the movie adaptation too. Cliff clearly had his eyes set on film, not TV. We went back to Judd Hirsch, who had previously turned us down. A real New Yorker, born in the Bronx, Judd knew how to play a hard-boiled member of the working class. He could see *Taxi*'s potential, and that was the problem: He didn't want to risk uprooting his family from New York, tying himself down for years to a sitcom that he thought might last two seasons at best. He was also a new father and had a great Broadway career going for him. No dummy he, Judd had his agent hit us up for a salary that we would surely refuse. We didn't. Judd was in.

The role of "John Burns" was central to the pilot. He was a sheepish young man from the Midwest who was driving a cab to pay his way through college. We cast Texas-born Randall Carver, who had mainly done TV guest appearances. *Taxi* was his big break. ABC and all the producers thought John Burns would be the one character the country those outside New York could identify with – a nice, normal, sweet, midwestern kid. Unfortunately, the writers were never able to figure out what to do with him, and with so many strong personalities in the cast, Randall's role kept diminishing until finally, at the end of season one, his character was dropped with no explanation.

The last part to be cast was that of "Bobby Wheeler", an eternally hopeful but insecure struggling actor. I had just finished my work on *Grease*, which was not yet released to theaters, and I knew how good Jeff Conaway was as Kenickie, the best friend of Danny Zuko (John Travolta). A cute, longhaired 1970s guy, Jeff was certain, I felt, to become a big movie star, and we'd be lucky to get him on *Taxi*. The one holdout against him was Jim Brooks. In an abrupt change of plan, Jim had decided that maybe Bobby should be black. Perhaps because I kept annoying everyone, saying how can we be authentic without one person of color in a New York taxi crew? Anyone who has spent any time in NYC knows that many taxi drivers hail from Bangladesh, India, Somalia, and all over the world – some not speaking a word of English. On the day of Jeff's final audition, Jim brought in Cleavon Little, best known for playing the black sheriff of an all-white Western town in Mel Brooks' *Blazing Saddles*. Conaway read very well; Little, not so well. Both were told to go home while we and the Paramount and ABC execs made the decision. Most everyone in the room lined up behind Jeff but Brooks would not give ground. In situations like these I can be very eloquent. Buzzing from a quick snort in the men's room, I went to bat for Jeff as persuasively as a televangelist. Jim caved, and Jeff got the part.

Unfortunately, I was very wrong. I knew that great actors often do lousy auditions but this time I didn't say that to the guys. I should have remembered how great Cleavon Little was in the Broadway musical *Purlie,* for which he won a Tony, *and* in the movie, *Blazing Saddles*. But I didn't speak up. While Jeff was very good, it became apparent to me within a few episodes that

Jeff's and Tony Danza's characters somewhat overlapped. After a few seasons, Jeff was unhappy; he complained to the producers about the writing of his part, which to him was nothing more than a heap of struggling-actor clichés. He asked to be let out of his contract after the third season. He had fired his good manager from *Grease* days, Bob LeMond, and had hired new managers who convinced him they could make him a movie star. This is a typical tactic used by agents and managers when they want to steal an actor away from his/her current representation. It was a stupid move which years later Jeff acknowledged and regretted.

His character "Bobby" wasn't missed, but he was personally missed because the cast of *Taxi,* like the cast of *Grease,* had become a true family. From there Jeff did TV guest shots and had roles on a few series including the space series *Babylon 5.* When an old back injury resurfaced, Jeff became opioid-addicted and began a downward spiral. Eventually he joined the lurid VH1 reality series *Celebrity Rehab with Dr. Drew.* The rehab attempts didn't work. On May 26, 2011, he died at sixty following an accidental overdose. This saddened everyone who knew him. He was the loveable bad boy whose trailer was constantly rocking with female companionship during the shoot of *Grease.* After the shoot was over, Jeff settled down and married Olivia Newton-John's sister, Rona. Jeff became a devoted stepdad to Rona's son, Emerson, and for a while it looked like things were going to go well for Jeff, but sadly that did not happen. Both Oliva and Rona are no longer with us, but Emerson remembers Jeff as his loving father. I wish I could tell you that the rest of *Taxi*'s dramas were confined to the screen. The show certainly got off to an encouraging start. It enchanted most of the critics. Wisely, ABC scheduled it for Tuesday nights at 9:30, right after *Three's Company*. *Taxi* held onto much of that audience, but it was always more of an artistic than a commercial success.

After four seasons, ABC canceled it. NBC picked it up for one last season, but the ratings were never good.

Along the way, we had Andy Kaufman's schizophrenic (in the most literal sense) behavior to deal with. One of Andy's "personalities" was "Tony Clifton", a comical cliché of an over-the-hill nightclub singer with ruffled shirts, huge rings, sunglasses, a shoe-polish black curly wig with matching 70's porn star mustache. Not only did we have to hire Mr. Kaufman, but we also had to "hire" Tony, whom Andy never acknowledged was actually him. That meant two separate contracts and paychecks. One clause in Andy's deal stated that should Clifton ever be fired; Andy's contract would be null and void. If we wanted Andy (and we did, badly), we had no choice but to comply with his wacky demands. Contractually bound to employ Tony Clifton in four episodes, the writers came up with the good idea of using Tony as Danny DeVito's brother. He showed up for the first rehearsal with a hooker on each arm and proceeded to be obnoxious to everyone. The cast members hated the way the boorish and bullying Tony was behaving on set and got very pissed off with Andy whom everyone thought was both nuts and a genius. Worse than that, Tony was unbelievably awful as an actor – so much so that he had to be fired in order for the episode to be completed. Ed. Weinberger (the period after his name all through this book is not a misprint – his name is actually, Edwin), who was the show runner for the group of its creators, called Andy's manager, George Shapiro. He explained the situation, and George said he'd get back to him. Meanwhile Ed. called me to line up a replacement actor. I hired Richard Feronjy, ironically the actor who I had in mind for *Starsky & Hutch* when he was displaced by Danny DeVito.

George called back and told Ed. that it was okay to fire Tony – on the condition that he get fired in a very public way. Ed. warned the cast that something bizarre was about to happen on set that afternoon and to just go along with it. Paramount's security guards were placed on standby. Word got around, and the bleachers where the audience would sit for tapings were filling up with Paramount employees who couldn't wait to watch the shenanigans begin. After the lunch break, Tony returned with the two hookers. Ed. told him, in full view of everyone, that things weren't working out and he had to let him go. Tony erupted in anger and began yelling: "WHAT DO YOU MEAN? I'M THE BEST ACTOR IN THIS BUNCH! YOU CAN'T DO THAT!". Judd Hirsch, who was finally fed up, walked over, and began shouting back at Tony/Andy. Just before they came to blows, three security guards grabbed Tony and dragged him, kicking and screaming, off the set and off the lot, leaving his two bewildered hookers behind. Later, Andy met George at a nearby restaurant. As George explained afterwards, Andy told him that this was the happiest day of his life for he had pulled off an incredible piece of performance art.

About this time, I got an interesting offer from Garry Marshall's company at Paramount. They wanted me to cast a spinoff from *Laverne & Shirley*, which itself was a spin off from *Happy Days*, as was Garry's latest smash hit, *Mork & Mindy*, starring Robin Williams. It was called *Big Rosie*. I read the script and thought it was barely okay, occasionally funny, but hardly the sophisticated comedy writing I was used to on *MTM* and *Newhart*; it was not the kind of material I wanted to work with. After all, hadn't I just cast the most successful movie musical ever, with the world's biggest film star? I said no and thanked them. The next day they called back and told me that Paramount would let me produce the pilot if I cast it. Without even thinking, I said no again. I then told some of my friend what I had just done. They all thought I was crazy and the nicest way they described me was "asshole," followed closely by, "How idiotic can you be? Don't you want to produce? Most people would kill to work with Garry Marshall." Of course, they were right. I sheepishly called back and confessed to my stupidity. If the job were still available, I said, I'd love to do it. Thank God, it was.

Unlike CBS Studio Center and 20th Century Fox, the Paramount lot was buzzing with activity. Paramount had begun to awaken from a long sleep. Under the leadership of Barry Diller (at the top) and Michael Eisner (just below) and the studio was hot. It had been about a while since I'd cast *Grease,* and the change was obvious. There was much renovation of the studio facilities, and new paint everywhere. As far as television was concerned, Paramount had the two most important suppliers of network comedy, with Garry Marshall's group (*Happy Days, Laverne & Shirley, Mork & Mindy*) and the John Charles Walters Company (*Taxi).* Garry's shows featured broad, populist humor. They were highly successful ratings-wise but were seldom well-reviewed or Emmy material. The John Charles Walters writers who were responsible for *Taxi,* wrote in a much more sophisticated manor and their offices ran out of room for their many nominations and awards. On the other hand, Garry's company's work was much more popular with the TV audience. My snobbery made me much less interested in working with Garry's shows, but once involved, I listened and learned from a master.

Garry believed in nepotism. His father, Tony Marshall (a.k.a Anthony Masciarelli) came to the office every day, and unlike the rest of Garry's staff was always dressed in a coat and tie. This look went perfectly with his role as head moneyman. He was responsible for overall budgeting, and when someone had to be let go, Tony was firer-in-chief. He was listed on all Garry's shows as an executive producer. Ronny Marshall Hallin, one of Garry's two sisters, worked as a producer, and was great with casting and post-production. His other sister, Penny Marshall, was Laverne on *Laverne & Shirley*. Garry worked with the same writers year after year and continued to do so even when he branched out very successfully into movies, including *Big*, *Beaches*, and *Prettty Woman*.

As for TV, Garry's first big hit was *The Odd Couple*; later he produced *Happy Days*, which ran for eleven seasons on ABC. Garry had been a writer on *Love, American Style*, a hit comedy anthology series. One of its segments, *Love and the Television Set*, had led to a pilot for a series about family life in the fifties. Its star was Ron Howard. The pilot didn't sell, but it was seen by George Lucas, who cast Ron in his hit film *American Graffiti*, also set in the fifties. The film's success made ABC take another look at the failed pilot. They asked Garry to broaden the humor and make another pilot with Ron. While the first pilot had been shot like a movie, the second was shot in front of a studio audience. A crucial new cast member, Henry Winkler, was added as biker Arthur "Fonzie" Fonzarelli. Henry had little TV experience prior to this; his only previous work was on *The Bob Newhart Show* and *The Mary Tyler Moore Show*. Before *Welcome Back, Kotter*, John Travolta had auditioned for Fonzie and thank goodness, didn't make it. Nevertheless, *Happy Days*, as the show was eventually called, ran eleven seasons.

There were many spinoffs (and spinoffs from spinoffs) from *Happy Days*: *Laverne & Shirley*, *Mork & Mindy*, *Joanie Loves Chachi*, *Blansky's Beauties*, *The Ugily Family*, and the one offered to me, *Big Rosie*. The character being spun off was "Big Rosie Greenbaum", played by the physically imposing and excellent actress, Carole Ita White. She was a co-worker and rival to Laverne and Shirley. Rosie gloated over how she had married a doctor while Laverne and Shirley were unhappily single. Why they were calling this a spinoff I'll never know, because Paramount wanted to a) tone down the character's obnoxiousness, b) find another actress to play Rosie; c) change the character's name to insure that Ms. White could claim no financial interest; and d) convert Rosie from Jewish to Italian. I went to a catalog of movie stars and thumbed my way through, looking for possible names. I got to the D's and saw Angie Dickinson's name. That's how *Rosie* became *Angie*.

The plot of the pilot was simple: A sweet waitress meets a handsome, wealthy doctor and they fall in love. John Travolta sent me our lead. Donna Pescow had appeared in *Saturday Night Fever* as "Annette", John's former dance partner, who winds up in the backseat of his car. Donna came to L.A. to seek further work, and John asked me to meet her. I loved her instantly. My two choices for her mother were Doris Roberts and Olympia Dukakis. Doris won out. This very Jewish actress then started her career as an Italian mother and later spent nine years playing one on *Everybody Loves Raymond*. Robert Hays rounded out the main cast as Angie's doctor boyfriend and a year or so later as the leading man in the movie *Airplane!*

During production, after casting was finished and we started rehearsing, Garry disappeared. He left the two writers, Alan

Eisenstock and Larry Mintz, and myself completely alone until the dress rehearsal with a small audience. The first thing he did was to tell us how happy he was with what he saw and to get rid of one of Donna's costumes. Since the Philadelphia coffee shop, she worked in had a Revolutionary War theme, I'd put Donna in a "bodacious wench" outfit. Wrong. The rest of his script and acting notes were also spot on. I remember there was one problem we could not resolve, and Garry said to "hang a lantern on it" meaning to *emphasize* it, not to hide it. I also asked him what to do about the audience laughing at an inappropriate time. He then asked me what an "inappropriate" laugh sounds like versus an appropriate one. "We're all here to make funny," he continued. I got the point and shut up.

Eisenstock, Mintz, and I were happy and proud of what we had created. The pilot was then "tested" by ABC, and we heard that Donna tested higher than any other female lead in recent years. Six episodes were ordered immediately. The story lines followed Angie's courtship and wedding and gave Doris lots of space to do her interfering mother shtick. *Angie* was scheduled to follow *Mork & Mindy* on Thursday nights and was an instant hit. Our ratings were in the top twenty shows on TV. All was great with the world, and I was a finally a real producer – and then I along with the writers were gone. I had never been fired before. I didn't realize this was nothing personal, just "showbiz." Eventually I did learn that we were let go so that Paramount could pay off an expensive deal with another producer, Lee Thuna , who was not only not funny in person but was severely lacking in comedy writing skills. Appealing to Garry Marshal was useless in that he was pretty much out of the TV business and fully involved with his feature film career.

ABC then made a schedule change by moving both *Mork* and *Angie* to Sunday nights at seven, directly opposite *60 Minutes*. Both shows tanked in the ratings and were cancelled: *Angie* was first and *Mork* soon afterward. *Angie* was just not funny anymore and probably deserved to be cancelled, but *Mork* did not, but no one asked my opinion. I was miserable. I didn't realize that none of this was personal, just "showbiz." I could still pay my mortgage and eat; thank you, unemployment insurance. I didn't understand, and never would until long after the fact, that I was suffering the same neurosis that all actors, writers, directors, etc., even the best ones, have between jobs: the fear of never working again. In my case, the scariest dry spells unfailingly gave way to some of the great opportunities.

PHOTOS

In 1940, my grandfather, Abe Balsam,
at his farm at 712 Hendrix St., Brooklyn, NY.

My mother and I....Love the hat!

The grand opening of my paternal grandfather's grocery store in Brownsville, Brooklyn. 4th from left, my Grandmother Nani, then Grandpa George, middle with elbow on counter, my father, Bernie and next to him, Uncle Leo.

Cam Walter, my very own "Auntie Mame"

My 1959 acne-free graduation photo from Samuel J. Tilden, High School in Brookyn.

My first show business job - Box Office Treasurer at Tappan Zee Playhouse in Nyack, NY.

Honey Waldman, Owner of the Tappan Zee Playhouse and the Bouwerie Lane Theatre.

Pearl Bailey "adopted" me when I was Company Manager and later Casting Director for her Broadway version of "Hello, Dolly!" She plucked me out of NY and she brought me to Hollywood to work on her short lived TV show. I owe my entire career in LA to her.

In 1971 at my just
purchased Laurel
Canyon house and '65
Mustang Convertible.

Unable to afford new siding, I am
installing shingles by myself.

Architect Peter Schneck (standing) at his house in Sardinia, Italy.
Photographer Michael Childers (seated).

All alone in the empty Coliseum at
dusk; fulfilling a fantasy being a lover
of sword, sandal and gladiator movies.
And yes, the tower is still leaning.

Ahhh... to be 19 and single in
the ruins of Herculaneum in the
shadow of Mt. Vesuvius

The Phoenix Family - left to right: Summer, Liberty, Rain, Leaf (later Joaquin), and River with parents John and Arlyn (later Heart) Phoenix.

Jeffrey Wiseman and Heart Phoenix on their wedding day in 2001.

In 1976 on set of THE BOY IN THE PLASTIC BUBBLE. From left: John Travolta, Diana Hyland, Glynnis O'Connor, Director Randal Kleiser, back row Joanie Stewart, Howard Platt, writer Douglas Day Stewart and Co-Producer, Cindy Dunne.

In December 2019 preparing for GREASE sing-a-long performances in Florida. From left: Angie Losito, myself, Randy Slovacek, Randal Kleiser, Olivia Newton-John, John Travolta, Michael Caprio and Jimmy Marino.

John Travolta, Costume Designer Albert Wosky, Choreographer Pat Birch and Producer Allan Carr. Albert is the unsung hero of the movie. Try to imagine it without his designs.

All in costume and makeup for our Florida sing-a-long shows: Kelly Ward, Barry Pearl, Olivia Newton-John, John Travolta and Michael Tucci. All still rock 40 years after making the movie.

Olivia and her husband, John Easterling (in back with hat) generously invited us to travel with them from city to city on her tour bus. In violation of the splendor of her bus, we acted like school kids on a day off. From Left to Right seated: Olivia, Barry Pearl, me, Kelly Ward and Paulina Calonoc. Back row: Martha Real, Michael Tucci, John Easterling and Randal Kleiser.

Randal Kleiser, Dame Olivia Newton-John and myself celebrating our
movie, IT'S MY PARTY.

Kareem Abdul-Jabbar, Rossie Harris and Peter Graves in AIRPLANE!s
cockpit. The most fun I had casting any project.

On the set of "Gimme a Break".
Left Kari Michaelson, myself Lara Jill Miller and Nell Carter.

Nell Carter and her brother Bernard on her wedding day. I performed the ceremony.

Nell Carter and then fiancé George Krynicki at my house in Laurel Canyon

Babysitting Nell's two sons: Daniel (L) and Joshua (R)

Danny DeVito giving me $18 for my 70'th Birthday. He had just told me that Jews traditionally give cash gifts in multiples of 18. I just finished asking why not $1800 or $18.000? L. Mariliu Henner, R. Yvans Jourdain

General Manager Brian Avnet with wife, musician Marcia Avnet. Brian was my boss at Westbury Music Fair and after he moved to Hollywood hired me to cast L.A. productions of TOMMY (with Teddy Neeley), THE ROCKY HORROR SHOW (with Tim Curry and Meat Loaf) and JESUS CHRIST SUPERSTAR (Teddy Neeley and Carl Anderson)

Judith Light and husband Robert Desidero and my first ex, Tony nominated actor Lou Libertore.

Both Loni Anderson (L) and Wonder Woman's Linda Carter (R) co-starred in a big NBC series, "Partners in Crime". It was an unexpected big flop.

With Barbara Eden after screening of "Harper Valley PTA" series.

Cliff Richard, England's Elvis Presley. Olivia Newton John got her start on his TV show.

I brought Christopher Meloni in for every role he was right for and he never got any of them. However his career turned out just fine.

My boss Brandon Tartikoff criticizing my modeling efforts at some NBC event

Cassandra Peterson aka Elvira out of costume and makeup. My sister Fran on right.

Lilly Tartikoff. In addition to having raised hundreds of millions of $ to fight cancer, she is also THE best person.

My former casting assistant Catherine Keener with Lou Liberatore. She asked if she could "read" for me to see if she could act. Obviously she could.

Actress and Director Jenny Sullivan and I at the Emmys. She was my "spouse" on Maui and at other NBC functions.

Casting Directors and best friends, Joan Barnett (L) and Linda Otto (R)

With good friends, Broadway stars Patti LuPone and Christine Ebersole. I put Christine on the '81-82 season of "Saturday Night Live". In 1987 I cast Patti as Lady Bird Johnson in our TV movie, "LBJ: The Early Years"

My next door neighbor and friend, "Full Service" author Scotty Bowers at 96 being interviewed at L.A's gay film festival, OUTFEST.

Nicole Scherzinger during tapings of POPSTARS which I cast.

My new staff at NBC. After three months all were gone except Steve Kolzak, far left on couch. After NBC he became a prominent AIDS activist.

My best friend, Manager Bob LeMond, who's clients included John Travolta, Patrick Swayze, Jeff Conaway, Marilu Henner, Katherine Helmond and Holland Taylor. He was the first of my many friends who died of AIDS.

Lea DeLaria as she first appeard on set and in second photo dressed up as the new Police Chief of Atlanta with Andy Griffith during shooting of a spin off of "Matlock" centered around Lea's character.

Warren Littlefield, myself, Tim Flack and Brandon Tartikioff all slightly toasted at Moroccan restaurant celebrating Tim's brithday.

This was the first production of the musical, THE ROCKY HORROR SHOW, in the U.S. It played at the Roxy nightclub rather than a theater. Also note that this was the first time that Casting Directors got credit on a cast album. This is the production that introduced Tim Curry and Meat Loaf. We made the movie immediately after this production closed.

Oscar winning actress
Marlee Matlin (left)
recording dialogue for my
1996 film IT'S MY PARTY.

My suggestion is a bowl of black bean soup (75¢), a hamburger or cheeseburger ($1.50/$1.65), and pecan pie (95¢)—or chocolate cake made by casting director Joel Thurm, which is chocolatey, moist, delicious (95¢).

From a 1970's issue of The Hollywood Reporter.
To supplement my meager CBS salary, I made
and sold cakes to Joe Allen's.

Producer/Director Lee Daniels and I un-dressed for a night out at a disco "Skirt Party".

With Jesse Tyler Ferguson and Richard Kind at the Hollywood Bowl after their performances in "The Producers"

With the brilliant Randy Rainbow at one of his early shows.

My first ex and still best friend, Tony nominated actor Lou Liberatore

My second ex, actor/director Yvans Jourdain with J. Karen and myself at Halloween. Spiderman sheets went back to Target the next day.

Me with three former assistants, who were then heads of talent at different studios: Standing, Lori Openden (CW), Seated Peter Golden(CBS), Bob Harbin (Fox)

After a performance of HAIRSPRAY starring Bruce Vilanch (center) with friends Jack Grossbart (L), Marc Schwartz (R)

Director James Burrows (center) accepting an award from The Hollywood Arts Council with myself and Ted Danson

Not so terrible for turning 70.

Ultimately it is all about family..... And this is mine!

CHAPTER 10

HOW *AIRPLANE!* BECAME AIRBORNE

Despite my not being asked back to *Angie,* the executives there clearly liked my work and was made head of V.P of Television Talent for the studio.

But just before that happened, an agent friend called and asked if he could suggest me to cast another Paramount project, a feature film called *Airplane!* I said of course. I was approved by the studio, but I had to meet the writers/directors. Once more I was about to get involved with motion-picture history. I read the script at my kitchen counter with my morning coffee on the same day I was scheduled to meet the three writers who were also going to direct the movie together – an unprecedented situation. Never before had three directors directed a movie together. I was almost embarrassed to bring that script with me, because by the time I'd finished reading it, it was covered with stains from spitting and spilling coffee all over the pages from laughing so hard.

This was 1979, and the decade-long disaster-film craze was winding down. *The Poseidon Adventure, The Towering Inferno, Earthquake,* and *Airport '70, '75, '77,* and *'79.* The genre had earned millions but had sunk into cliché. Burning skyscrapers, sinking ships, and emergency rescues and airplane landings were getting spoofed on TV comedy specials and in Johnny Carson monologues. Brothers David and Jerry Zucker and Jim Abrahams knew this, and they saw possibilities. They had grown up as best friends in Milwaukee then moved to L.A., where they wrote, directed, and performed in an improv comedy group called Kentucky Fried Theater. Out of that came *Kentucky Fried Movie*, a low-budget film of satirical sketches. It was a surprise hit.

Now the trio had written the ultimate takedown of the disaster flick. They turned all the panic and destruction that moviegoers had endured for years into a welcome release of belly-laughs. *Airplane!* was a *Mad Magazine* movie parody come to life. Every conceivable element and much more in an airplane disaster story became an object of hilarity. There was: the leading man, an inept former Air Force pilot who is terrified of flying; a possible pedophile in the cockpit; the airline fish dinner that gave all the passengers and crew food poisoning; the plane's backup "autopilot," a life-size, inflatable doll named Otto; a guitar-playing singing nun; and, of course, a sick little girl who needs emergency surgery. This was not sophisticated or even original humor; Roger Ebert would later praise *Airplane!* for its "utter willingness to steal, beg, borrow, and rewrite from anywhere."

The Boys, as the Zuckers and Abrahams were now called, had stumbled upon a 1957 black-and-white B-movie melodrama called *Zero Hour*, about an emergency airplane landing. They fell upon this movie by accident. In order to find commercials to parody at Kentucky Fried Theater, they left their video recorder on all night and in the morning in addition to commercials, was *Zero Hour* In it they saw potential comic riches. Much of the *Airplane!* dialogue, played straight, was taken directly from *Zero Hour*. They then got the rights to the movie from Warner Bros. and Paramount for $2500.00 which in 2022 dollars is about $11,000. The price turned out to be a bargain.

Jim, David, and Jerry successfully fought to direct *Airplane!* together, something that had never been permitted by the all-powerful Directors Guild of America. Jim even filed court paperwork to get his name officially changed to "Abrahams N. Zuckers", thus combining the partner's three names into one that the Guild would accept as a "single" director. That was the name listed on all reports and documents for the first several weeks of the shoot.

Paramount gave the Boys an extraordinary ally (and watchdog) in Howard Koch, a well-respected veteran producer who had worked at Paramount for years in several capacities, including head of production. Even though Paramount had said yes to the project with The Boys directing, the higher-up execs didn't know what they had on their hands. Koch was to be the one to keep the Boys on time and budget, but he did much more than that. Robert Stack was not at all sure he wanted this job until Koch called him with a "you've got to trust me on this one" message. It worked. All Paramount's casting suggestions were the opposite of what was needed and what we wanted that is, serious dramatic actors who would play their roles straight, thus creating the humor. Instead, the studio pushed comedic celebrities on us like Sonny Bono, David Letterman, and Dom DeLuise. Although he denies it today, I was told by The Boys that Mike Eisner, the studio's President suggested Barry Manilow for the leading man, a former Air Force pilot. Fortunately, Paramount's executives were distracted by the production of another comedy, *Serial*, their big-budget, hoped-for summer blockbuster. With the TV movie-size budget we'd been allotted of $3.5 million, we were cheap enough to fail, and inconsequential enough to be left alone. Alas, *Serial*, which starred Martin Mull and Tuesday Weld, opened to bad reviews and no audience.

During our first casting discussion, I found I was totally in synch with the three creators when I suggested bygone movie stars like Lloyd Bridges, Robert Stack, and Peter Graves. Graves, who became the plane's Captain Clarence Oveur (pronounced "over"), was known mainly for his work on TV's *Mission: Impossible*. Initially he thought that the script was the worst piece of garbage he had ever read. Fortunately, his wife and kids disagreed and talked him into it. Graves was a figure from my Saturday morning childhood TV viewing. He starred in a half hour black-and-white series called "*Fury,* a story about a horse and the boy who loved him" was the title and the long voiceover description that followed. Seriously. Graves played a western ranch owner with a son who had a great horse, of course, named Fury. I had an all-consuming crush on him and desperately wished I could be his son on the series or, better still, in real life. When I told this story to The Boys, they roared with laughter. It fit right in with one of the movie's most famous moments, when a little boy visits the cockpit. The pilot asks, "Joey … you ever seen a grown man naked? Joey, you ever hang around the gymnasium? Joey … you like movies about gladiators? Joey … you ever been in a Turkish prison?" I checked all the boxes except the Turkish prison one.

The role of copilot Roger Murdock had been written for baseball star Pete Rose, but he wasn't available because the shooting clashed with playing season. I became obsessed with the idea of getting another sports idol to say yes. Next on my list was Bruce Jenner, winner of the Olympic decathlon, which in turn had made him famous as "the world's greatest athlete" and landed him on Wheaties cereal boxes. Jenner read for several roles, and his agent told me that he would do the role of Murdock, but a week later he pulled out so that he could play a starring role in *Can't Stop the Music*, the Village People's camp musical and one of Allan Carr's series of flop movies after *Grease*. I thought it was a career-killing move, especially when I saw him in the micro-Daisy Duke cutoff jeans that he wears throughout the film. Decades later, after he'd transitioned to Caitlin, those sexually ambiguous shorts made sense.

Next on the list was basketball hero Kareem Abdul-Jabbar. The salary for him and all the other "name" actors was "favored nations," which means they all got the same modest deal; what clinched his deal was a small but pricey Persian rug that was discretely bought for him. Though not an actor, Kareem gave us the perfect performance we wanted.

The Boys had a special casting concern. Who could we possibly get to play the small role of Lt. Hurwitz, a soldier with PTSD who thinks he is Broadway's legendary Ethel Merman and sings a few lines of the song from her starring role in the Broadway musical, *Gypsy,* "Everything's Coming up Roses." "Why don't we just ask Ethel Merman," I said. They were thunderstruck. "Wow," said one of them. "Do you think we can get her?" I laughed. Hollywood and TV were hardly knocking down her door, although she'd begun making campy TV appearances as she did on *The Love Boat.* I told The Boys that if we offered her the low salary in the budget but treated her like the star she was – flying her in first-class, setting her up in a suite someplace like the Beverly Hills Hotel with a welcoming bouquet of flowers and champagne, etc. – she would "be in make-up and circling the studio." Needless to say, we got her and, rather than acting like a diva, she was grateful we asked. Her only requests were not to have an early call time and for a specific hairdresser. She got both and we got a great moment. In case she didn't work out my backups were Carol Channing and Eartha Kitt singing their signature songs: "Hello, Dolly! for Channing and "Santa Baby" for Kitt.

Casting the part of handsome, shell-shocked young pilot Ted Striker was a headache. Scores of the hot, up-and-coming actors we pursued turned it down, including Harrison Ford, who was fresh out of the biggest action-adventure hit in years, *Star Wars*, and did not need to accept our chump-change offer. Finally, after Paramount let us go after "unknown" actors instead of movie stars, I was able to get the actor I'd always wanted, Robert Hays, who I had cast in and was currently shooting the second season of *Angie* on the same lot. Because he was rehearsing and shooting *Angie* at the same time, we were casting, he could not come in until several weeks into the process. At last he found the time to come in and audition. With his quasi-vacant demeanor, I knew Bobby could play the jittery pilot straight and get all the laughs. The Boys loved him.

Throughout the film, his character "Ted" tries hilariously to win back his ex-girlfriend, "Elaine", the flight's beautiful and prim head stewardess. I know, they are flight attendants now, but then they were stewardesses. Our New York casting director, Gretchen Renell, brought her in. When Jerry Zucker, who had gone to NYC representing the rest of the trio laid eyes on her in the Paramount Building's elevator, he prayed that she was on her way to the auditions and if so, her reading would be at least halfway decent. The moment she began to read, he knew we had our Elaine.

Barbara Billingsley was not our first choice to play "Jive Lady", the character who translates two black passengers' jive talk. The joke in casting this role was that the whitest woman on the plane offers to interpret the blackest of "jive." Currently, the movie has been criticized for this joke. #BlackLivesMatter has changed us all to finally acknowledge our unconscious biases. Thinking back on all my casting in the '70s and '80s, my biases were definitely there, as they were throughout all of the TV and movie business as well as throughout all professions in the U.S. at that time. I think that in this case the criticism is unfair. There was no actual jive dialogue written in the script. The two guys who got the roles, Norman Alexander Gibbs and Al White, met for the first time outside the audition room and came up with that dialogue themselves. And it was and still is today hysterically funny. These kinds of moments should be interpreted in the context of their time and not by current standards.

For years Barbara Billingsley played June Cleaver, the super-mom on *Leave It to Beaver*, America's second-biggest suburban-family sitcom of the 1950s. But we wanted to go straight to the top and sign Harriet Nelson, costar of the number-one '50s domestic sitcom, *The Adventures of Ozzie and Harriet.* Both women essentially played the same role – that of the housewife who vacuums while wearing high heels and pearls. Harriett's son David Nelson (brother of pop idol Ricky Nelson) desperately tried to convince his mother to take the role but failed. He told me she could not bring herself to utter the word "muthafucka" onscreen. June Cleaver had no such problem. Barbara said later that *Airplane!* has done as much if not more for her career than *Beaver*; ironically, her muthafucka line never made the final cut.

The role of Dr. Rumack, a passenger, in keeping with our casting plan was offered to just about every famous actor who had ever played a doctor in film or on TV. All of them – including Robert Young, Jack Klugman, and Richard Chamberlain – or their agents - turned it down. And thank goodness they did, because that allowed our Plan B actor, Leslie Nielsen, whom The Boys always favored, to become our Plan A. Nielsen was best-known for playing rich, white-collar villains. Later on, critics suggested that our use of him in *Airplane!* was a great example of casting against type. Nielsen always responded that comedy *was* his true nature, and that he had been cast against type in all those dramatic roles. To prove it, he made himself notorious on the set for his "fart" machine: a little handheld device that he used to make flatulence sounds at the most inappropriate times, mostly when he was off camera delivering lines to the other unsuspecting actors. Robert Hays has laughed ever since about how he would hear a fart noise every time the camera pulled in on him for a close-up. The fart machine now sits in a trophy case in the Boys' office. Leslie Nielsen's career, more than anyone else's in *Airplane!*, benefited from the film's success. He went on to make three *Naked Gun* movies (with O.J. Simpson as his sidekick), and a *Naked Gun* spinoff TV series, *Police Squad*. In him, The Boys found their perfect muse. Sadly, both he and Peter Graves died within weeks of each other in 2010.

As for me, I can't help but burst with pride every time *Airplane!* is mentioned – and it is, quite a lot. Several actors who held smaller roles went on to bigger things: Jonathan Banks earned two Emmy nominations for playing a private investigator in *Breaking Bad* and *Better Call Saul*. Michael Warren became Officer Bobby Hill on *Hill Street Blues*. Lorna Patterson played three seasons as the star of TV's *Private Benjamin*. David Leisure was the fictional shyster automobile spokesman Joe Isuzu in a famous series of commercials ("If I'm lying, may lightning hit my mother") and a regular on the sitcom *Empty Nest*.

Airplane! is acknowledged as having been a game-changer in comedy. The format of relentless jokes and sight-gags had a big influence in film and TV. Director brothers Bobby and Peter Farrelly (*There's Something About Mary, Dumb and Dumber*) acknowledge their debt to Jim Abrahms & David and Jerry Zucker as do Matt Groening (*The Simpsons*), Comedy Central stars Key & Peele, and Amy Schumer. Though it did not win any Oscars or Golden Globes, *Airplane!* was later included on numerous lists of all-time best film comedies; it even topped polls by *People* magazine and ABC. Dialogue from the film is still quoted today.

"Surely you can't be serious."
"I *am* serious, and don't call me Shirley."

*****

Once more, post movie-casting letdown set in. But *Airplane!* had given me the confidence that I might actually work again. At least I wasn't terribly concerned about paying the mortgage. I had made one of my smartest business moves by refinancing my house, which enabled me to buy a larger one directly across the Canyon from my little cabin. The new house was a very simple, one-story ranch house on a dirt road with not a speck of gentrification: no stainless steel, marble or granite. When I pulled up the carpeting I found only plywood, not the oak hardwood I was hoping for. I just painted all the floors with epoxy white paint every couple of years. What it did have was sliding glass doors facing incredible views of the city and, on very clear days, the Pacific Ocean.

The house was divided into two distinct spaces; I moved into the larger one and rented the other to wickedly funny and smart comedy writer and TV personality, Bruce Vilanch. Bruce, who bears a direct resemblance to *Sesame Street's* Cookie Monster, would soon be writing Bette Midler's jokes, appearing as a panelist on Whoopi Goldberg's re-boot of *Hollywood Squares*, and writing for the Oscars, Tonys, Emmys, and Grammys and eventually playing "Edna Turnblad" in *Hairspray* on Broadway. Bruce lived in my house with his boyfriend, an aspiring punk-rock singer named Michael Muffins. Michael is short, cute, and totally bald. He wore a series of different wigs, changing them almost daily. Bruce is tall and rotund, so he and Michael made an interesting-looking pair. With those guys around, the laughs kept coming.

The laughs continued into the 2000s when I rented the same space to comedian/singer Lea DeLaria, who went on to play "Big Boo" in *Orange is the New Black*. She and I met in 1994 at the Montreal Comedy Festival where I was scouting, and she was performing. Lea was one of the first "out" female comics and certainly the first butch one. I had never met her and confess to being slightly put off because of her then ferocious head-shot photograph. But after seeing her hilarious act I approached her the next morning I found her to be warm, wonderful and hysterically funny. We became and still are best friends to this day.

I pitched her an idea to play the Don Rickles role in a remake of a 70's sitcom *CPO Sharkey*. Meanwhile I had partnered with my former uber- boss at both CBS and later NBC, Fred Silverman. He was now an independent producer with several very successful shows on the air including *In the Heat of the Night* starring Carol O'Connor (*All in the Family*) *Diagnosis Murder* starring Dick Van Dyke and *Matlock* starring Andy Griffith. As the producer of *Matlock,* Fred was guaranteed one spin-off episode per year and wanted to try spinning Lea off into her own one-hour series as the Police Chief of Atlanta. I did not think this was the greatest idea but in that it would cost him nothing, it made sense to try. He asked me to one thing - to make sure that the audience knew she was a woman. We had a great time shooting in Wilmington, N.C., but again no sale.

The little dirt road my new house was on had a few fascinating residents, including Katherine Helmond from *Soap* and *Who's the Boss,* Jennifer Aniston , (pre-*Friends)* and Tea Leoni (pre-*Madame Secretary).* The last two were both live-in girlfriends (at different times) of a wonderful young actor who has since passed, Daniel McDonald. Also on this street was the now notorious Scotty Bowers, whose book *Full Service* details his exploits as a gay Hollywood Madam for closeted movie stars and other celebrities from 1945 into the 1980s. His book was later made into a fascinating documentary and used as inspiration for Ryan Murphy's limited series, *Hollywood.* Scotty's clients ranged from Spencer Tracy and Katharine Hepburn to the Duke and Duchess of Windsor. Scotty, who did all sorts of odd jobs, also trimmed my Eucalyptus trees with his assistant, Marlon Brando's son, Christian – the one who went to prison for killing his half-sister's abusive boyfriend.

Life at work seemed equally sweet. Shortly after *Airplane!* finished shooting, *Taxi's* first year of episodes went into production. In those first few episodes, two new characters were introduced, and I cast them with Christopher Lloyd as "Reverend Jim" and Carol Kane as Latka's wife, "Simka". Both became series regulars. With Jimmy Burrows as the director, tapings went very fast. Every Friday night, after taping, there was a party paid for and thrown by the cast. Anyone and everyone could attend. Friends of the cast, including John Travolta, Jack Nicholson, and Francis Ford Coppola, stopped by and mingled. Yet it didn't feel like a business party, just a pleasant hang after a long workweek.

Paramount took a look at my recent projects – *Grease, Angie, Taxi, Airplane!* and I guessed realized I knew my stuff. I was offered the job of head of TV Talent along with a generous salary and full benefits. They even agreed to my request for a royalty for every episode of *Taxi.* No casting director I know of, before or since, has ever received a royalty for casting a pilot.

The only downside was that there was very little for me to do. However, that also enabled me to leave my office and go to various stages to watch the shows being rehearsed. On the *Mork & Mindy* stage I saw Robin Williams riffing on the script with one terrific stream-of-consciousness improvisation after another. In real life, Penny Marshall was a bit of a grouch, but to see how she morphed into the breathlessly enthusiastic can-do Laverne of *Laverne & Shirley* was fascinating. While the Garry Marshall group, which produced it, had lots of shows in varying stages of development, that unit was self-contained and knew what they were doing, and the last thing they needed or wanted was my "interference." But they did call on me to help in dealing with ABC when I was needed. Often, I got them stars for special episodes or cash to fly in interesting new actors from New York. My favorite guest casting episode was a two-part *Mork & Mindy,* with the guest-star role of a villainess from outer space who comes to Earth to screw with Mork. The series was hot then, largely because of its star, Robin Williams. Jane Fonda agreed to do the part because it was her kids' favorite show. Unfortunately, her schedule changed at the last minute, and she became unavailable.

The day was saved when we went to Raquel Welch and she said yes. Welch was then on the downslide from movie stardom to TV roles. This would have been an unsettling time for anyone in her position, and she acted out a bit during shooting, taking up extra time in hair and makeup, staying in her trailer a bit longer than necessary, and one day flat-out refusing to wear a certain costume. She did look spectacular, however, in her main outfit, a silver skintight cat suit. After the shooting of her second episode, at the small wrap party I was talking with one of the producers, Bob Boyett, when Raquel, now out of costume but still gorgeously made up, sidled up to us. "Look," she said, "I know I was a bit of a pain in the ass, but wasn't I worth it?" It was very funny and also very true.

Otherwise, I can't claim that my reign as Paramount's head of TV Talent was among my greatest periods. For the next couple of years, fate was not in Paramount TV's corner. In 1977 and for the next couple of years we immersed ourselves in planning the long-awaited sequel to the *Star Trek* TV series, to be called *Star Trek: Phase II*. I think the biggest problem was that Leonard Nimoy (Spock) did not want to be part of it. There were countless business problems as well, and it was decided that it made much more sense as a feature film. It was a great decision because 1979's *Star Trek: The Motion Picture* completely revived the franchise and led to endless new TV series and a slew of feature films.

The new *Star Trek* series idea tanked, but how could we go possibly wrong with a new series from the John Charles Walters Company of *Taxi* fame? The multi-award-winning writing quartet had undertaken a new show, and all of us were excited. *The Associates* was, like *Taxi*, a gang comedy, only this time a white-collar one, set in a law firm with three new associates fresh out of law school: a gorgeous, smart, and tough Ivy League woman, a female scholarship student from the wrong side of the tracks, and a quiet Midwestern guy who is always a bit out of step with the others.

To play the latter, we zeroed in quickly on Martin Short, a star of *SCTV*. This would be his first scripted series role, and he read for it terrifically. Next came Alley Mills (later to play the mom in *The Wonder Years*) as the scholarship student. She, too, was just what we'd hoped to find. Unfortunately the Ivy League toughie was miscast. I had gone crazy for an actress I didn't know who taped or filmed an audition for us in New York, Kathleen Turner. But I couldn't get anyone to see what I saw in her and this audition tape or film eventually disappeared. At the last minute a beautiful former model, Shelly Smith, came in, gave a great funny reading, and got the part. Sadly, that reading was the high point of her performance in this role. Thereafter she was not funny nor good. This happens all too often when an actor does a great audition in a room and then tanks on film. Part of my job was to know how to avoid this. I failed this time. Despite the talents of Martin and Alley, a great performance from John Houseman (*The Paper Chase*) and a scene stealing turn by British character Wilfred Hyde-White, *The Associates* limped along for thirteen episodes and was cancelled. A major problem I think was that the John Charles Walters Company was beginning to fray. Jim Brooks was moving into features, and Davis was about to quit the rat race and enjoy life with his new love, Julie Kavner, famous as Rhoda's sister Brenda on *Rhoda* and later as the voice of Marge on *The Simpsons*.

But two new sitcoms were in the works, and their unknown but sensational actors promised much. *Bosom Buddies* and *Good-time Girls* were the brainchildren of a new producing entity, Miller-Milkis-Boyett Productions. Tom Miller and Ed Milkis were longtime Garry Marshall executive producers, and Bob Boyett had recently resigned (wisely) from his executive position at

Paramount. They charged right out of the box with these pilots. In *The Some Like It Hot* rip-off, (oops, I mean inspired) *Bosom Buddies*, two men (played by brand new and very young Tom Hanks and Peter Scolari (later from the second *Newhart* series) get themselves dressed up as women in order to live in the one apartment they can afford, which happens to be an all-girl residence. Donna Dixon, in the Marilyn Monroe part, was the sexy blonde and Holland Taylor (Charlie Sheen's mother in *Two and a Half Men)*, their boss. Disappointingly, *Bosom Buddies* never jelled, and it lasted just two seasons. Tom Hanks, Peter Scolari, and Holland Taylor were terrific and went on to much better things, but who can replace Miss Monroe? Donna Dixon tried very hard but it didn't quite work. However she, too, found success when she married Dan Ackroyd.

Goodtime Girls did not fare much better, but Miller-Milkis-Boyett didn't look back. In their future were years of hit sitcoms, notably *Family Matters, Step by Step, Full House,* and *Fuller House* on Netflix. Back at Paramount, I turned my attentions to *Allison Sydney Harrison*, a dramatic TV movie and "back-door pilot" for NBC. A back-door-pilot is when a pilot is made in a two-hour TV movie format, and if it does not sell as a pilot, it can air as a TV movie and recoup most of its costs. *Allison Sydney Harrison* was about the adventures of a high-school girl (Katy Kurtzman) and her private-detective father (Ted Danson) who work together to solve crimes. This was a few years before I cast Ted in his signature role, the lead in *Cheers*. Having met and been wowed by him a year earlier, I was always on the lookout for roles for him.

Pretty, heart-tugging Katy Kurtzman was the best kid actress around. She had caught everyone's eye on *Little House in the Prairie*, where she played a stuttering child who was treated meanly by another little girl. After that she starred in a hugely popular made-for-TV children's movie, *The New Adventures of Heidi*. Word had come to us from NBC that Fred Silverman, now the network's CEO, having left ABC, adored Katy and wanted her for the show. But Katy was having a tough adolescence and her entire physicality was rapidly changing; no longer was she super-cute and petite. What Fred saw on film was not what he had anticipated. Ted did a yeoman's job and Katy tried her best, but her awkward adolescence and their lack of chemistry put the piece in the toilet.

Typical of Fred, he blamed the show's failure entirely on Ted. From that time on I could not get Ted into any Paramount/NBC project. Timing was on Ted's side, however, because by the time we were casting *Cheers* and I was at NBC Fred Silverman had been fired and replaced by Grant Tinker, thus clearing the way for Ted to be considered

My job at Paramount had become no fun but I was staying put for the time being. But once again, fate smiled upon me just when I needed it. I got a call from my old CBS boss and mentor, Ethel Winant. We had remained friends even though she had wisely ushered me out of CBS. Ethel had become a producer with Children's Television Workshop, a company whose big show was *Sesame Street*. CTW's way-too-ambitious production schedule had sent it financially over the edge, and a disheartened Ethel had quit and gone back into casting at NBC.

Fred Silverman, her longtime boss at CBS, had taken over NBC in 1978, when it was drowning in horrible ratings. After two years, Fred's miracle-working reputation was not producing any miracles. He promised Ethel that in a couple of years, after she had reorganized NBC's casting department, she could leave casting and head the miniseries department. The catch was that she had to find her own replacement. She called me. I was immediately intrigued. NBC was in such bad shape, the only way it could go was up – but to get it there would require tremendous work. I had acquired a solid group of credits and hoped I could be up to the job. Also, with all the ups and downs of being independent, and my parents' depression era unconscious influence, I longed for the security that this job could bring.

I said yes. NBC would be paying me nicely above my Paramount salary. My boss, Gary Nardino, was horrified when I told him I was leaving. I tried to reassure him that there was very little work for me there and that my assistant, Mary Buck, could easily take over what little I was doing. He would not take no for an answer. The next day I got a call from Gary's boss, Michael Eisner. He had never called me before, and we had only interacted during occasional large staff meetings. Eisner asked if there were anything Paramount and he in particular could do to keep me there. Foolishly, without thinking what great timing I had stumbled into and what great cards I was now holding, said that I had already made a deal and could not go back on it. Of course, I could have gotten out of the deal. I should have met with Eisner and told him that I eventually wanted to produce or write or whatever I truly wanted to do with the rest of my life. But at that moment, I really didn't know what I wanted anymore.

CHAPTER 11

NBC, BILL COSBY, &
THE CASTING COUCH

I arrived at NBC in the middle of pilot season in early 1981, when the network's ratings were in the toilet, where they'd been for most of the seventies. All around us, TV was becoming edgier and more permissive. But NBC had remained stodgy, old-fashioned, and conservative, full of variations on the same old cop shows and a slew of "country/heartland" shows that did not at all appeal to the more advertiser-important and bigger audiences in the big cities: *B.J. and the Bear* (truckers and a chimpanzee); its spinoff, *The Misadventures of Sheriff Lobo* (reformed corrupt lawman's comic adventures); *Barbara Mandrell and the Mandrell Sisters* (country music variety); Dennis Weaver in *McCloud* (hick detective on horseback in the big city); Jack Klugman in *Quincy, M.E.*; and Michael Landon's *Little House on the Prairie.* Only two of the above survived, *Quincy* and *Little House.* Universal was the production company that supplied many of the network's primetime shows, and it had NBC in a stranglehold. Each year when it came time to negotiate with them for renewals, Universal would demand a few more series and TV-movie commitments in exchange for not upping the licensing fee for the existing ones on the air. There was hardly any room on NBC's schedule for new blood, meaning talented writer/producers, nor was there was any money to pay for them.

NBC's president, Fred Silverman, stuck with this bad hand, was at a loss. That wasn't typical for one of the acknowledged geniuses of network TV. As the former head and boy wonder of CBS and later ABC, he had boosted both networks to their peak of prosperity and popularity. In 1978, Fred had accepted a huge financial offer to come over to NBC and try for the trifecta.

He didn't make it. Fred was expected to turn things around, to solve every problem, as he had in the past. He soon found that he couldn't, perhaps because he had no money to pay for new programming? During his rocky three-year stay, Fred managed to push through a few substantial hits, notably *Diff'rent Strokes*, *The Facts of Life*, *Hill Street Blues*, and *Gimme a Break!* But he was mostly frustrated and expressed it by drinking a lot and yelling; one did not want to deal with Fred in the late afternoon or early evening. He also made gaffes that got him publicly ridiculed. One of Fred's desperate efforts was *Pink Lady and Jeff*, a 1980 variety series that starred a hugely popular (in all of Asia but not the U.S.) Japanese pop-singing girl duo named Pink Lady and a sweet young comic under contract to the NBC, Jeff Altman. The real problem was that Pink Lady could not speak or understand a word of English, and after five disastrous episodes, the show was yanked.

Fred's good friend Ethel Winant, now head of talent at NBC, who had saved his ass at CBS with her casting ability, could hardly do the same at NBC if there wasn't any fresh programming to cast. That's one reason that Ethel yearned to get out of casting. Her other reason was that her casting department was not only not in good shape, but it was also a disaster. For the moment I decided to leave everyone in place and learn this group of people for the next few months before making any changes. Three months later, I knew enough. Three of the four members of my department were less than useless. One did nothing but bluster, one was incompetent in that every suggestion made was bad, one was there via nepotism but was sweet and good at clerical work, and the last and only good one was my former assistant from *Starsky & Hutch,* Steve Kolzak.

Coincidentally my friend Linda Otto, who had returned to casting, had a new and equally talented partner, Joan Barnett. They were disbanding their casting company, this time because Linda was now firmly into producing documentaries. I had worked with this group many times and their four younger casting associates were enormously talented, too. I offered Joan and all four associates jobs at NBC. Only Joan and one associate, Vicki Rosenberg, accepted. The other three preferred to open their own independent casting offices. Joan Barnett came in as a vice president dealing with movies and miniseries. Vicki Rosenberg came in as a corporate level director, and I elevated Steve Kolzak to the same corporate status.

Among my newly hired staff was a casting assistant I poached from my New York casting consultants Julie Hughes and Barry Moss. The poached one was one of their assistants who was smart, had a sense of humor and great phone manner. When I met her in person, she was also uniquely beautiful and sexy. I then did something unheard of, I offered her a job as a casting assistant in L.A and to pay for her air fare and some relocation expenses. She was shocked but she said yes immediately. She turned out to be as good if not better than I expected. But…isn't there always a but? About a year after she came to NBC, she asked if she could see me privately in my office. Once inside she made me promise not to yell. I did have somewhat of a reputation for phone yelling when agents and managers would make truly ridiculous suggestions. She told me that while she was enjoying her job in casting, she realized that what she really wanted to do was to act. She offered to do a monologue for me and wanted my advice. She did her monologue and I told her that she was more than very good and she should definitely go after an acting career. I went on to tell her that she would have great success not only because of her acting ability but because she was unique, very likeable and was adored by all the women she worked with and every man in the building wanted to fuck her. She roared with laughter and hugged me. Her name was and still is Catherine Keener. She went on to star or co-star in the following: Jordan Peele's horror comedy *Get Out* as the woman always noisily stirring her tea cup, "*Being John Malkovich, The 40-Year-Old- Virgin* with Steve Carell and the 2005 movie *Capote* . She received Oscar nominations for *Malkovich and* Capote. In total she's made and about 65 other feature films, 26 TV projects and received 59 various award nominations with 17 wins. She did reject one piece of my advice out of hand. Catherine had a space between her upper front teeth much like model, Lauren Hutton. On film close-ups the space would appear much larger than in real life. I suggested she get a dental device called a "flipper" that she could take in and out to close this space. She said that it would not be natural, and she was all about being natural. P.S. After the first time she saw herself on screen, she had dental work and the space never was seen again.

The blusterer had wisely left NBC. The sweet and good nephew was put in charge of our videotape library and other clerical duties. The last and worst filed official sexual favoritism charges against me, saying that she deserved to be elevated to vice president and should have been given Joan's job. She said the only reason this did not happen was because I was homosexual, and Joan got the job because she was my friend and a lesbian. Directly below Fred

Silverman was a new young TV genius in charge of programming, Brandon Tartikoff. He was my immediate boss. Tartikoff in serious mode called me to his office to show me these charges. I knew nothing about them until he explained them to me. My reaction was to burst out laughing. Joan Barnett, who sadly passed away a few years ago, was a short, stout woman from Queens, N.Y., with a deep voice, who gave great New York attitude. But as I explained to Brandon, "While Joan may look like a duck, walk like a duck, and quack like a duck, she ain't a duck. Not only is she not gay, but she has had the same handsome and much younger boyfriend for the last ten years." Brandon then began to laugh, too, and told me to go back to work and not worry. I did and didn't. The complainer left my department for some other job in the bowels of NBC and I never saw or heard from her again.

As NBC's new Vice President of Talent and Casting, it was up to me to supervise the casting of all network programming from Daytime through Late Night. No more did I cast individual shows. Instead, I acted as a kind of actor quality-control for the network, trying to make sure every role was properly cast. For me, "properly" meant balancing what the writers and directors wanted with what the "network" wants, and needs were. Factor my own opinion into the equation and you can imagine the balancing job necessary. One thing I did learn over time was which writers/producers/show runners knew their stuff and did not need any "help" from us. But if I did have a good idea or two, they would not dismiss it out of hand simply because it came from "the network".

When pilots were in production, I'd approve and often disapprove casting directors chosen by production companies; I knew who were good and who weren't. This did not make me overly popular. The pilot casting directors and I would then meet and exchange ideas, and then they would send me progress reports on every actor they'd auditioned. Intellectually I knew the power of that job but not until being in it did I fully realize it. I was not always comfortable exercising that power because sometimes I had to turn down friends for certain roles that I knew were not right for them.

But I had to jump right in and swim. I had to deal with the shows that were already there. But there wasn't much I could do at the time to liven up that largely stale programming schedule. I managed to thrive, because even the smallest improvements helped. I joined my colleagues in helping save *The Facts of Life* from its sad position as NBC's lowest-rated series. Set in a boarding school for girls, the show focused on seven of them – way too many, and not all were interesting. A mass overhaul was needed, and it took place at the beginning of season two. Future movie star Molly Ringwald, who was a few years away from her breakthrough success in *Sixteen Candles* and other "brat-pack" movies, was the youngest of the seven girls living in a dorm supervised by Mrs. Garrett, played by the wonderful character actress Charlotte Rae. We dropped Molly, along with three others. There were just too many to write for. Wisely, we decided to keep the most obvious ones with the strongest personalities: the blond, beautiful Blair (Lisa Welchel), chunky Natalie (Mindy Cohn), and the sweet and tiny Tootie (Kim Fields). Yet something still felt missing. That gap was filled when I suggested we take fourteen-year-old Nancy McKeon, who had been in a pilot we'd just rejected, and add her to the three remaining girls. "You need a tough girl with New York attitude," I told the team. I had used Nancy in many guest roles and knew she was a terrific actress who could play both sweet and hard. The production company approved Nancy, who came aboard as motorcycle-riding Jo from the Bronx. At the same time, the show's writers changed Blair's character to a wealthy snob, setting up believable comic conflict between her and McKeon. Thus, streamlined and spiced-up, *The Facts of Life* showed an immediate spike in the ratings. By season three, it was NBC's second highest-rated show.

But NBC lingered at the bottom of the network ladder. In June 1981, Fred Silverman was fired. In came Grant Tinker, who had left his own company, MTM Productions, to become NBC's new chairman and CEO. Brandon Tartikoff, the thirty-two-year-old program executive, got bumped up to President of NBC. I now had a great boss; an extremely capable one who was a sheer pleasure to work with. Brandon was very, very good to me. A wonderful human being, he had the ability to make you want to be on his side. For me, a totally non-athletic boy from Brooklyn who was always chosen last, it felt wonderful to be on the team of an attractive (I would call him Jewish-cute), talented, charismatic Yale grad. He was smart, warm, and had a wicked sense of humor. He knew how to interact with creative people, and which writers and producers could make the most of his excellent ideas. Unlike many execs in similar jobs, he knew that his great ideas would be best served by giving them to others. Michael Mann, for instance, was a writer with a few good episodes of *Starsky & Hutch* and *Police Story* on his resumé. Around 1983, Brandon suggested a new type of cop show, to be produced by Mann and written by Tony Yerkovich, another *Starsky & Hutch* graduate. MTV was exploding, and Brandon suggested an MTV-like cop show – quick cuts and current popular music. Michael ran with that idea and turned it into *Miami Vice*.

Everybody at the network was pushing for more eyeballs, and while still under Fred's watch and Brandon's guidance, NBC had begun inching its way toward the long-awaited resurrection. One of our hottest shows of the decade, which influenced all subsequent cop shows, was *Hill Street Blues*, set in an inner-city police precinct.

From the time of show's premiere on January 15, 1981, the two writers, Steven Bochko and Michael Kozoll, began pushing the envelope in terms of sex, violence, and daring storylines. There were recurring guest characters, story arcs that played out over several episodes, and the use of handheld cameras that were constantly in motion. We were giving people what they wanted to watch. But it was a slow process. There was an FCC rule in place that eight p.m. to nine p.m. was reserved for family viewing. That hour was tame. As the decade went on, it became less so, but the network "censors" would go over *Hill Street* scripts with a fine-tooth comb, searching for improper language and images. Fortunately, more often than not, *Hill Street* won these battles.

But television evolved as society evolved. The man who had triggered this process was Norman Lear. On *All in the Family* and *Maude*, he took cutting-edge social issues and presented them in very funny ways. "Maude" has an abortion. "Archie Bunker" discovers that one of his drinking buddies is gay, and Sammy Davis, Jr., visits the bigot, Archie, with surprising results.

With the rise of regular cable followed by pay cable, audiences saw how much titillation they'd been missing. Broadcast TV had to compete. It became all right to say "ass" in the eighties. In 1993, *NYPD Blue* broke the network taboo on nudity by having Dennis Franz and Sharon Lawrence bare their butts. In Dennis's case I'm not sure that was a great idea. Sharon's however was superb.

Mild nudity became commonplace on primetime and daytime. Now you can pretty much say anything on network TV except "fuck" and "cunt." And on many late-night shows, though the word "fuck" itself is not heard, you can clearly read an actor's lips and just a tease of the "f" sound.

In the early '80s, all we dreamed for at NBC was to put on shows that somebody would watch. We were desperate, and some of our efforts crashed and burned – literally. In 1982, we ordered from Paramount TV a science-fiction show inspired by *Superman*, called *The Powers of Matthew Star*, in which a teenager finds out he's a prince from another planet and has superhuman powers. Paramount tested three male-female pairings of actors. One of them was Tom Cruise and Heather Locklear. I had met her in my office and thought, jeez, this is a junior Farrah Fawcett, but not quite ready yet for primetime. I had not met Cruise in person, but had seen him in *Taps*, a hit movie that came out that year. Cruise's agent and manager did not want him anywhere near our project, but he liked the script and wanted to do it, even if he had to tape a screen test. The results were god-awful. But Mary Buck, my former assistant and now head of Paramount TV Talent, said, "Joel, he is going to be a movie star. You taught me not to judge by one screen test. Let's get him now." Foolishly I didn't listen to her, and we passed. It was a stupid mistake on my part. If you want to see the test, just go to YouTube and judge for yourself.

We gave the female lead to a young woman named Amy Steel, the heroine of *Friday the 13th Part 2*. As Matthew, we cast an actor from *The Young and the Restless*, Peter Barton, who was even prettier than Cruise. *Matthew Star* must have been cursed, because shortly into shooting, Peter fell on his ass onto a lighted road flare during shooting. He was rushed to the hospital burn unit with second- and third-degree burns on his back and buttocks. Shooting was interrupted; the show aired for a few episodes, then had to vanish and come back months later. It was a disaster. Peter and Amy were neither good nor bad, just uninteresting, and bland. About the only good thing in the show was the performance of Louis Gossett, Jr., in the Morgan Freeman-like, older-and-wiser man role. The series died at the end of the season. *TV Guide* later ranked it twenty-two among the 50 Worst TV Shows of All Time.

But 1982 also brought two promising signs that NBC might be on the mend. Former MTM comedy writers the Charles brothers (Glen and Les) and director Jimmy Burrows were flying high thanks to the success of *Taxi*, and had formed their own company, Charles-Burrows-Charles, under Paramount's large umbrella. They came to NBC to pitch a new show. *Cheers* was set in an imaginary Boston bar that attracted all kinds of local characters and their stories. The idea, combined with the track record of the creators, equaled an easy sell. Right after their meeting with Brandon, Jimmy and the Charles brothers came into my office and announced that they'd been given a green light for an initial six episodes. No pilot, just straight into production.

Remembering how fruitfully we'd worked together at MTM, Glen and Les and Jimmy asked if I would handle the casting myself as Ethel Winant had done at CBS with *The Mary Tyler Moore Show*. I loved the script and badly wanted to do this. They were willing to pay NBC for the services of me and my department just as outside companies had paid CBS for Ethel and her staff's services. The CBS casting department was actually a profit center for them, and this, I hoped, would give me the opportunity to do the same at NBC. Unfortunately, RCA, NBC's corporate owner, was in bad financial straits, as was NBC itself. Every department had to make cuts, and I had to lose one member of mine. Instead of losing the last to be hired, who I knew would not survive outside the nest, I went to the best person I had, Steve Kolzak, my former *Starsky* assistant. I explained to him that I was being forced to ax someone, and that I'd picked him – but hastened to add that I was going to give him *Cheers*. "This will set you up as your own independent casting company, with an office on the Paramount lot and benefits. "You can then do feature films and whatever else you want in addition to *Cheers*." Jimmy and the Charles brothers agreed to this after I explained that if you go with Steve "you will also have me available 24/7 as well."

Now that Fred Silverman was gone, Ted Danson was about to get his chance to break out. *Cheers* had a lead character, Sam Malone, an over-the-hill, former Red Sox baseball player who had to quit the sport when his drinking got in the way. He now owns a bar and has a sporadic relationship with the female lead, Diane Chambers, a smart, sophisticated, pretentious grad student at Boston University. To pay her tuition Diane works as a cocktail waitress at the bar.

As casting began, I told Jimmy and the Charles Brothers: "I'll just give you two names: Ted Danson and Shelley Long. I know you're gonna see everyone in town, but I promise you will wind up with them." Blond, pretty, and slightly neurotic, Shelley was busy filming the female lead in a comedy directed by Ron Howard, *Night Shift*. I was certain that she and Diane Chambers would make an ideal match.

Many other actors were seen and the finalists were: Ted and Shelley, William Devane (JFK in *The Missiles of October)*, paired with Lisa Eichhorn (*Yanks,* opposite Richard Gere), and the former NFL player Fred Dryer, paired with Julia Duffy (*Newhart*). Each auditioning couple performed two scenes live on the stage with the folks from Paramount, and the NBC execs sitting in the bleachers overlooking the stage. After the actor pairs had read, all of us – a grand total of about 18 people, none of whom were women, black, or anything but white men decamped to a conference room behind the bleachers and discussed what we'd seen. Typically, at these meetings, no one wanted to speak first until they had seen which way the metaphorical wind was blowing.

But since casting was my job and I was getting paid for my opinion, I started the conversation by saying, "Guys, I don't know about you all, but for me it's no contest. Ted and Shelley are the best couple. They're funny, they're attractive, they're likable." But a consensus wasn't forming. This was Grant's first casting session at NBC, and he did not want to lose the upper hand. He said he thought William Devane and Lisa Eichorn were the best couple. I held my ground and pointed out that they were not very funny. Grant said, "How can you dismiss Bill Devane? He's one of our great actors!" I said, "Yes, Grant, I know that and agree with you but *not* for this project. Many more women out there will want to fuck Ted Danson than Bill Devane." Grant blanched as if he had just been slapped in the face and gesticulated as if he were a society matron clutching her pearls and had no retort. We went around the room a couple of times, and just like a jury coming to consensus, Ted and Shelley were chosen.

I think Grant, who was a very proper gentleman with excellent manners, was truly shocked by my crude remark. Except for *St. Elsewhere*, a show from his former company, MTM Productions, which his sons Mark and John were writing and directing, he never came to another casting session. To this day I don't know if what I did in that room turned him off or showed him I could do my job well. In retrospect, Grant was not totally wrong about Bill Devane. He was exactly what the script description called for. But often during the casting process if you look a bit outside the box you find gold.

Cheers premiered on September 20, 1982, and the reviews heralded a smash. But the ratings were a disaster. Brandon and the network stuck with it not just because it was a great show but also because we *had* to. There was no other choice. We had nothing else to put on the air, so we were forced to stick with what we had. But when *Cheers* swept the 1983 Emmys – Shelley, the Charles Brothers, and director Jimmy all won, and the show was named Outstanding Comedy Series – its fortunes turned. It lasted for eleven seasons.

Cheers gave NBC a strong upward push. So did *Family Ties*, which launched Michael J. Fox. Then, in September 1984, NBC saw the premiere of *The Cosby Show*, the series that singlehandedly revived the half-hour sitcom, which for years had been a floundering genre. In its eight-season run, it broke ground in all sorts of ways. For the first time, TV viewers saw an achieving, non-stereotypical, African Amercan family: a doctor, his lawyer wife, and their five children, all of whom had the same problems as a typical family of the white, upper middle-class.

The masterminds behind this show were a duo of former ABC executives, Marcy Carsey and Tom Werner, who when there had helped launch *Mork & Mindy*, *Three's Company*, and *Welcome Back, Kotter*. Now they had their own production company, and they needed product to sell. At the time, Bill Cosby's career was in a slump, and apart from talk-show guest spots, TV had not quite taken to him. Two sitcom efforts, *The Bill Cosby Show* and *The New Bill Cosby Show*, had failed. Carsey and Werner pitched ABC on a new Cosby series, and got a no. Years later, after Cosby had become huge on NBC, Tom and Marcy did the same thing with another show, but in reverse: They offered NBC *Roseanne*, and this time NBC said no and ABC said yes. You know what happened after that.

But in this case, NBC approved the taping of a pilot. It had to be cast in less than two weeks in order for the show to be shot, edited, and presented to advertisers in time for a possible slot the next season. I quickly assembled a team and had casting directors working simultaneously in L.A., New York, and Chicago. Three or four finalists were chosen for each part, with the out-of-towners flown to L.A., where the deciding auditions would be held in my office in front of Bill, Marcy, Tom, Brandon, director Jay Sandrich, and myself, along with a host of other NBC executives. Bill read with the actors. He was very much in command, with a specific vision for each character.

To play his wife, Clair Huxtable, Bill wanted a woman who was like his real-life wife, Camille – beautiful, light-skinned, with the ability to speak Spanish. Why? He thought it would be funny to have a show wife who could break into Spanish in times of stress, like a female Ricky Ricardo. I remembered a woman whom I had met a year before in L.A at a party Nell Carter gave for the touring cast of *Dreamgirls*, which had just arrived. Nell grabbed my hand and said, "You've got to meet Debbie's sister," then dragged me all over until she introduced me to a beautiful woman who just radiated gentility and class. It turned out that she was Debbie Allen's sister, Phylicia Ayers-Allen, later to become Phylicia Rashad. She was understudying the lead in

Dreamgirls. After using my bad Spanish to thank a server passing some food, I giggled at how badly I spoke. She differed, saying I was pretty good, and that she spoke Spanish because she'd spent a few years in school in Mexico. I also found out she had graduated magna cum laude from Howard University in Washington, D.C. I remembered everything about meeting this woman – except her name. I spoke to our NY casting director Lois Planco and told her to find Debbie Allen's sister who understudied the role of "Dena" in the last touring company of *Dreamgirls* to play Los Angeles and to put her at the top of the list.

Bill was striving for authenticity. In real life, he had a dyslexic son, Ennis. At his insistence, his son on *The Cosby Show* had dyslexia, too. Our candidates for that character (Theodore Aloysius "Theo" Huxtable) included a promising New York kid actor, Malcolm-Jamal Warner, then thirteen. He was the last actor to audition. In his scene, a confrontation with his father, he went for a laugh by acting sassy and rolling his eyes. We all thought he was funny, except Bill. In a stern, fatherly voice, he asked Malcolm if he would behave like that with his real father. No, he said quietly. Bill sent him out of the room to rethink his approach. His second try reminded Bill so much of his own son Ennis that he knew he'd found his Theo.

The Clair candidates auditioned with a scene in which she and Theo have an argument. As actress after actress read, Bill seemed unimpressed; all of them adopted typical scolding-mom body language – finger-wagging, hand on hip. But Phylicia caught his eye. At a certain point, she went silent and gave Theo a burning glare that let him know who was boss. That stare was what won her the part. After having dismissed or eliminated all those women who did not speak Spanish, it turned out that Clair

Huxtable was never asked to do so during the entire life of the series.

My associates in Chicago had sent us ten-year-old Tempestt Bledsoe, a child model and jingle singer, to audition for the role of the smart but boy-crazy daughter Vanessa. Tempestt had only acted in a few commercials. But she brimmed with personality, and Bill liked her high-pitched voice, which to him suggested both girlishness and intelligence. Tempestt was chosen.

From the moment Bill saw Lisa Bonet, he knew that she had to play daughter Denise. He wanted Denise to be a hip but spacy, fashion-loving, downtown Bohemian-type. Lisa, then fifteen, had shown up with only one side of her face made up – and when they read together he felt that she *was* that character, without trying. In 1987 Bill reversed course and was happy to be rid of her by spinning her character off as a student at a historically Black college in *A Different World*. She was on that show for a season when a feature film starring her, and Mickey Roarke was released. No longer daddy's little girl, in the movie, she was nude and fairly frisky. Bill was not pleased, and she subsequently disappeared from both *Cosby* and *A Different World*. Sabrina LaBoeuf and Keisha Knight Pulliam as the oldest and the youngest rounded out the original Cosby family.

Bill's instincts were consistently on the money; neither I nor any other executive felt we could have picked better. We finished the pilot on time and on September 20, 1984, *The Cosby Show* premiered. America, of course, fell in love with the Huxtables, the Black family that served as role models for the entire country. The series was television's biggest ratings hit of the decade. It was No. 1 for five years, and in its eight-season run it never fell out of the top 20.

In light of Cosby's downfall and imprisonment in 2017 for sexual abuse and his subsequent release in 2021on a legal technicality, everyone asks me what I knew of his behavior at that time. I knew nothing – nor did any of my fellow execs at NBC. What I did hear was that he flirted a lot and because he was rich and famous, and not a troll like Harvey Weinstein, sometimes women came on to him. Even so, the power dynamics were so lopsided that anything sexual would have been inappropriate. All that being said, it would have been very hard to refuse his attentions if a woman was genuinely attracted to him. More importantly, drugging women escalated his behavior to a wholly inexcusable and criminal level.

Culturally, Cosby showed that black people are just like white people *if* they have money and education. He was considered the epitome of what any great father should be. I never knew him well; our relationship consisted of casting sessions in my office and one or two visits to the set in Brooklyn, but what I saw of him impressed me. Most important, his show had done wonders to drag NBC out of the doldrums.

This seems as good a time as any to discuss the most notorious aspect of my profession, the one that pops into nearly everyone's mind upon hearing the term "Casting Director." The casting couch has been around in show business in some form or other since way before Shakespeare, and it exists in other industries, too, as long as a less powerful person wants or needs something from someone with more power who can make that something happen.

With my job came an automatic presumption that I was a participant in this behavior. But something inside me knew this was wrong. Maybe that had to do with the fact that I was relatively young, in good physical condition, reasonably attractive, and didn't *have* to stoop to that to get laid. Further, I was not interested in the "chase" or the game of seduction or proving my "power." My rule was that anyone I met my office or at an industry function was off limits. However, if we met in a gay bar or other gay-oriented event, it was okay to take it from there and I always took no for an answer.

There was one time, however, when I almost slipped. Thinking I had a problem being obsessed by sex, I went to a Sexual Compulsives Anonymous meeting. Having earlier attended a week's worth of Narcotics Anonymous meetings to deal with cocaine, I knew the drill. Among those at the meeting was an actor I knew. He, along with others there, shared their stories. As with the NA meetings, I realized my "addictions" were small potatoes compared to the others. After the meeting the actor and I chatted for a while and I suggested we go out for coffee or a drink. He was a lot smarter than I; he declined my invitation. Unconsciously or somewhat consciously I was hitting on him. This story made it into an episode of *Cheers* when Ted goes to an SCA meeting and hits on one of the group. It was very accurate and very funny.

When certain agents and casting directors bragged to me about the actors with whom they'd slept in exchange for preferential treatment, I was appalled, and would never deal with them professionally again. When I first met him, agent David Graham worked for Peter Witt Associates, which represented many distinguished actors such as Maggie Smith. David left agenting to become a casting director, and a pretty good one. We worked together to cast the multi-award-winning TV movie, *The Gathering*. The director, Randal Kleiser wanted me to do the casting, but the producer had worked with David before and wanted him. I suggested a compromise in which we would do it together out of my office. The movie was nominated for seven Emmys and won two.

A year or so after the success of the movie, David, who was not a physically attractive man but did have the gift of gab, proudly told me his method for coming on sexually to aspiring actors, both as an agent and a casting director. Being a "gentleman," he would invite them to dinner – always at a restaurant near his home in West Hollywood. Then he would ask them back to his house for a nightcap. A polite refusal would have been appropriate. But either out of naïveté or opportunism, quite a few of them said yes.

Once home, David would try to kiss or fondle the guy to see where it would lead. He told me that he scored about one time out of four. This scenario was confirmed to me by one of David's clients, a wonderful actor with a very imposing name, Granville Van Dusen. Tall, handsome, heterosexual Granville – known as Sonny – had racked up an impressive theater resumé before turning to David for representation. David suggested dinner, and the evening played out just as I described. When David hit on him, Sonny said, "Why are you doing this? You know I'm straight!" He laughed it off and went home. A more insecure actor would have probably let David blow him.

I told David I thought his actions were despicable. He disagreed, explaining that all these men were old enough to make up their own minds. When I pointed out the uneven power dynamic, he pooh-poohed it. From that day on I would not approve him as a casting director for any NBC project. Perhaps others were on to him as well, because his casting career dwindled. He then tried his hand unsuccessfully at acting. David died in 2015.

Another in my rogues' gallery was J. Michael Bloom. Michael ran one of the most successful commercial talent agencies in New York, representing children, models, and sports figures. At some point he added a theatrical department and handled the early careers of several big stars, including Tom Hanks and Alec Baldwin. Baldwin stayed with the Bloom agency until well into his Hollywood stardom. After Bloom died in 2008, Baldwin wrote a virtual love-letter to his former agent in the Huffington Post. His praise was deserved in that Michael was a terrific agent with a great ability to spot talent. But how could Baldwin not have known about Bloom's sleezier side? As I had discovered, it was fairly well-known in the biz.

One night over dinner, when Michael and I were celebrating the hiring of one of his clients, he boasted to me about how he went about seducing young wannabe actors. He would look at all the unsolicited photos and resumés that were sent to his office and pick out some handsome men. Then he would ask a member of his staff to contact them and set up office meetings. Bloom would then call to "cancel" these meetings for various excuses and suggest that the meeting be re-scheduled at his town house in New York or to his Hollywood Hills home. Bloom would promise to represent the actor as a "hip-pocket" client – one who wasn't signed to the agency but who would be sent out as if he were. Then came the pass, which started by asking the guy to take his shirt off so he could judge the body and then the pants....etc. Bloom told me it worked more often than not.

He had tried this routine on an actor friend I know, Joel Polis. Joel was not a photo sent in the mail but an established theater actor. He got dinner and the invitation to the townhouse. Like Sonny Van Dusen, he was straight, and when Michael made his move, Joel said, "Cut it out, Michael!" and he stopped. Bloom was even brazen enough to hit on the boyfriend of one of his female staff. She quit soon afterward. After his stories, I neither spoke to Bloom again nor returned his calls. Not wanting his clients to suffer at NBC, I simply dealt with other agents in his office.

Next on this list was one of the most important agents in Hollywood, whose clients included many A+ movie stars. I won't name him here. Our careers started about the same time but we diverged, him to movies, me to TV. With the then almost total separation of movies and television, we saw little of each other. But every now and then he would call me to see one of his clients for a TV project. Invariably they were male and gorgeous. One of those actors read so well for me that I sent him to one of our pilot's casting directors and the actor tested for and got the role and the pilot went to series. Only later did I learn that this actor, who is straight and married with a family, got his start on this agent's casting couch. At least he was a man of his word: If you cooperated, he got you the audition or the meeting. His shenanigans were no secret at his office, where his many secretaries knew how to schedule visits to his office in ways that he thought would escape notice, but everyone knew. Even more appalling was that this agent gave big parties with lots of handsome young men and a few of his friends. Should one of these young men pass out from booze and/or drugs, this guy would invite his friends to have their ways with the passed out young man. What made this even stranger was that this agent was an extremely handsome man, who would have had no problem meeting guys. I guess the same could be said about heterosexual sexual abuser Jeffrey Epstein, who was also a very handsome man. I guess it is more a power than a sexual thing.

One day I got a call from a producer of a series I was casting. He asked me to schedule a certain actress – let's call her Jennifer – for a role we were casting at an afternoon session that week. He asked that I schedule her last in the day. I said sure, thinking nothing of it. I gave the list of actors to my assistant to schedule the auditions. When a couple of actors cancelled, she did the correct thing – although she didn't ask me first – by moving Jennifer into a now-vacant earlier slot. I showed up at the production office with the final list for the auditions. The producers asked why Jennifer wasn't last. I explained what had happened. He and his partner exchanged a dejected glance. Only then did I learn that Jennifer was known to offer blowjobs to producers and the casting directors in hopes of increasing her chances. Not surprisingly, her reading was terrible. But the guys kept talking to her – and Jennifer offered to blow all three of us. With her offer on the table, the two producers, both husbands and fathers, began to appear more embarrassed than stimulated. I saved the day by announcing how late we were running, and said we had to move on. They ended the session by halfheartedly promising to see Jennifer some other time. I got the sense that they were relieved not to have to go through with their plan. As far as I know, they were good boys from that day on.

Obviously, this is a loaded topic. Harvey Weinstein is now in jail, probably for life, as is R. Kelly. CBS's Les Moonves, who ironically did more to promote women executives up the corporate ladder than any of his predecessors, was fired and disgraced. Gone from their jobs and status are newscasters Matt Lauer, Bill O'Reilly, and Charlie Rose, chef Mario Batali, Kevin Spacey, opera star Placido Domingo, Senator Al Franken, Jeffrey Tambour, directors Bryan Singer and Brett Ratner, singer Ryan Adams, etc.

And on the cusp, Russell Simmons. Apparently forgiven, or at least still working after allegations were made against them, are: Woody Allen, Martin Lawrence, Mike Tyson, Pixar's John Lassiter, and of course Mr. Trump. The list of others accused is endless. Why are some forgiven? Why do some of those accused, like Al Franken, become victims of our current cancel culture; where all the good works they did before are suddenly forgotten and not viewed through the era when their misdeeds happened but judged by our currently hyper politically correct moment? I have no answers to these questions, but hope is in sight. Al Franken has appeared on *The Jimmy Kimmel Show* and is doing a concert tour.

CHAPTER 12

BEAUTIFUL DOWNTOWN BURBANK
and THE GOLDEN GIRLS

I was told recently by actress Lorna Luft, Judy Garland's "other" and extremely funny and talented daughter, that I was "the most powerful and feared casting director working in television." Perhaps this was because I had no time for small talk. My often-used first phone call words would be, "Hi, what's up," thereby getting to the point right away with zero small talk. But unlike many in my position, I would talk to any manager or agent at least once. If I thought, they were smart, made good casting suggestions or had good gossip, I would always take their calls. Unlike many in my industry, I would return every single phone call from both the powerful and the powerless every day – and not just at lunchtime to avoid them.

I'd become a TV bigshot although I don't think I behaved like one. My friends were not A-list celebrities, and the only openings and red-carpet functions I went to were the ones I *had* to attend. Once while in the hospital for minor surgery I asked the doctor to keep me there one more day so I could have a good excuse for not going to the Emmys! At these functions, I always self-parked my car to avoid having to make conversation with people I didn't recognize but who knew me while waiting for the valet parking attendant. During pilot season, most all final casting sessions were done in my office with many writers, directors, and studio executives present. The highest recorded number reached sixteen people at one time. With often two or three final casting sessions a day during pilot season, there would have been no way I could remember all those who attended. Yet at that particular moment, to them I was the most important person in the room and they definitely remembered me. At Christmastime my room was filled with gifts from every talent agency and manager in Hollywood. Most of these presents went straight to Goodwill, and those with JT initials were forwarded to John Travolta. I was invited everywhere but sometimes I would accept a party invitation from a studio executive or powerful agent and at the last minute make some lame excuse and not show up. I remember when I accepted an invitation to a New Year's Eve party given by prolific TV movie producer, Chuck Fries and his wife Ava. At the last minute, when the time came to get dressed, I just could not do it and called and left word I would not be there. I felt there would have no joy attending. I never received another very sought-after invitation to this affair.

Meanwhile at NBC, my life was terrific. When I left the studio, I got into the very same '65 Mustang convertible I bought on arrival to L.A., lit up a joint, and headed home. But this was the 1980s, and weed had become passé. Coke was at its height of social acceptability, and lots of NBC's executives, myself included, used. Another NBC exec with the office next to mine and I had a secret word, "sneep." We would call one another and say, "I think it's sneep time." We'd meet in one of our offices, have a few snorts, and get on with things. We were not hopping around like a crazed Al Pacino from *Scarface*. It was more like a slight boost in spirits. I could easily work on a small amount of coke, something I could never do with weed. That was strictly for after work.

Coke and other drugs were sent between offices on each coast via "the pouch," which transported mail between NBC's East and

West Coast offices. We did giggle when really stoned over the image of a giant kangaroo hopping over the Rocky Mountains. The goods would arrive in a VHS cassette box on my desk with other east coast mail, thanks to that kangaroo.

At that time I often carried around a little coke vial that looked like a glass bullet. These were ubiquitous, so much so that once, I was having a celebratory lunch for *Airplane!* at a prominent New York restaurant with the leading lady, Julie Haggerty, and my fellow casting director on the film, Gretchen Renell. The hostess came up to us with a coke vial in her hand and said, "I think one of you dropped this." I took the vial and thanked her; not another word was said by anyone.

Eventually I decided I was doing too much of it. I began to test myself by taking the vial with me to work and telling myself, "It's in my pocket, but I'm not going to use it." That never worked. One holiday weekend I was in Hawaii, and I took some coke with me. I sniffed it and it burned my nostrils up to my eyeballs to the point of tears. I thought to myself, "Why am I doing this shit for the 15 second high it's giving me, when it really hurts?" I flushed it down the toilet and immediately regretted it. When I came back to L.A., I called some friends who were in recovery and said, "I want to go to a meeting. I've got to stop this." I went with a friend to NA meetings for about a week and listened to members' horror stories. I hated the tobacco smell that permeated those rooms and the coffee-time socializing afterward even more than I'd grown to hate coke. But I did manage to quit for good. I have the innate ability to walk up to the line, lean all the way over it, but not cross it.

Work went on and kept getting better. Brandon remained a close-to-ideal boss, and we never had a cross word. My casting decisions were much more often right than wrong. In return, he gave me almost total autonomy and an almost unrestricted budget to travel to New York, London, and elsewhere to see new actors and plays. NBC was raking in so much advertising money that no one cared about what was going out I was also now in the beginning of what would be a twelve-year relationship with a wonderfully talented and handsome New York actor, Lou Liberatore. Because he was recreating his Tony Award-nominated role in the Broadway play *Burn This* (written by my old N.Y. Caffe Cino friend Lanford Wison) opposite John Malkovich on stage in London, the travel perk helped a lot. I spent a lot of time in the air in first class, reading upcoming NBC scripts, and getting triple mileage from a mileage war between United and American Airlines. I even lucked into a ride on the supersonic Concorde when the regular flight was cancelled.

In 1985, Tony Masucci, then head of the movie department, came into my office with a script. He asked for my help in getting it a green light. I read it, loved it, and knew that we had to do this movie. It was the first AIDS movie ever. *An Early Frost*, written by Ron Cowen and Daniel Lipman, told of a closeted young attorney who has to find a way to tell his parents he's gay, has a lover, and has contracted AIDS. Tony told me that Brandon was very wary of the movie and of the all-powerful and fearsome and conservative advertising sales department in New York; Brandon was leaning toward not giving a go. Please remember that all programming on a network exists to bring eyeballs to the tube to fill the space between the commercials. To this day, network sales departments have tremendous power over what gets on the air or doesn't.

I called Brandon's wife Lilly, a beautiful, vivacious, and former dancer with the New York City Ballet. I said, "Lilly, I'm gonna send you this script. You're gonna read this, and you are not gonna sleep with your husband again until he gives this project a go." She laughed and said, "What's it about?" I said, "I don't want to say anything. Please read it." She listened. I sent it over by messenger and a few hours thereafter, she called me and said, "It's extraordinary. We *must* do this." That expression is her mantra when she gets behind a cause. She has raised hundreds of millions of dollars through her fundraising for breast cancer research. Lilly encouraged Brandon to give it a go, and I don't think she had to withhold sex.

You must understand what a breakthrough this was on 1980s TV. Up to then, there had been only two gay characters on any series. On the ABC sitcom *Soap* (1977-1981), Billy Crystal played Jodie Campbell, the scion of a mafia family. His persona was a bit muddled and cliché; Jodie was having a secret fling with a pro football quarterback, but also considering a sex-change operation. Later the writers had him father a child with a woman who seduces him. Way over the top, hardly real and very funny. Yet it was heavily self-censored by ABC and pilloried by every conservative and religious organization. In 1982, Tony Randall had starred in the short-lived sitcom *Love, Sidney*, the story of a lonely older man who bonds with a single mom over their shared love of old movies. Sidney's gayness was never explicitly stated, just implied. In years past, of course, television had its share of gay personalities – Paul Lynde, Charles Nelson Reilly, *Laugh-In*'s Alan Sues. Seen today, they look unmistakably like life-of-the-party camp queens. But in the '70s, most of America probably saw them as funny oddball characters of no particular leaning.

An Early Frost, however, was very serious. AIDS was with us; you couldn't hide it. It had become a huge national story. John

Erman, who had directed many of the most acclaimed "quality" TV movies, episodic shows, and miniseries, including *Roots*, signed on. He was openly gay. I was so fired up about the potential of this film that I aimed for the stars, literally. "We need people to watch this," I said, "and one way for them to watch it is to have the biggest star we can find to play the mother. I suggest two: Audrey Hepburn and Julie Andrews. So let's start with Audrey Hepburn." But John feared that either choice would result in a Hollywood-style production – not a "real" one.

The parents in *An Early Frost* were successful working-class, and we needed actors who could play them believably. I totally understood his concerns. Ironically, six years later, Erman directed another TV movie about AIDS, *Our Son,* starring Julie Andrews, Ann-Margret, and Hugh Grant. The role of the brave and compassionate mother in our movie went to Gena Rowlands: a perfect choice we all agreed on. Gena was raw, she was real – an actress who could depict everything from intense pain to euphoria, and who was adept at playing mother lionesses, as she had in her Oscar-nominated turn in *Gloria*, directed by her husband, John Cassavetes.

Erman and I did disagree on the casting of the father, a lumber-business owner who struggles with his son's revelations. John wanted Richard Kiley, the stentorian baritone actor who had originated the role of Don Quixote in *Man of La Mancha*. To me, Kiley, with his cultivated speech, seemed too upper crust.

I argued: "You put Richard Kiley into this and you're not gonna get a salt-of-the-earth character. I want viewers to relate to this guy as one of them." My choice was New York-born, street-smart Ben Gazzara, the original Brick in *Cat on a Hot Tin Roof*. I held my ground, and happily John came around. The next week, while conveniently vacationing in Rome, where Gazzara lived, I hand-delivered the script to him. A week later he called my hotel and said he was in.

Unavoidably in its day, *An Early Frost* was slightly sanitized – the men didn't kiss or embrace, as any straight couple on TV would have done. Standards and Practices, our in-house censor, demanded about a dozen rewrites but none of them affected the movie, and the film did incredible raatings numbers. There were no angry protest calls and letters. I'm sure there were no dissenters because the movie was about universal human emotions – a loving mother and father caring for their dying son. The film broke important ground. Within the next few months, various series including *St. Elsewhere* and *Mr. Belvedere* addressed AIDS.

As for our two young stars, who along with their agents might well have been concerned about the possible damaging effects of playing gay, *An Early Frost* brought Aidan Quinn an Emmy nomination and he has done prestigious work ever since. The film gave his onscreen boyfriend, D.W. Moffett, his first major TV exposure, and D.W. has stayed busy to this day as an actor and director. After the movie aired, Brandon asked me if D.W. was gay. My answer was "I don't know. Why don't you ask him? For the record he's straight.

Unlike in New York theater, there was and still is much more homophobia in Hollywood. Neil Patrick Harris does not count since he grew up in front of our eyes and is, I think, considered family. Out lesbians seem to have better luck there than men but don't look for their names here. Television has been much kinder and there are out leading men on cable and streaming services. At NBC, homophobic jokes were common, but not told in my presence. I only heard about then afterward. None of the higher-ups there or at CBS, Paramount, or Spelling-Goldberg asked me to keep quiet about my sexuality. Instinctively I obeyed and had no problem with the unspoken code that if there was a business event you came single or with a woman. That was easy enough and not trouble for me to do. Every single person I worked with closely knew I was gay. My former boss Ethel Winant met me because I was her best friend's boyfriend. Now I was at the height of my career. How was it going to harm me? I was never going to be president of the network, nor did I want that job. Those who aspired to that were not out. "Everyone" believed that Barry Diller, who was head of ABC then Paramount and then started The Fox Network, was gay and in the closet before he married Diane von Furstenberg, I frequently saw him at gay parties in L.A. with a small, close-knit group of gay friends, including David Geffen, Sandy Gallin (Cher's and Dolly Parton's manager). I have no idea if he is or isn't or was and isn't now - and I don't care. He and his wife, Diane Von Furstenberg have been extremely generous with their vast fortune; including donating over 100 million dollars the building of "Little Island" and its adjacent public parts on the Hudson River in downtown NYC. A wonderful place to visit next time you are in NY.

There were at least ten other gay men and one lesbian in the programming department at NBC. Yet I was one of only three who were out. The closeted ones included Garth Ancier, a smart, cute young man who had started his NBC career as an assistant to Brandon. He felt rightly or wrongly that Barry Diller would never have asked him to leave NBC for Fox and help create The Fox Network if Diller had known he was gay. Garth told me he came out to one of his contemporary young gay executives at NBC with the expectation that the exec would come out to him as well. It didn't happen.

Certainly, you would hear actors referred to as "too gay" or "light in the loafers" or having "a hint of mint." Agents at the time avoided signing them. Known gay actors were at a disadvantage; their futures depended on how straight they seemed. Super-agent and friend Ed Limato once told me that actors should never let casting directors, producers, or anyone in a hiring position know their sexuality. Like in a courtroom when a judge orders a jury to disregard a previous statement, how can one not hear the already rung bell? Subliminally some people cannot help but let that tiny bit of knowledge influence a decision. Of course, this flies in the face of modern thinking that says that everyone should be honest and out, but even today there are *zero* out leading men in movies. On television there are several. I can't explain this except for the huge amounts of cash involved in movie production and feature film requires complete suspension of disbelief. That is much easier to do watching a play or a musical

Once the age of AIDS dawned, gay TV actors who had the disease faced another form of discrimination: They couldn't get cast in series roles because it was believed that they were not going to outlive a long running series. According to Steven Bochco, one of the creators of *Hill Street Blues,* the show's beautiful and classy Veronica Hamel came to him asking for no more kissing scenes with the shows gay but closeted leading man, Daniel J. Travanti. There was that much fear and lack of knowledge about the disease at that time. Many agents called to tell me that a client of theirs needed one or two more days work in order to meet the minimum amount of union earned salary for Screen Actors Guild health insurance. If I had nothing to offer, I would call producers or other casting directors and make a strong plea to hire those guys – for they were all men. One day Julie Hughes, my

New York casting representative, called to tell me she was taping an audition by a handsome and talented actor, Court Miller, for a romantic role in one of our pilots. Julie knew that Court had HIV, and she honestly didn't know if what she was doing was right or wrong. I assured her that she'd made the right choice and urged her to keep doing it for others like him. Court, who was not gay, got the part. He came to my office and thanked me in person. It was all I could do to hold back the tears until he left. Sadly, he passed away in 1986.

Lilly Tartikoff helped me circumvent the system in one more way. As mentioned, there still was a lingering custom in the entertainment industry that if you went to a business function you brought a woman or went alone. The matter arose in 1986, when a milestone occurred in NBC's history: General Electric bought our parent company, RCA. GE then went to Universal and paid them a lump sum and canceled all those future commitments that NBC had been roped into giving them. The cash floodgates were finally open for Brandon to bring in new writers and bolder concepts. NBC rose to number two in the ratings, just a hair's breadth from No. 1. Most of our shows were not only commercial successes but critics' favorites and award-winners.

To celebrate this and to thank the affiliates (the locally owned TV stations mostly in the smaller cities) who had remained loyal to NBC during its dark days, we were informed that the annual Affiliates Convention would be held at the Hyatt Regency Hotel in Maui, rather than in a hotel ballroom in L.A. We were told we could bring our spouses on NBC's dime. I immediately called my best gal-pal, actress-turned-director Jenny Sullivan, and asked if she wanted to be Mrs. Thurm for a long weekend on Maui. Of course, she said yes.

Just before the trip, I fell in love and was living with the actor Lou Liberatore, as mentioned. A New Yorker by way of Leonia, New Jersey, Lou had never been to Hawaii. I suggested that instead of the room that NBC would pay for, I would get a one-bedroom suite and pay the difference. Then something came up that changed our plans slightly.

My friend Tim Flack, who died of AIDS in 1995, worked with me at NBC as my v.p. level assistant for a couple of years. Tim was the funniest man I have ever met. He was also whatever the opposite of being in the closet is; "gay as a goose" comes to mind. He was adored by all who knew and worked with him. After he left NBC, he put together and was going to produce TV movie for us about a couple stranded on a tropical island starring Loni Anderson (*WKRP in Cincinnati* and Bert Reynolds' then wife) and Perry King, a wonderful and gorgeous leading man, but not yet a "real" star.

Tim had heard that Loni was a bit difficult. This was not true at all and was so typical of those times and also true right now; in that if a woman questioned anything she was "difficult" but if a man did the same thing he was merely being "professional." A great example of this was when Loni was starring in a TV movie about the very blond, 1950s bombshell movie star, Jayne Mansfield. Loni "complained" to the producer and the director (both men) that the cheap dynel wigs they bought for her were terrible and asked for new ones. Fortunately, the woman running our movie department, Joan Barnett, went to the set and nicely explained that the movie was selling glamour and you don't get glamour with dime-store wigs. Loni got the new wigs and looked great. The movie was a big success both with critics and ratings. This was possibly helped by her co-star

Arnold Schwarzenegger, who played Mansfield's body builder husband, Mickey Hargitay.

Tim asked if I could come to the set for the first few days since I knew Loni well. Coincidentally, NBC had a planned retreat for all the programming department at a nearby Lake Arrowhead. The aim of the retreat was to get to know one another, share our feelings, and thereby work better with one another. I don't do well at those things. I went to Brandon and asked if I could miss the Lake Arrowhead retreat because Tim asked for help on our movie. He asked where the movie was being shot. "Tahiti," I replied. He then said, "And you are telling me this with a straight face?" To which I said, "With the straightest one I can manage." He laughed and okayed the trip with the caveat that if anyone found out about it, he would kill me. So instead of flying from L.A. together with Lou and Jenny, I would get there a day early – flying from Tahiti to Maui – and meet them at the airport.

Lou and I had discussed that the three of us would hang out for a few days before the affiliate convention started. Then when the convention began, Jenny and I would do the business stuff and Lou would take our rental car and explore other parts of Maui, namely the less touristy but equally stunning side of the island called Hana.

We had a great time for a few days, although each time I asked Lou what his plans were or if he had called any of the hotels in Hana, he said, "Oh, I forgot – I'll do it tomorrow." A few days later, on Friday, the day of the first convention event – a cocktail party followed by a sit-down dinner – "tomorrow" had yet to come. Most of that day Jenny played tennis while I took surfing lessons at the beach and Lou hung out at the pool.

It was there that he met Lilly Tartikoff. They hit it off instantly. Late that afternoon, both Brandon and I arrived at the pool; Brandon to pick up Lilly to get ready for the party, I to see if Lou had left for Hana. Brandon, who had previously met Lou, said hi, then told Lilly they'd be late unless they left now. As she got up to leave, Lilly turned to Lou and said how wonderful it had been to meet him, and that she looked forward to seeing us at the party. "Well, sorry, but you won't," said Lou. "Joel is here with his spouse, Jenny, so I'll be up in the room watching *Matlock* on closed circuit." Lilly a former ballet dancer correctly sized up the situation. She turned to her husband and said, "Brandon, this is ridiculous. Call someone and tell them that Lou is going to sit with us." Brandon made the call, and Lou sat at their table for every convention event, including being entertained by Liza Minnelli, while Jenny and I sat halfway back with the masses. Thereafter, at every NBC function where spouses were invited, Lou and I were invited as NBC's only out gay couple. The best part of all this is no one cared.

Will & Grace was still a dozen years away, but a campy comedy evergreen had taken its place among NBC's hits. Its four female stars, all over fifty, were adored by straights, gays, drag queens, and very demographic group from the very young to the very old. Much has been written about *The Golden Girls*, notably in Jim Colucci's *New York Times* bestseller, *Golden Girls Forever*. It was one of the best sitcoms of all time, as funny today as it was when it premiered in 1985. It won countless awards, including Outstanding Lead Actress in a Comedy Series for each of its stars – a first in Emmy history. The idea for *The Golden Girls* happened at the filming of a promotional special showcasing NBC's schedule for the following year. The youth-oriented *Miami Vice* portion of the show was introduced by two of the network's funniest and oldest supporting actresses: Doris Roberts of *Remington Steele* and Selma Diamond of *Night Court*. What better choices? They were hysterical in their ogling of Don Johnson's butt and got a huge laugh when they called the new show *Miami Nice*.

Seeing the two women together gave Brandon the idea, and he directed his head of comedy, Warren Littlefield, to follow through. What happened next is one of the great accidents in TV history. Producer Paul Junger Witt and his business partner Tony Thomas (son of Danny and brother of Marlo) came into NBC to pitch a series about two young sisters who live together. They had brought the writer with them. Littlefield wasn't interested in their premise; instead, he remembered Brandon's idea for a series about older women who share a house. He suggested that alternative idea to the writer, who turned it down. Witt, Thomas, and the writer left. A few moments later, Paul and Tony came back into Warren's office and said that if Warren was serious, no one could execute that concept better than Paul's wife, Susan Harris. This enormously talented woman had created and written every episode of another groundbreaking comedy series, *Soap*. But Susan had been lying low and recuperating physically and emotionally after her exhausting work on that show, which was forced off the air by conservative watchdog groups who were appalled by its frank though totally silly and not at all lascivious sexual content.

The idea of writing about older women appealed to her, and she said yes to the project. It was she who came up with the format of three single women roommates plus the mother of one of them. NBC's dubious contribution to the mix was to ask for a gay houseboy – ironic recompense after what Susan had gone through with *Soap*. Paul and Tony hired a superb casting director, Judith Weiner, who had done a first-rate job with *Family Ties*. Weiner and her assistant Alison Jones (later to become a top casting director herself) began auditioning countless women for the roles.

For Sophia, the only actress to hit all the marks was Estelle Getty. Estelle's resumé had been slim until she got the role of Harvey Fierstein's mother in the original off-Broadway production of *Torch Song Trilogy*. Her first audition for *The Golden Girls* was sensational, but she had a month's worth of callback auditions to go. Finally, Estelle, the youngest of all the women who were eventually cast, came into my office with sprayed gray hair, a professionally done makeup job to give her an old-lady look, a thrift-shop dress, hat, and shoes, and most important, a tacky straw pocketbook. From the moment she opened her mouth, she had the dozen of us laughing so hard we were gasping for breath.

The next two roles were harder to cast. Many "unknown" women of a certain age in both New York and Los Angeles just didn't make the cut, so the producers decided to go for known personalities. "Rose" (the naïve one) was offered to Rue McClanahan (*Maude's* clueless next-door neighbor), "Blanche" (the hyper-sexual one) to Betty White. Though not thrilled with the character of Rose, Rue saw how good the writing was. She agreed to do the part, but first she had to read with Betty White for Jay Sandrich, the pilot's director. Since Jay had never met Rue, he asked her read Rose for him alone. He told Rue that while the reading was good, he just did not believe her as this character. With divine inspiration, Jay asked if she would be interested in playing Blanche – the role she was dying to do.

Betty White, who had already agreed to play Blanche, came in to read with Rue. Jay knew Betty very well, since he had directed

most of the episodes of *The Mary Tyler Moore Show*. He asked
Betty if she might consider playing Rose, a homespun and naïve
former farm girl. At first she was wary, but she warmed to the
idea of playing a character totally different from the man-hungry
Sue Ann Nivens of *The Mary Tyler Moore Show.* Rue and Betty
read together. It was magic.

Then the real drama happened. I didn't know at the time that
Susan Harris had written the role of Dorothy specifically and
only for Bea Arthur; had she or anyone else told me, the following would never have happened. Brandon Tartikoff did not like
Bea and could quote her TVQ score by heart. This system, a bible
in the industry, is a measurement, based on polling, of how many
people recognized an actor, and more important, how many liked
that actor. Bea's score indicated that she had a high recognition
factor but a very low likeability score. Likeability was at that time
considered by most anyone with the power to hire, *the* qualifica-
tion for an actor needed above all; screw talent. The theory was
that if the audience liked the you, you would be invited into their
homes on a weekly basis. Likeability became less important as
the years went by with cable and streaming giving us a multitude
of anti-heroes: Bryan Cranston on *Breaking Bad,* Kevin Spacey in
House of Cards, and Viola Davis in *How to Get Away with Murder,* to name a few.

Brandon asked me if I knew anyone else who could do the
role. While disagreeing with his feelings about Bea Arthur, I said
that I did know another woman who could play Dorothy. She was
the Tony-winning Elaine Stritch, famous for her rough edges and
fierce comedic delivery. At that time, she was best-known for her
biting performance of "The Ladies Who Lunch" song from the
Stephen Sondheim musical *Company* on Broadway. I explained

to Brandon that Stritch would be a discovery to the TV audience, a new old face, since she had done little television work. I did not mention that Elaine liked her liquor a bit too much.

I met Stritch (as she was always referred to) in my office a few years back, and I told her I was dying to find something for her on NBC. She was eager for me to do just that. Brandon hadn't heard of her, but he told me to fly her out and present her to Susan Harris and Tony and Paul and the all the NBC executives. I overnighted a script to her, and after she read it, she called and asked if I had any tips for her. I told her who else had been cast and that "Dorothy was strong-willed, obstinate and doesn't take shit from anyone but can be a marshmallow inside at times, just like you." She laughed, coughed, and hung up. She really wanted this gig. On Broadway, even in leading roles, she never earned anywhere near a TV salary, and she needed the dough. A couple of mornings later, Stritch arrived at NBC for her reading. My assistant buzzed to say that Stritch had arrived and had gone to the ladies' room to freshen up. I didn't find out until later that freshening up meant taking a fortifying nip or two of vodka.

I still didn't know that Susan Harris had Bea and only Bea in mind for the part. But I sensed something was wrong when Witt, Thomas, Harris, Jay Sandrich, Warren Littlefield, and Brandon filed into my office with no small talk and with very serious looks on their faces. The room was colder than the proverbial witch's tit. I brought in Elaine and introduced her to everyone in my office. I tried to start a bit of small talk to make the atmosphere more comfortable, but it went nowhere. Then Stritch and I began to read. Needless to say, she was very nervous and when she got no laughs she asked to do it over. The sound of no laughter is frightening, and even the best actors tend to compensate by pushing harder, which only makes things worse. So it was with Stritch. In her desperation, she added a "fuck" to Susan's writing, then apologized. Again, silence.

Finally someone said thank you, and she left the room. It was only then that Susan spoke up and explained how she had written the part for Bea Arthur, and there was no reason not to offer it to her. Brandon defended his position that Bea was the TV equivalent of box office poison at the movies. But Susan, Paul, and Tony persisted. They made headway only when they pointed out that Bea would not be the sole star of this series but part of an ensemble with one of the most likeable women on TV, Betty White. Brandon gave in.

Last to be cast was a gay houseboy, Coco. Susan and the director, Jay Sandrich, insisted they did not want a stereotypical gay performance. All the actors brought in for final auditions played it "straight", but none were funny. Brandon then suggested Charles Levin, who had played a flamboyant gay character called Eddie Gregg on *Hill Street Blues*. Levin, who was straight, came in prepared to read Coco as he had played Eddie. But before his reading, Jay told him not to camp it up. There wasn't one laugh and he was sent home. At Brandon's instruction, I called Levin that night and told him to come back tomorrow and try again – but this time to camp it up and do "Eddie Gregg." He got loads of laughs, and the part was his. Susan tried, but the "straight" gay character she wanted just didn't work.

Unfortunately, it became apparent after we'd done the pilot that his character was superfluous. Even though he got a few laughs, there was no way he could compete for screen time with those four women. So out with Coco, and good news for Estelle Getty; whereas Sophia had been initially conceived as a recurring character, now she became the bona fide equal of the big three. As for Elaine Stritch, she survived her *Golden Girls* debacle to become an ever-more-beloved fixture of the theater. Ultimately, she got her TV role: that of Alec Baldwin's mother on NBC's *30 Rock*. In 2001, she devoted a considerable chunk of her Tony-winning, autobiographical, one-woman Broadway show *Elaine Stritch at Liberty* to this audition disaster. Almost everything she said was accurate, down to quoting Susan Harris' response when Stritch asked if she could change "a few things in one particular line." Susan's answer: "Hopefully just the punctuation." Stritch went on to blame her loss of the part on that slug or two of vodka. The incident, she said, brought home the extent of her drinking problem and convinced her to stop, which she did. I never told her the truth.

The last remaining and the oldest – and arguably the most loved of the quartet – Betty White, passed away December 31, 2021. Tributes and adulation poured all over the press and TV, all very well-deserved. But no one is perfect. We all have a side that we'd rather not show to others. Betty was not loved by her *Golden Girls* co-stars, especially by Bea Arthur, and not exactly adored by Rue McClanahan. When Estelle would forget lines, Betty would go out of character and keep the audience laughing by making a gesture with her thumb to her mouth and point to Estelle as if she had been drinking. I don't think she was intentionally making fun of Estelle but rather trying to keep the audience laughing between takes. Nonetheless, Rue and Bea thought this was very unkind. Betty's feuding with Bea is well-documented, and during the production of a Showtime series I cast in 1999, *Beggars and Choosers,* Bea, who on the series was playing an exaggerated version of herself, referred to Betty, off-camera, as a cunt. Whatever disagreements these women had in private, they never interfered with the show itself. Indeed, *The Golden Girls* has become 2022's version of the 1950 black-and-white *I Love Lucy* shows. Like the *Lucy* episodes, you can find *The Golden Girls* still airing all over the world in English and dubbed versions – and still as funny as if the show was taped just yesterday.

CHAPTER 13

THE PHOENIXES: TRUE FAMILY VALUES

The day I began working at NBC, a pile of press releases was on my desk. One of them was about me. Whenever a new executive came aboard, an announcement was generated and distributed to everyone in the programming department. They, in turn, welcomed you by writing something clever or nice on your press release and then forwarded it to you through interoffice mail. One of those messages was from the head of daytime TV, Earl Greenberg, who offered help to the newbie. He listed several mutual friends, all of whom were gay. I guess this was his subtle way of letting me know he was, too. Earl, who left NBC a few years later and made a fortune in infomercials, dropped by to introduce himself and ask if I needed anything. "Yes," I said. "A really good assistant." Earl advised me not to go with any of the HR suggestions and told me about a woman who had worked a temp for him a few weeks earlier. Her name was Arlyn Phoenix.

I arranged to meet her the next day. Immediately I saw why Earl had recommended her so highly. Empathy flowed from her every pore; Arlyn's whole demeanor was gentle and warm. It turned out that she was married and had five kids and a dog. The family had moved, via Winnebago, from Florida to Los Angeles. Arlyn and her husband John were hoping to get their unique children into showbiz. Arlyn had a tenuous connection to none other than Penny Marshall, aka Laverne of *Laverne & Shirley*, and her brother, Garry Marshall, *Happy Days* creator. They were friends of a friend of Arlyn's – all being residents of the same

Bronx neighborhood. Arlyn got in touch with Penny's sister, producer Ronny Hallin, who arranged a meeting with the Marshalls' casting director, Bobby Hoffman.

It was a disaster. Hoffman, who was obviously just doing a favor for Penny, handed "sides" (a couple of pages of a script without context) to her two oldest kids, River and Rain, and asked them to read the scene with him. To put this in perspective, adults who have been doing these types of readings for years have problems with this practice, so just imagine what this must have been like for ten- and eight-year-olds who did not have a clue.

Arlyn Dunetz, I learned, had met John Bottom in 1968 while hitchhiking on Santa Monica Blvd. in L.A. after she had just arrived from the Bronx. They shared the same spiritual ideals and soon became a couple traveling through the Pacific Northwest, earning a meager living by picking fruit along the way to Canada so John could avoid the draft. After arriving in Eugene, Oregon, they found out that John's draft number was very high and in all likelihood, he would never be called up. Looking for a milder climate, they wound up in Phoenix, Arizona, and it was there that they met members of a Christian movement called the Children of God (COG). This was a bit extraordinary in that Arlyn was born and raised Jewish. But it was also the first time they met folks like themselves – people living communally and with goals to spread peace, joy, love, and understanding through song and prayer.

Several years passed and they found themselves in Puerto Rico, Mexico, and Venezuela with four children and one on the way and a growing realization that COG was not living up to what they expected. They became totally disillusioned with the group, which had begun espousing using sex to acquire new members.

That, and the increasing difficulty crossing borders with their growing brood caused them to move back to the U.S. in 1977. As part of their "rebirth," they changed their last name to Phoenix, after the mythical bird that rises from the ashes.

When I met Arlyn, they were living in Sun Valley, located in the foothills of the mountains on the northern edge of the San Fernando Valley, not too far from NBC in Burbank. Real estate prices in Sun Valley are about ninety percent less than they are in the foothills of the southern mountains, more commonly known as the Hollywood Hills. In short, Sun Valley has pretty hills, but they ain't the Hollywood ones.

It was an interesting job interview, because whatever I told Arlyn I would need, she replied that she couldn't do it. For example, I told her that her hours would be from about 10 a.m. until she finished anything that needed doing. She said that with five kids, staying late would be difficult. I then suggested that if she had to work late, her husband could drive the kids to the studio and have dinner for free at the NBC commissary. She countered that they were all vegan – to which I said that the commissary served vegetarian food and if necessary we could order from the local "natural" food place nearby that could prepare vegan. Her kids, I explained, could stay in a conference room, watch TV and eat, which later, in practice, they loved to do. Joaquin told me years later that one of the reasons they liked this so much was that television was strictly limited at home, and there definitely were no large bowls of candy to be gobbled up either. My fellow execs loved seeing and interacting with them. Their great energy was catching.

Next I asked if I could dictate some data for her to put into business-letter form, something I am not great at doing. It took her all of three seconds to write the letter. I read it quickly, crumpled it up, and asked her when she could start. She later told me that when I had crumpled the letter and tossed into the trash, her heart had sunk, thinking she failed. While the job paid more than she expected, it seems that her pay level would depend on her having already been a secretary/assistant to a show business vice president. I then said, "That's nuts and of course you've worked for a vice president before." And with a wink-wink I named a couple of V.P friends she had "worked" for. She got my innuendo, thanked me, but insisted she could not lie. I said, "Well, I can and will because I think you will be great in this job and I really need you." And I did just that.

Two days later, Arlyn started working for me, while the kids pursued their performing careers. That consisted solely of playing guitars and singing for tips in Westwood Village, a busy area near the UCLA campus. That year, 1981, the children in descending age order were River (11), Rain (9), Leaf, later to reclaim his birth name of Joaquin, (7), Liberty (5), and Summer (3). And oh, the dog was called And Justice for All. There was something magical about these kids. River, with his beautiful tan and naturally blond-streaked hair, was like a sun god with rays of light emanating from him. He was a natural leader for his siblings and had the most warm and genuine smile, which he gave, along with a hug, to everyone he met. Rain, the oldest daughter, was fierce and determined. Leaf was so dear, with his father's soulful and mesmerizing eyes and a quiet yet very subversive sense of humor. I never imagined what was to be in store for him in the future; all I wanted to do was hug him and tell him everything would be all right. Liberty and Summer, the two youngest sisters, were terrific little kids, too.

Rarely do I encourage adults, and never kids, to try their luck in showbiz. One night I went to see them working a street corner in Westwood. They were dressed in matching tank tops and shorts. Their singing and guitar-playing was just okay, yet something about them attracted groups of passers-by to stop, listen, and throw green bills into the open guitar cases. The kids' joy at just being there to sing for the crowd came through strongly. Clearly River, Rain, and Leaf were talented while the two youngest, Summer and Liberty, were just super adorable. I videotaped their performance, and a clip of it was used in an Anderson Cooper interview with Joaquin on *60 Minutes.*

Not too long after that night, I asked Arlyn if she would like me to arrange for her children to meet the best kids' talent agent in L.A. Of course she said, if it was no problem or unethical. I then called Iris Burton, a woman of a certain age with jet black hair, a tan developed from way too many hours at her pool, and a gravelly cigarette voice. "Meet a whole fuckin' family," she asked. "You mean I gotta sign all of 'em even if I only want one?" "Yup," I said.

After the meeting, she called and said, "Ya didn't tell me they won't do commercials for meat, dairy, or junk food. What the fuck am I supposed to do with 'em? But you know what, the oldest one, what's his name – *Rivah*– is *gaw-jus,* and where the hell do those names come from? But they got somethin' goin' on, and so what the hell, I said I'd send 'em out and see what happens." Like me, Iris was foul-mouthed and able to see those special things that separated stars from ordinary people like us. Little by little, having learned how to handle reading "sides," River began landing guest parts on TV while Leaf and Rain started working in commercials. Eventually, Leaf got a small role on *Hill Street*

Blues, and according to casting director Simon Ayr, blew the roof off the part.

Things at NBC were not going so well. At the time, the early '80s, the network was sinking lower and lower in the ratings, and the pressure on me and the programming department was enormous. One day Arlyn invited me for a home-cooked meal. From the minute I walked in their house, my blood pressure dropped. I got hugs from John, Arlyn, and all the kids and licks from the dog. It was my first vegan dinner, and I loved it: celery stalks filled with "nutritious yeast" for a starter, then sautéed millet burgers and salad, followed by "banini," made by taking frozen pieces of banana and putting them through a Champion Juicer. The final product had the consistency of and tasted exactly like banana-flavored Carvel. After the kids had gone to bed, a joint appeared from my pocket, and I went home emotionally renewed and stress-free. Well, almost. I had decided to leave my car at a service station just down the street from their house and take a taxi home. The next day when I called the station, my '65 Mustang convertible was "stolen" from the locked garage. It did turn up a few days later unscathed. The police figured it was taken for a joy ride.

The children by this time had become fixtures at NBC; everyone who met them loved them. With the network failing in all time slots except for *The Tonight Show with Johnny Carson,* Earl Greenberg asked what I thought of a morning or daytime show featuring the kids. We did some test tapings of them singing and dancing, but their technical skills were just not there. When I suggested to Arlyn that they could benefit from professional instruction, she demurred and said they could not afford it. I said that NBC would pay for it, but she then told me that her husband,

John, was teaching these skills to the kids and at this point that's the route they wanted to take for now.

But River was definitely going places very fast. As the oldest and most obviously "commercial" of the kids, he quickly became that season's go-to, in-demand kid actor. His breakout came when he was cast in the film *Stand by Me* (directed by Ron Reiner), in which he played one of four troubled boys in a small town in Oregon. Two years later, River was nominated for an Academy Award for *Running on Empty*, in which he had met and begun a relationship with his co-star Martha Plimpton. He didn't win but attended the ceremony with his mother. I kvelled at home in front of the TV.

Arlyn worked with me for five years. She left only because the family was moving from Sun Valley to a beautiful little town, Murphys, in the Gold Rush country of the Sierra Nevada Mountains in Northern California. The family moved there because River had been cast as the youngest brother in a TV series version of the old MGM musical *Seven Brides for Seven Brothers*, which was being shot on location there. Richard Dean Anderson, later to become *MacGyver* was also cast as the oldest brother. In addition to its natural beauty, I'm sure that this location was chosen because the producer, David Gerber, a pussycat-like bear of a man, not only owned the hotel where most of the cast and crew stayed, but just about every other commercial enterprise in the town. I guess that since he was making money from every direction, he even agreed to provide River with a rubber saddle – leather is not vegan and rubber saddles are not cheap.

I had spent a few weeks in this area years before when my friends actors Jenny Sullivan and John Ritter (pre-*Three's Company)* were on location for a movie based on Tom Tryon's novel,

The Other. Tom had been a teen-aged crush of mine when he played the title role in the Disney TV series *Texas John Slaughter.* Tom, who never really enjoyed acting, had reinvented himself with this novel and was now a best-selling author. We met at a party in L.A., locked eyes, and a few weeks later I found myself on location, too.

A few months after the Phoenixes had moved to Murphys, I entered my first midlife crisis. I was depressed, anxious, and in a bad place. I called Arlyn, and she said that since pilot season was about to end and if I had some free time, why not come up and stay with them for a while? In a repeat of what I'd experienced at my first dinner with them, I felt at peace from the moment they welcomed me in. Google Murphys, California, and you will see what a magical place it is: snow-capped mountains, small rivers and creeks, and most of all giant redwood and sequoia forests. River had a light shooting schedule that week, so we all went tubing, which meant getting into a rubber-tire inner tube and floating down the the Stanislaus River, a new experience for this city boy. As I said, the Phoenix energy was catching, so their place became the drop-in-and-hang house for other cast members. The day after our tubing, Peter Horton and his then-wife Michelle Pfeiffer and a few others dropped by for some wine and snacks. Sadly, I had to get back to L.A. and work, but my midlife crisis had been nipped in the bud.

Arlyn's last assignment for me had been to find a replacement for herself, and she did: Lillie Robertson, who in many ways was the same as well as the opposite of Arlyn. She and her husband Don, who lived nearby in Burbank, were a "straight" churchgoing couple with three kids, in contrast to the hippie-like Phoenix family. But underneath the obvious and unimportant surface differences, both Lillie and Arlyn had their families as their first priorities. Lillie stayed with me for five years. After a difficult day I asked her how she put up with me. "Easy," she said. "I raised three children."

River's star kept rising, and Leaf began to work as well. Arlyn told me Leaf was up for a role in a movie to be directed by my old friend Randal Kleiser, the director of *Grease*. The film was called *Flight of the Navigator* – a sci-fi space flick. Arlyn asked if I could call Randal and put in a good word for Leaf. I did, but unfortunately it did no good. He had seen Leaf's television work and thought he was a terrific actor, but he also thought that Leaf's face wouldn't look good in close-ups on a big movie theater screen because of a small scar on his upper lip. But that didn't stop Leaf. That year he was cast as one of the leads in a similar movie, *Space Camp*. Neither of these space pics was successful, but Leaf was wonderful, lip scar and all. A few years later, when he was of high-school age, he got cast in the movie *To Die For*. Leaf played a horny teenager who, along with two schoolmates (Casey Affleck and Alison Folland), is manipulated by a sexy, aspiring local newscaster (Nicole Kidman) to kill her interfering husband (Matt Dillon). *To Die For* was a hit. By now Leaf had changed his name back to his given one, Joaquin. He was totally different from his star brother but equally as talented. Later he played a tortured monk who worked for the Marquis de Sade in the movie *Quills*. During the years after, he earned Oscar nominations for his performances in *Gladiator*, *The Master*, and for playing Johnny Cash in *Walk the Line*. His co-star, Reese Witherspoon, won an Oscar for her performance – which was terrific – but he was robbed for not winning one too especially because he did his own singing where he absolutely nailed Cash's voice.

He went on to do many movies playing wonderfully eccentric characters, but it was not until *The Joker* that he became recognized as arguably the best actor of his generation. He received overwhelming positive critical response even from those who did not like the movie. He won a Golden Globe, a slew of other awards, and as was widely predicted, the best actor Oscar for 2019. Many times in the past when speaking with Arlyn, I joked that Joaquin was a great actor but a terrible movie star. I said this because being the very private person he is and preferring to let his work speak for itself, he did not do things like giving interviews or showing up for photo-ops at red-carpet premieres, etc., I also gave this comment to 60 *Minutes* which Anderson Cooper used when interviewing Joaquin in the weeks leading up to the Academy Awards broadcast. Joaquin roared with laughter and I am pretty sure he knew where that line originated.

He is still a very genuine and unspoiled person and I believe he is perceived as mildly eccentric within appropriate bounds. He has become an articulate, activist movie star, and he got street cred when he was arrested along with Jane Fonda and Martin Sheen in Washington, D.C., protesting inaction by the federal government on global warming.

I'm guessing that River's and Joaquin's success helped buy the family a homestead in a small town outside Gainesville, Florida. This generosity did not surprise me, because the family was and still is like the Musketeers – all for one and one for all. The family moved into its own kind of Kennedy Compound, albeit on much cheaper land than Cape Cod. Their place consists of a few houses on a few acres of beautiful land with a small pond that becomes a lake during rainy seasons, often inhabited by an alligator or two. Gainesville is home to the University of Florida, which makes that central Florida region a very interesting redneck/liberal place. Arlyn became very involved working as a community organizer specializing in environmental causes.

All the while River and Rain continued to develop their musical talent by starting a band and touring the east coast. Rain toured with the Red Hot Chili Peppers and appeared in several movies including *Even Cowgirls Get the Blues*.

River's death on October 31, 1993, outside the Sunset Strip club the Viper Room at the age of twenty-three, was shocking to me and to the rest of the world. For one thing, he was not into the club scene and all his co-workers, friends, and family knew he was not a regular drug user. His image was not in the John Belushi mold. Clean-cut and healthy was a more apt description. That night, he, Joaquin, and Rain went to the club to check out its music scene for he was as much into his music as he was his acting. They were definitely not club kids. I don't think that anyone, with the possible exception of his two siblings, knows exactly what happened and. Indeed. I'm not certain that even they know for sure. Bad things happen to good kids, and River was no exception. I have been in similar bad situations, but I have been lucky. River was not. He died with his brother and sister standing helplessly by his side – something unimaginable to me.

I next saw Arlyn, Summer, and Liberty at River's memorial service in Hollywood. Summer had grown into a beautiful young woman, and Liberty looked amazing. Arlyn was strong, and her talk about River was very emotional and healing. I continue to see her from time to time in L.A. and when I visit Florida. After River's death, she founded the River Phoenix Center for Peace Building in Gainesville. It combats police brutality, school bullying, and other forms of violence.

About this time or earlier, John Phoenix went to Costa Rica to develop a piece of family-owned property as an eco-resort. Time and distance did not help their already strained marriage, and he and Arlyn divorced. The divorce did not sit well with the kids; even adult children have a tough time dealing with parents divorcing. A few years later, Arlyn changed her name to Heart and married a terrific younger man, Jeffrey Weissberg, whom she had met and worked with years before. It was my first vegan destination wedding, and it was a blast. Who knew that vegan lasagna could taste exactly like the real thing – and thank goodness wine is vegan, because I drank plenty of it.

God doesn't give with both hands, and the good fortune of the Phoenix family has been greatly challenged by tragedy. While staying with her father in rural Costa Rica, Liberty's middle son came down with what was thought to be meningitis. With no hospitals nearby and a rising fever, he needed emergency care. They had to make their way to the nearest hospital by car and boat; a helicopter airlift was impossible because the air pressure would have killed him instantly. But luck wasn't with them. Imagine holding your son and watching him slowly pass away on the long trip to the hospital, which is what happened. Liberty recovered. She has incredible spirit and entrepreneurial gifts and eventually opened Indigo Green Store in Gainesville, where she sold environmentally safe cleaning and building products. She is convinced that it was toxins that compromised her son Indigo's health. I had dinner at her sweet and oh-so-comfortable house in Gainesville and met her now teen-aged other sons. She was as sharp and vital as ever.

Summer continued acting. She was stunning in the London West End production of the Kenneth Lonergan play, *This Is Our*

Youth. Her co-stars were Matt Damon and her boyfriend and eventual husband, Casey Affleck. The day after I saw the play, we all went to the Victoria and Albert museum to see an exhibit of British and other European royal tiaras. How gay was that? Back in New York, Summer and two friends opened a boutique on the lower East Side, selling Liberty's own hand sewn mash-ups of vintage clothing and fabrics.

Now let's talk about Joaquin's infamous David Letterman appearance in 2009 and the subsequent production and fall-out from his and Casey Affleck's "mockumentary" *I'm Still Here,* which was about Joaquin's "choice" to give up acting and become a hip-hop artist. The piece when it was released in 2010 was disastrously unfunny. Unfortunately, neither Phoenix nor Affleck possessed the comedic chops of mockumentary filmmaker and actor Christopher Guest (*Spinal Tap, Best in Show*). Satire without humor is doomed.

But the Letterman interview, which was planned as the first part of their project, came off brilliantly thanks to Joaquin's performance, for it *was* a performance. Ostensibly he was on Letterman to promote a film he had made with Gwyneth Paltrow. The first noticeably odd thing was his showing up sporting a beard looking like the fourth member of ZZ Top. He then answered Letterman's interview questions with one-word or no answers and became the best straight man Letter ever had on show. Joaquin's silence allowed Letterman to be wild and funny at his expense. I had heard about his appearance in advance and recorded it. The next day I called Heart and asked what Joaquin was doing. She told me to watch it again, especially at the end when he leans over and whispers in Letterman's ear and a look of recognition appears on Letterman's face as if to say, "Oh, now I get it." The stunt was brilliant but went over far too well, in that no one in the TV audience got that what Joaquin was doing was intentional and wildly funny. Everyone thought he had gone nuts, and the subsequent announcement of his retiring from acting pushed that idea even further. I was so hoping that the movie would be good enough to show how well thought-out all this was; but alas it was not. Another casualty of this project was Casey Affleck, now Joaquin's brother-in-law, being sued for sexual misconduct by two women on the project.

The suit was settled out of court and several years later, Summer and Affleck divorced. She has survived a very rough patch and is now thriving with her kids, now teen-agers. Joaquin lives right up the hill from me with his fiancé, the wonderful actress Rooney Mara, who starred in *The Girl with the Dragon Tattoo*. Heart told me that this is the best thing that has ever happened to him. Seeing them together, I realize Heart was absolutely correct. She is her ying to his yang – or is it her yang to his ying? Either way, they are obviously very much in love and have had their first child, a boy whom they named River Lee Phoenix. Rain continues to make music, including a video of one of her songs, a duet with Michael Stipe.

John Phoenix continued living in Costa Rica and when he was diagnosed with cancer about 10 years ago. His children brought him to Los Angeles and cared for him until his passing several months later. Knowing these folks has given me insight into the true meaning of family values. Not having children of my own, River, Rain, Joaquin, Liberty, and Summer became kind of surrogate children/nieces/nephews for me. It has given me enormous pleasure to watch them physically grow up into the smart and talented adults they have become. My heart swells with each good review they receive, and I am awed by Liberty's incredible strength in the face of much sorrow. I admire Rain's tenacity regarding the music business and delight in Summer's evolving not only into a wonderful actress but a terrific mother. Lastly I am happy that Heart has found her calling in life running the River Phoenix Center and love in her marriage to Jeffrey.

CHAPTER 14

NELL CARTER: A MOST UNUSUAL FRIENDSHIP

The first talent deal I made at NBC was with a woman I had never met, but who was destined to play an important part in my life. I first heard about Nell Carter from director Tom O'Horgan. He correctly described this four-foot-eleven singing dynamo as wildly talented and wildly crazed – a not-unusual combination in show business. I got my first look at Nell in 1978 when she played one of the stepsisters in *Cindy*, an all-black TV version of Cinderella. *Cindy* was not great, but Nell was sensational. That same year she opened on Broadway in *Ain't Misbehavin'*. Her performance won her a Tony, and from then on, I began seeing her a lot on talk shows. I always loved her flirty, sassy personality and of course her extraordinary talent.

When I met her, Nell had just passed thirty. She had a round, pretty face with big, wide, expressive eyes that could make you feel protected or, when she narrowed them, very afraid. She was 4'11' and her weight varied through the years from the low 100s to well over 250 pounds. Even heavy, Nell could dance as well as anyone, which was one of her assets as a performer. Her real-life persona was as strong as her professional one; like the great movie stars of the 1940s, she essentially played herself in all her roles. Her singing voice, though, was her ticket to stardom. She could go from a low whisper to powerful high notes, with an overlay of nasality that helped you identify her instantly. Listen to her on the soundtrack of *Hair*. The cast was full of wonderful actors who weren't the greatest singers. The movie used Nell's voice to sail and wail way above all other voices. For me, I could see that Nell could be plugged into any number of our existing shows and future pilots. To me, it was a no-brainer to try and get her exclusively on NBC. I called her agent, and he was thrilled with the offer. So was Nell. A year or so earlier, in order to get some good-paying, steady work on the soap opera *Ryan's Hope*, Nell had given up the part of "Effie" in the early workshops of the musical *Dreamgirls*, originally called *One Night Only*. That's right: If it were not for that damned soap, you might have heard Nell singing "And I Am Telling You I'm Not Going" over and over and over. Both Jennifers: Hudson and Holliday should be eternally grateful to Mr. Ryan's soap. On YouTube you can listen to an early recording during the workshops of *Dreamgirls* of Nell singing "One Night Only" slowly and beautifully.

Nell Ruth Hardy came from Birmingham, Alabama. She endured a horrific childhood that affected her for years. Her father, Horace Hardy, died when she was two. At fifteen Nell saw the smoke from the bombing that killed four little girls in a Birmingham church. A couple of years later, she survived a rape at gunpoint, and became pregnant. Not only was Nell victimized by the assault itself but by members of her own family when she refused an abortion. Nell gave birth to a baby girl and attempted to raise her child but found it overwhelming. She left her daughter in care of her trusted older sister, whom Nell called Aunt Willie. She then changed her last name to Carter and moved to New York City. Nell began working almost immediately – this despite an almost instant reputation for being "difficult." As Viola Davis said in a *Vanity Fair* article, "We know as women when we speak up, you're labeled a bitch immediately…as a woman of color all you have to do is roll your eyes and that's it." Nell rolled them a lot. Nell's reputation didn't bother me; I'd been through something similar with Pearl Bailey. I'd found out that most of Pearl's reputed diva-dom was false. All I had to do with Pearl was listen to what she had to say and give an honest answer. The same held true with Nell, despite an issue I hadn't faced with Pearl. After a relatively short time in New York, Nell had become known for using cocaine, but it rarely, if ever, affected her performances. Coke use was hardly unheard of in show business at that time, and not until the early '80s did her use become abuse for Nell.

Once she had been signed, NBC bought the rights to televise *Ain't Misbehavin'*. It was nominated for six Emmys and won three, including one for Nell. At that point, NBC should have developed a new show for her or added her to an existing "good" show. But in a desperation move, those above me stuck her in a piece of on-air crap called *The Misadventures of Sheriff Lobo* playing a deputy sheriff. Already on life support, it did not survive the season. When pilot season rolled around and the series development was looking as bad as it had the previous year, I got a call from an anxious Brandon Tartikoff. His boss, Fred Silverman, was tearing out what was left of his hair in frustration. Brandon told me that one pilot was worse than the next. Who, he asked, did we have under contract who could center a half-hour comedy? Not wanting to sound like a broken record, since I had been pushing this to him for a while, "What about Nell Carter?" I said. He asked me what she could play. My immediate response was, "Well, she could always be a maid." Why didn't I say she could be a nurse or a doctor or a lawyer or a singer who has a family and has to juggle home and career? No, I went there. A better example of unconscious bias has never existed. "Yeah," said Brandon, a black *Hazel*. He was referring to the 1960s sitcom about a white housekeeper, played by Shirley Booth, who was smarter than the family she worked for. He then asked me what sort of character Nell would work for. I said, "Some authority figure, like a cop or a fireman." He asked if I had anyone in mind for that role. What happened to me then is something that often happens when I'm under extreme pressure. I instantly came up with the name of Dolph Sweet, an actor whom I had met when I cast one of my first shows for David Merrick. I described Dolph as a man in his fifties, with a prizefighter's bashed-in looking face and a bit of a gut; a classic redneck type, but with a very sweet quality. Great, said Brandon. He hung up and called Fred. A day later, Brandon gave me the news: NBC would go ahead and do a pilot based on my premise. Brandon then asked me to ask Nell if she would play a maid, ahem, a "housekeeper." But this was 1982 and we'd entered the Reagan years; culturally and in many ways the country was sliding backward. I was going to a party with Nell that night and sitting her car and doing a hit of her coke before we went in, I popped the question. "Here's the good news and here's the bad news. We want you to star in your own sitcom pilot, but the character is a maid." She sat quietly and thought-fully for a moment. Then she quoted Hattie McDaniel, who was the first African American to win an Academy Award; she'd won it for her performance as the slave "Mammy" in *Gone with the Wind*. Oscar and all, for the rest of her career she played mostly domestics, including the title character of *Beulah*, an early-'50s sitcom. Reportedly McDaniel had said: "I'd rather play a maid than *be* a maid."

Psychologically this must have weighed on Nell because it began to weigh on me. Throughout all my career unless a role was described in the script as Black or Asian, it was always cast white. I thought of all the times I had suggested that a particular role could also be played by a black actor. Invariably the answer from the always white producers was that "they couldn't see it that way". But when it came to smaller roles that were there to give exposition like, "Yes, I saw the man run down the street," or, "I'm sorry, Mr. Smith, your wife is still in intensive care," I had a lot of leeway and I always tried to use persons of color if only to make the role a bit more interesting. I found out that most all my fellow casting directors tried to do the same thing, some with greater success than others. At the very least, this was a pragmatic decision for Nell; if the show clicked, she could, financially, set up herself and her daughter for life.

We needed a script fast, so the project was given to Mort Lachman, who was Bob Hope's main joke writer. Though very old-school, Mort had a reputation for turning out scripts quickly. He wrote a serviceable pilot in a very short amount of time, and it clicked. On October 29, 1981, the series, entitled *Gimme a Break!*, began its first of six seasons. Mort and his co-producer, Sy Rosen, were also the show runners, he people who manage the show's needs and hold creative control. They did an adequate but unremarkable job. Things ran fairly smoothly for most of the first season. The ratings were nothing to be proud of, nor the critical response, although Nell herself got great reviews and an Emmy nomination. *Gimme a Break!* hung in there on the schedule because there were no other shows to replace it. A year later, *Cheers* and *Hill Street Blues* also remained on the schedule for the same reason.

By the end of the first season though trouble had started; due mostly to Mort. Nell told me that any suggestions she made regarding her character, or the script were either ignored or scoffed at. She begged for the opportunity to sing more often on the show; obviously that was her strongest suit. Not only did Mort completely disrespect his star, but he was also diabolical in that he learned how to push Nell's buttons and when those buttons were pushed, she reacted by falling into old bad habits. Nell responded to his abuse through acting out and engaging in self-destructive behavior, such as heavy drug use.

I tried to help by going over Mort's head to Alan Landsburg, the executive producer whose independent production company was financing the show. Alan was sympathetic but said that even he could not control this aspect of Mort and that getting rid of him was not going to happen. I tried talking to Brandon. But since the show appeared to be working well and had settled into not-terrible ratings, he did nothing either. I brought the matter up to a few other executives at NBC. While they had no love for Mort, they did not understand that his browbeating and disrespectful treatment of the star were not in anyone's best interest.

Up to now, I had not become real friends with many of the actors I'd met on a professional basis, but Nell was an exception. Often, we were each other's plus-one at industry events like the Emmys and, on one occasion, the Oscars. Nell was my date at one of the first screenings of *Mommie Dearest*, the movie based on movie star Joan Crawford's daughter's tell-all book about her mother's abuse. Cast in the role of Miss Crawford was Faye Dunaway, whose way-over-the-top histrionics turned the movie into a camp classic. That is not how this major Paramount dramatic feature film was supposed to turn out. But as I sat in Paramount's screening room next to Nell, I could not contain my chuckling. Nell kept poking me in the arm and saying, "Shhhhh!"

However, I completely lost it at the notorious scene in which Faye waves a wire hanger at Christina and shrieks, "NO WIRE HANGERS EVER!" I burst into laughter, as did Nell. The rest of the audience then exploded along with us. There were other good times, too. Nell attended a Seder (Passover dinner) at my house along with seven others. To give the event a novel twist, I had replaced the usual Seder requirement, a lengthy reading of the Haggadah which tells the story of the Torah's Exodus chapter, with a screening of Cecil B. DeMille's *The Ten Commandments*, starring Charlton Heston, which tells the same story. With me controlling the remote for the VCR, I skipped from hilarious chapter to chapter. It was a riot to watch the overacting and listen to the overwrought lines, and we all got drunk on Manischewitz and some good wine too, and screamed with laughter. Things turned serious and stirring when Nell sang an á cappella version of "Let My People Go" which is included in all written copies of the Haggadah and boy did she kill.

But Nell's demons were taking over. Her weight was ballooning dangerously. She had no doctor, so I sent her to mine, Dr. Larry Siegler, whose diagnosis was that she was pre-diabetic. She liked him and for a while heeded his counsel, and her weight gain stopped. But her cocaine consumption increased. Her spending on coke and other luxuries was out of control but her salary though very good, was not huge by TV standards of the day. Right after she started working on *The Misadventures of Sheriff Lobo*, Nell bought a custom 1981 BMW 528I, with charcoal paint and a red-leather interior. It was not an excessive choice, considering that Beamers, Mercs, Jags, and Porsches were de rigueur for anyone in L.A. who was successful or wished to appear that way. About four months later, she drove up to my house in a brand-new Mercedes with a backseat as big as my bedroom. I said that the car was beautiful, but why? Wasn't the BMW good enough? She said she'd had some trouble with it and, besides, this was a much better car. I then bought the Beamer from her. She was right. There was always some trouble with it – expensive trouble. Not long after that, when the Mercedes was no longer sufficient, she bought a gorgeous Maserati sedan upholstered with the leather soft as butter and a backseat the size of a living room.

Around this time, Nell told me she had been dating someone, and was bringing him over to meet me. He was a "businessman" from Vienna, Dr. George Krynicki. I never did find out exactly what "doctor" meant or what kind of business he was in. Younger than Nell, he was bearlike, bearded, and about six feet tall, with a girth not unlike Nell's. Appropriately they had met at a Jewish deli in San Francisco. According to her he came from a Viennese bourgeois Jewish family that had somehow escaped the Holocaust with its fortune intact. When I asked her about George's assets, she told me all his money was in his family's name, and so well-hidden that even the Nazis could not find it. George was a good-looking guy, intelligent, well-read, and pleasant. Nell told me (even though I put my hands over my ears and did the Pee Wee Herman *lalalalalala* thing) that both he and she loved oral sex. They began a super long-distance relationship, with him in Vienna and she in L.A. It seemed to work, and I was glad that at least some of her life was going nicely. Then I got a call from the set telling me that Nell had not shown up for work and was not answering repeated phone calls. Her agent knew nothing. I went to her house. The door was unlocked. There was Nell, passed out naked on the living-room floor, with an empty bottle of Jim Beam within arm's reach. I found out later that after having done coke all night, she had finished off that bottle to come down. This went a long way toward explaining some of her weight gain. I knew she wasn't dead because she was loudly snoring. Instead of calling 911, which I knew would never be private, I called Dr. Siegler who thought it best to let her sleep it off. There was not much I could do besides cover her with a blanket and close and lock the door. Next, I called the set and told them she was not well, and that I had spoken to her doctor. He felt sure that she would be able to work the next day. And the next day there she was, right on time. The amazing thing about Nell was that with all this chaos going on, she somehow always managed to be brilliant on tape night, when the show was recorded in front of a live audience. She could miss three days of rehearsal and still be electric in front of the cameras. Just like Ethel Waters and Pearl Bailey, when the fucking began, Nell showed up and wowed everyone.

Still, something had to be done. Dr. Siegler suggested a four-week mini-rehab program at Century City Hospital. The show was scheduled to take a two-week hiatus, and that break was extended by a couple of weeks to allow her to complete rehab. Four weeks later she came out of rehab looking better than she had when she'd gone in, and the show continued without much drama.

Sometime around 1983, during season two of *Gimme,* Nell decided to become a Jew, and began conversion classes. She told me it would stand her in good graces with George's family. I thought, it would probably take a lot more than converting to please George's family. In two visits with George in Vienna, one of them as his houseguest, I never met any of them. Later that year, George was in Vienna and Nell was performing in London. Her drug cycle had resumed, and she overdosed and/or tried suicide or something equally dramatic. All I know is what I read in the papers or saw on tabloid TV shows. Whatever had happened, Nell realized she had to do something. She got in touch with Liza Minnelli, with whom she'd been friendly in her New York days and who was also in London. Then Liza and her sister Lorna pulled some strings and got Nell into Hazelden, one of the best rehab places in the U.S. It is a very important thing to note that this was *the* first time that Nell herself, not a doctor, nor a family member, nor I, was asking her to get help with her addiction. She told Lorna that she just couldn't handle things as they were and for the first time *she* realized *she* needed to help herself. Lorna told me in the world of addiction that is a momentous step. It was good timing, because her show was to be on hiatus for several months and there was no urgent pressure for her to get back to work.

When she came back to L.A. after Hazeldon, she looked fantastic. Not only had she lost almost a hundred pounds, but her skin glowed; at least for a while, she was off drugs and seemed genuinely happy. She presented me with a set of handmade coffee mugs that she'd made in the arts-and-crafts portion of her rehab. Nell was feeling good; good enough to want to marry George. She asked if I would perform the ceremony and host the reception at my new house, which was located on top of one of the highest ridges in Laurel Canyon, with spectacular views of the city which could have provided magnificent backdrop for the ceremony if it was not on a smoggy day. If one believes in omens, that day was very smoggy. As for officiating, why not? We already had an unusual relationship. I became a minister in the Universal Life Church, a mail-order ministry. I still have my certificate. I rehearsed my lines thoroughly and even grew my beard back so I could look more rabbinical. The night before the wedding, Nell called and said she and George had had a fight (not an unusual occurrence) and that she wanted to call the wedding off. I encouraged her to do just that. But she began to waffle, asking what people might think. I said, "They would think you came to your senses." As for the florist, caterer, and so on, I said we would turn it into a big, wonderful afternoon party. Unfortunately, Nell went through with the wedding. I told her I would not send the marriage certificate with my signature to the city, which was needed to make it legal, but would hold on to it for a few days in case she changed her mind. She did change her mind a few weeks later, but by then I had already filed the papers.

When *Gimme* resumed production, there were some major changes. Her salary was renegotiated; finally, she was making closer to what she deserved: well over a million dollars a year. With lots of encouragement from me and her agents, Mort Lachman was replaced by Rod Parker and Hal Cooper, who had held that position on *All in the Family* and *Maude*. Hal directed and was the "good cop"; Rod produced and was the "bad cop" authority figure. They began to write the show with broader humor which was a better fit for her personality and to incorporate more of her singing. Most important, they treated her as the star; while they didn't always agree with her, they listened to what she had to say.

At NBC, whatever Nell was asked to do to promote the show, she did without hesitation or complaining, unlike many other stars. Nell was also asked to do numerous benefits for AIDS and other worthy causes, and I don't think she refused a single one. One of the things that NBC asked of its stars was to attend the gala banquet and show that the network put on once a year for its affiliates, just like the one in Maui only this time in an L.A. hotel ballroom. At these events, we announced the shows on the schedule for the coming season. In addition, through major manipulation of numbers, we tried to show the affiliates how well NBC was doing when it was actually not. These banquets always included top talent; at the one I attended with Nell, Frank Sinatra was the talent. Nell and I were seated with the owner of an affiliate station from somewhere in the south. With him were his wife, two of his grown children and their spouses. Mrs. Affiliate began to show signs of having had way too much of NBC's champagne. She started telling Nell how much she reminded her of "a girl" we used to have." I almost choked on whatever I was eating. I was about to launch World War III when I felt Nell kicking me under the table. I looked at her and her eyes said, let me handle this. She said to the woman something like, "That's nice, what was her name?" One of the grown children chimed in with the name, then changed the subject and asked Nell if she were going to perform. Nell said, "Just Sinatra tonight, baby." The tension disappeared. She had lived with racism all her life and had learned how to respond without using a salad fork as a weapon. Another time Nell was asked to perform at a birthday party for Grant Tinker, then Chairman of the Board of NBC, at the Rainbow Room, which is on the 65th floor of the GE building (the former RCA building) in Rockefeller Center in New York. This required her to fly in and stay overnight for no pay; NBC would pick up the expenses. I called Kathy Tucci, NBC's head of Talent Relations, whose job it was to keep our stars happy and to get them to do publicity, talk shows, and the like. I told Kathy that Nell was being taken advantage of and we should figure out how to get her some cash. Kathy agreed, but for some corporate reason no direct payment could be approved. However, they did give us permission to buy her a gift for up to $10,000. Did I have any ideas? Of course, I did. I said, let's go to West 47th Street (the jewelry center of Manhattan) and buy her the biggest diamond we could find for that money. Nell liked big. Kathy and I spent a very fun couple of hours shopping, and finally wound up with a pear-shaped diamond about the size of my thumb, which came with a "free" gold chain. Nell was thrilled and wore it that night when she sang for her supper – or in this case, her diamond. Years later, I was going to an AIDS benefit on Valentine's Day where guests had to show up in drag wearing red. I had the dress but needed accessories, like jewelry. I called Nell and asked if I could borrow some large costume jewelry that she wore in her nightclub act. I went over to her house, and while looking through a few boxes of junk jewelry I saw that diamond on its chain, surrounded by large pieces of plastic crap. I took it out, reminded her of what it was and how much it had cost and how it must be worth a bit more now. She just shrugged. I did borrow and return it. Eventually it wound up in storage in a box she never claimed. Someone who bought items from unpaid-for storage units must have had a very big surprise. During the financially good years, Nell bought a house just off scenic Mulholland Drive in Beverly Hills. It was relatively modest, with a small pool and a nice view of the city. It was a prudent investment at a time when her life was otherwise in upheaval. Nell's marriage to George was in a particularly rocky stage. She had tired of Judaism and was in a born-again Christian phase; meanwhile she was living a life of dangerous extravagance. One of the people she met in this period was what I would call a dreck-orator. That is an interior decorator whose tastes were in line Saddam Hussein's palaces or Donald Trump's apartment.

She spared no expense as long as Nell was paying. The hideous décor could not ruin the good bones of the house, and Nell was very proud of it. But her coke habit was taking a major toll on her earnings. Subsequently in interviews she copped to having spent up to $2,000 per day on the drugs. At that time, she also told me that she was sending money to her family in addition to the financial support she had always sent home for her daughter's care.

Gimme was having its own problems. The ratings, which had never been great, had dipped even further. To give them a hoped-for boost, we added another cast member. I had signed seven-year-old Joey Lawrence to NBC after seeing him in two adorable film clips: one a Zest soap commercial in which he splashed around in a bubble bath, the other of him singing and dancing in top hat and tails to the George M. Cohan song, "Give My Regards to Broadway." I sent these tapes to Johnny Carson's talent coordinator, Jim McCawley, who booked him on *Tonight*. Joey was the only person I ever could get on *The Tonight Show*. After singing that song, Carson did something rare and coveted when he invited Joey to sit down on the couch with him. He asked if Joey had ever seen his show. Joey responded, "Yes, when I was sick and throwing up." The audience went wild.

But the atmosphere backstage was turning dark. In 1984, during the show's fourth season, Dolph Sweet, her co-star, was diagnosed with cancer. He lost a tremendous amount of weight, and his scenes had to be minimized.

1985, Dolph died in the hospital with his wife at his bedside and Nell there too, singing to him. In the effort to figure out how to handle Dolph's death on the show, reality took a backseat. Nell, adopted his children, and the show limped along for another two years. Around this time, *Gimme* was sold into syndication for a reported $70 million. Nell took a $6 million one-time payout for all future residuals. Those are the figures she gave me when we had a serious conversation about her finances. Nell also told me about some smart, low-risk investments that her New York business manager had made for her: she owned a couple of small apartment buildings and several launderettes. Unfortunately, these investments had never been made. The guy had just out-and-out lied and robbed his clients. Nell had zero investments. He did go to jail, but that didn't help Nell in the years after *Gimme* was over.

I had always tried to help Nell find proper theatrical management. When *Gimme* had become a modest hit, she needed an agency big enough to represent her in TV, film, concerts, and nightclubs, which her small but good agent in New York could not handle. I introduced her to a friend of mine, John Kimble, an agent at one of the then three biggest agencies in Hollywood, the William Morris Agency. I thought he might be different, but when the show was over and the money stopped coming in, she was dropped. This is not an unusual practice. Ultimately, money rules, and when it stops, so does the care. At her request, I introduced Nell to a music-oriented manager, Steve Jensen, who at the time was handling Kenny Loggins, the B-52s, and Orchestral Manoeuvres in the Dark (OMD). Later he acquired Katy Perry, k.d. Lang, and Adam Lambert. Nell hired Steve and his business partner, Martin Kirkup, to help her shape her nightclub act. She opened in Las Vegas for Joan Rivers and other stars of the day and headlined in Reno and in large nightclubs like the Venetian Room of the Fairmont Hotel in San Francisco. Sadly, she did not listen to Steve's advice about watching her budget or to incorporate more contemporary music into her act. In addition to her three musicians and a musical director, Nell insisted on having three backup singers; she paid everyone's salary, travel and lodging expenses. All that, combined with expensive costumes for everyone and new arrangements for the songs, meant that Nell was losing a lot of money on each engagement. Opening acts, even in Vegas, don't get paid that much. Steve and Nell came to an amicable parting of the ways when it became clear that he was not able to help her, and she could no longer afford his commissions. That said, Joan Rivers told me many times about how much she adored Nell and used her as much as possible. Nell was also having a great time doing this act and loved the change of pace during down-time from the series. Money be damned.

She was still in her Born-Again phase, and from what I could see and from what others told me at the time, she was clean and sober. But throughout my years with Nell, I could never tell when she was high. Perhaps she was on best behavior with me, but when I like someone, I become clueless. Things were okay with the series, except that NBC kept changing its time slot. During its six seasons on the air, *Gimme a Break!* had ten different ones. This might be a record. But by the last two seasons, NBC didn't really need the show anymore. The network had risen from last place to a strong second with hit series like *The Cosby Show, Family Ties, Hill Street Blues, Cheers, Night Rider, The A-Team, Alf, The Golden Girls, Night Court,* and *Fame.* In order to renew the series for the 1986-1987 season, NBC demanded sweeping changes. All the previous supporting characters were no longer series regulars. Joey Lawrence's younger and almost identical looking brother, Matthew, was added as Joey's younger brother. Don't ask how or why but Nell adopts them, and they all move to an apartment in Manhattan. To replace her former best friend and neighbor, Telma Hopkins, I suggested a new find, Rosie O'Donnell. I had seen a tape of her standup and immediately realized her potential. We met in my office, laughed a lot and I sent her to meet *Gimme's* casting director, Randy Stone, who immediately sent her to the show's producers that day and Rosie's TV career was on its way. Unfortunately, while she was very good, there was no on-screen chemistry between she and Nell. Another problem had started. The Lawrence brothers' parents complained to me that Nell was not treating the kids well. This was exactly the opposite of what she had been doing before, when she went overboard in her care and affection, even going trick or treating with them on Halloween in costume as the biggest bumblebee they'd ever seen.

It got to the point where the parents were considering pulling their boys off the show. In an act of inspired lunacy, Kathy Tucci, my diamond shopping co-worker, and I went to the set and tried to be psychological mediators, with the Lawrence parents at one side of a conference table and Nell at the other. We had no idea what we were doing, but while the Lawrences were still grumbling a bit, Nell promised to be more aware of how she acted around the kids. But the show was already on its way out. On May 12, 1987, *Gimme a Break!* ended after 136 episodes.

Nell suffered an even more painful blow when her brother Bernard died of AIDS. He was a terrific guy, smart, caring, and one of the few people she relied upon constantly for emotional support. But Nell's timing was impeccably wrong. She had reconciled with George and had already started plans to adopt children as a single mom; George was not to be a legally adoptive father. At that time, she could afford hot and cold running nannies; this would change as her income drastically fell. She began an open adoption process, by which the birth mother knows who is adopting her child, and some financial arrangement is put in place to "support" the birth mother during pregnancy. This is a popular method of adoption for celebrities. I don't know how I got roped into it, but as I was preparing to meet Nell and George for dinner, I got a call from her asking me to join them at a hospital forty miles away in Pomona, where the birth mother was in labor. I wound up in the room at the moment of birth, some place I never wish to be again. I didn't know that birthing gives one the munchies but right delivery at the birth mother's request, I went out and bought her a Big Mac and a shake. Nell named her newborn son, Joshua. During his first few weeks home, he needed a tracheotomy to ease an obstruction in his breathing. A metal tube was inserted into his windpipe through his neck. The tube needed suctioning many times a day for about a month. Nell was very dutiful. About ten weeks after Joshua, the adoption agency told Nell that one of the agency's planned adoptions had fallen through and another baby boy was available. Nell said yes immediately. Nell then chose me as godfather to Joshua and his new brother, Daniel. I, who was kicked out of Yeshiva, would be looking after the spiritual lives of the kids should something happen to Nell.

Now gone from NBC and working as an independent producer, I came up with a few ideas for half-hour sitcoms for Nell. In one, which I sold to CBS, she and Jackée, who had played sexy foil to Marla Gibbs on the NBC series *227*, were to be a Laverne & Shirley/Lucy & Ethel pair of friends who worked as nurses. I felt the idea had a strong chance of being successful, but fate intervened. Redd Foxx, who was then starring in a low-rated CBS sitcom with Della Reese, decided to die, and in a Hail Mary pass, the powers that be at the CBS replaced him with Jackée. This was even more ridiculous than it sounds. The Nell/Jackée idea was dropped, and Jackée's new show quickly expired. Another of my ideas actually came to fruition, but in a disappointing way. It was a *Brady Bunch* theme with a twist: Nell, who is raising several kids alone, marries a white guy in the same situation, but the blending of families is not simple – funny ensues. Nell, who since I'd met her had shown no romantic interest whatsoever in black men, was excited about this possibility. CBS bought my idea, and we agreed that I would pick a writer to refine the concept into a script as soon as I returned from a three-and-a-half-week-long, off-the-grid vacation in Thailand. This was before cell phones and e-mails, and for most of this time I was incommunicado. I returned to a very odd situation. CBS, which was temporarily bereft of hits and a bit desperate to put something/anything on the air, had ordered six episodes of the series, with no pilot. The show runner was not going to be me, but a CBS favorite writer named Paul Haggis. He was brought in with his own concept, which Nell had agreed to before I could come home and try to convince her otherwise. I could have and should have left the whole project, but I needed the money. I think Paul was in the same situation, for he had just gone through an expensive divorce. Paul, who by his own admission bore an uncanny resemblance to Bozo the Clown; tall and bald, with a ring of light reddish-brown curly hair on the sides and back of his head was and is an excellent writer. In 2004 he won an Academy Award for writing the screenplay of *Million Dollar Baby* and two more for his work on *Crash*, which won Best Picture of the Year. But although Paul had written a few episodes of *Diff'rent Strokes* and *The Facts of Life*, comedy, especially broad comedy, was not his strong suit. In my absence, CBS had agreed to his "new" idea for the show, *You Take the Kids.* The pitch was essentially *Roseanne* in black. It was about a working-class family with a stay-at-home mom (Nell), a teenage son and daughter, and a live-in mother-in-law. However instead of being like *Roseanne,* it came across like an extremely poor copy of Norman Lear's *Good Times.* It was exactly the same! But *Good Times* was both funny and real. This one was neither. However, our teenage boy was a very funny and talented young man, then named Dante Béze who became the movie star Mos Def; currently he is a hip-hopper known as Yasiin Bey. Unfortunately, the show was terrible. The six episodes got made, but I'm not sure CBS aired all of them. When I asked Nell why she had agreed to do the show without at least talking to me, she said she needed the money and could not pass up an on the air series. Paul, Nell, and I, were doing something we did not believe in just for the cash. I made a huge mistake by never sitting down with Paul in the beginning and discussing the situation. Who knows, he might have agreed with me about my concept. Instead, I cast the series and deposited my checks. Paul Haggis currently has been "cancelled" after multiple sexual allegations. He denies them.

After that experience, Nell and I began to drift apart. In her life, money was still rolling out, but no longer rolling in. Divorce proceedings were filed in California; according to Nell, George cited community property laws and asked for half their "joint earnings." According to Nell, he made out very well. Recently, I found George on Facebook and sent him at least 3 "friend" requests, but he has never responded, so I have no idea if Nell's version of these stories are correct. Most of Nell's money had gone out to George, to overpriced and exploitative decorators, her agent, managers, and publicists, to the U.S. government, and to her dealers. There wasn't much left. She had way more debts than cash, and there were a couple of bankruptcy episodes. She sold the house on Java Drive and moved into a smaller but still beautiful rental house in Beverly Hills. Luckily, Nell could still make a good living; she could sing and entertain better than almost anyone. In addition to a few guest appearances on TV, she went out of town for concert and nightclub appearances. Often, I babysat the boys. Sometimes I had them at my house for a weekend, sometimes for as long as a week. I loved being with them. They were about four years old at the time and extremely adorable. But things were not great once they started pre-school. Nell decided it was much better to separate them than have them in the same class. She even sent Daniel, the younger boy, to her new girlfriend's parents' place in Wisconsin. YES, GIRLFRIEND!! Nell, it seemed, had always been bisexual, something many people knew but I didn't. Anne Kaiser was a smart and pretty woman in her thirties with a very sly sense of humor. She didn't talk much but when she did, it was on the mark. She worked in TV production as a stage manager, a very demanding job. How she ever managed work and Nell and the kids the same time, I will never know. Having someone this wonderful in her life, like Annie, was great for Nell and vice versa for Annie. Their relationship lasted for more than ten years, so lots of things must have gone right.

Unfortunately, Nell clearly favored Joshua, maybe because the tracheotomy he'd had as an infant had left him so needy, or perhaps because he showed signs of musical talent. Meanwhile, she was sending Daniel away for increasingly long periods of time. It was not a great situation. I think she tried to be a good mother, but it wasn't in her DNA. She had not raised her first child, and

Joshua and Daniel were parented mainly by Annie and her parents and one particular close friend. Nell even gave away the cute little fluff-ball dog that her former manager Steve Jensen had given to her. Annie's job required her to be on TV sets as early as six a.m., and the day could last into dinnertime. Nell could not deal simultaneously with being a mother (or pet owner) and making a living.

In 1997, Nell was cast as "Miss Hannigan" in a Broadway revival of *Annie*, the musical version of the comic strip *Little Orphan Annie*. It was there that she met fellow cast member, Jimmy Ryan, who became that "close friend" who moved in with Nell and Annie when he came to L.A. Miss Hannigan is a great comic villain role; she is the drunken, child-hating caretaker of the orphanage where the character "Annie" lives, and arguably has the best adult song in the show, "Easy Street". This should have given Nell's career the boost it needed, but it didn't. I went to New York to see the show. She was very good in the role, but I expected her to be great, not just good. I couldn't put my finger on it, but something was off. One of the producers and the show's general manager was Marvin Krauss, an old boss of mine from my Westbury Music Fair days. He knew of my connection to Nell and told me of the show's problems with her and asked for advice. Since she and I were planning to spend the next day together, I told him I would try to help. Our day together revolved around Nell getting hair extensions. This is a very time-consuming process, and therefore a fine opportunity to sit and chat and ignore the person extending the hair. But all Nell could talk about was what "they" – the producers, directors, stagehands, etc. were "doing" to her - like purposely turning off the power in her dressing room so that her diabetes medicine would spoil in the refrigerator. I had heard this kind of story from her before and usually took her side, but not this time. I told her I knew Marvin from way back and that he was a kind man who would never do something like that. But what I did find out was that Nell was not entirely wrong.

In a complete re-run of how she was treated during the first and second seasons of *Gimme a Break,* once again, from the beginning of *Annie's* rehearsals, she was totally disrespected and any idea she had would be immediately discarded. Her wonderfully funny and creative instincts were always cut down right in front of the cast and crew. But according to Jimmy, every time she was unfairly stifled, Nell would apologize and simply move on. All through my stage experience, the creatives in charge do their best to make a new star coming into an existing show comfortable and to incorporate what makes the new one special. That's probably why *Hello, Dolly!,* which has had at seven different stars on Broadway was so successful. Each woman was encouraged to bring what makes her special to the role. When I told this to Marvin, he had kind of an "ah ha" moment. Most of his information about Nell had come from those who stifled her. He went on to tell me that the money producers wanted to cast Nell, but the creatives were dead-set against it. Now it all made sense, including her performance. If there was one good thing to come out of this, Nell did not return to drugs to deal with the situation. This was a major step for her. There was little that I could to in New York to help Nell or Marvin, so I went back to California to continue my post-NBC midlife crisis. I was also in financial difficulties, and the easiest way out of it was to temporarily rent out my house, take my dog and the both of us move in with my good friend Jenny Sullivan, my Maui "spouse." Through a mutual friend, a possible renter came to see my house. It was Brian Cox, the great Scottish actor who after years of great supporting work has finally become an "overnight" star on HBO's *Succession*. He loved my house immediately and we made a deal. The house was to be for he and his pregnant wife.

So off I went to Jenny's with my dog Saki, a very sweet, young, runt of the litter, Rottweiler rescue dog weighing in at perhaps fifty pounds at most. Unfortunately, Jenny had a huge Newfoundland, well over 125 pounds. Newfies, as they are called, look exactly like St. Bernard dogs, only all-black with a few patches of white. The dogs got along great, except each time her Newfie playfully jumped on my dog, he screamed in pain. Had I left him there, Saki would have had his back broken in no time. Not knowing what to do, I took Saki and went up to meet Brian's pregnant wife, Nicole Ansari, who had arrived from Britain that day just when Brian was leaving L.A. for a movie location. The minute I walked in Saki jumped onto the couch where Nicole was sitting and stretched out with his head on Nicole's lap. Nicole was and still is a beautiful and talented actress/director. She fell in love with Saki at first sight and asked if I could leave the dog with her. Being pregnant and in a fairly isolated house, she said it would make her feel more comfortable when Brian was not around. And so, my house and dog were rented to a great couple, and we began a friendship that exists to this day. In the years to come I saw Nell and Annie only sporadically. Our last meaningful visit took place after Brian and Nicole and baby Orson had moved out and I was preparing the house for sale. It had a very large garage, and Nell had stored many boxes there as she'd moved from place to place. She and Annie came up for the boxes. It was a sad day for me because I was very attached to both the house and our friendship. Nell continued to work doing concerts and guest-starring on various TV shows including *Ally McBeal*, and had a reoccurring role as Reba McIntyre's therapist on her show, *Reba*.

The next time I saw Nell was at her funeral. It was 2003, and about five years had passed since she and Annie got the boxes. The boys were about thirteen, with Joshua living with Nell and Annie in a nice condo near Century City in L.A. Daniel had been sent off to St. John's Northwestern Military Academy, located near Annie's parents in Wisconsin. Early on the morning of January 23, 2003, Daniel was called into the principal's office. Anne Kaiser was on the phone to telling him that Joshua had found their mother lying on the bathroom floor not breathing and had called 911. Emergency workers pronounced her dead at the scene. There was no autopsy, but the presumed cause of death was a massive heart attack likely brought on by her diabetes, years of dramatic weight gain and loss, and a host of other body-destroying acts and illnesses. Although she and Annie were still living together, they had broken up as a couple, and Annie was preparing to move into an apartment with her new girlfriend. Ironically, Nell had cleaned up her act, was drug-free, on a strict diet, and was preparing to start a new and much better phase of her life. Both Daniel and Joshua remember the cheerful Nell going to and from rehearsals for a revival of the seldom seen musical version of *A Raisin in the Sun* called *Raisin*. This would have been a great singing role for her; something pushing her dramatic chops, not the comedy ones she was known for. Unfortunately, this new phase did not continue for long. I regret not having been in much contact with her those last few years. I was working out of town a lot on a new reality show called *Popstars* and doing other casting work. Nell's will stipulate Annie as the kids' legal guardian. This was a job Annie did not want but accepted for a time. Nell had managed to shake off most of her debts and her financial future had been once again optimistic; but there was no real money lying around. Had she lived, I'm sure she would have gone out on the road and resumed her singing career, and who knows, a return to Broadway in *Raisin* or series television. Unfortunately, we'll never know.

But she did leave behind trust funds set up for the boys' education and of course, years of wonderful performances and memories for those who loved her. Joshua has transitioned into being Tiffany Carter and Daniel Carter is now the father of a beautiful little girl, Anastasia Michele Carter. Annie is still with the same girlfriend, and they are now married with a little girl of their own. I miss them all.

CHAPTER 15

LIFE IS EASY, REALITY TV IS HARD

It was the end of 1989 and I'd been at NBC for almost ten years. I had gone as far as I could go as a casting director; but still I desperately wanted to be a full-time producer. I was tired of watching former TV network executives, many of whom I thought were tasteless and supremely untalented, make millions by producing their own shows. Boy, did I underestimate them. Brandon was encouraging. He had allowed me to take short leaves of absence from my casting duties to produce in-house for NBC, and I'd done well. In 1986 I'd produced a successful Nell Carter special, *Never Too Old to Dream*, with guests Phylicia Rashad and the Four Tops. It was nominated for one Emmy nomination. It was for lighting design, but hell, at least we were noticed. Two years later I worked with Peter Douglas (one of Kirk's sons) to produce a TV remake of the 1960 courtroom movie *Inherit the Wind*, which had starred Spencer Tracy and Frederic March in the infamous story of the 1925 Scopes Monkey Trial, in which a Tennessee high-school teacher was brought to trial for violating a law against teaching evolution in state-funded schools. Our version starred Kirk and Jason Robards. It won three Emmys: for best movie, best actor in a movie or miniseries (Robards), and best cinematography. A promising start, I thought, to my future career as a full-time producer. Also in 1988, Brandon called me into his office. He had renegotiated his NBC contract to allow him to make feature films that would play in theaters first then air on NBC. This was a first for any network head. He said, "Do you think your friend Elvira would be interested in making in a feature film about her character?" I answered his inquiry with my usual answer to questions like that: "Are you kidding? She's in make-up and circling the building!" Elvira was the comically ghoulish creation of Cassandra Peterson, a Las Vegas show-girl turned comedienne. Cassandra had joined an L.A. comedy troupe, the Groundlings, whose members included Paul Reubens (Pee-Wee Herman), Kathy Griffin, Phil Hartman, Jon Lovitz, Julia Sweeney, Maya Rudolph, and Will Ferrell. In 1981, Cassandra had answered a casting call from a local TV station for the job of hosting *Fright Night*, a series of campy "B" horror flicks. Cassandra got the job. She and her best friend, Robert Redding, whipped up the persona of Elvira, a vampire-ish sex-bomb in a skintight black dress, with outrageous and real cleavage and two bouffant wigs resting on her head. Elvira spoke like the bastard child of Mae West and a Valley Girl and became a sensation. She graduated to her own series, *Elvira's Movie Macabre*, and triggered a merchandising bonanza. The character inspired Halloween costumes, perfumes, action figures, comic books, and even a wine, Elvira's Macabrenet. We'd gotten to know each other over the years through several friends – including two mutual boy-friends! Cassandra had been dying, no pun intended, for a film vehicle for her character and already had a script she had written with a Groundlings bud, John Paragon (Jambi the Genie on *Pee-Wee's Playhouse*), and another writer, Sam Egan. Brandon and I liked the script a lot. It starts with a #MeToo moment thirty years ahead of the its time: Elvira quits her TV hosting job after the head of the station sexually harasses her. From there, *Elvira, Mistress of the Dark* is a madcap comedy, but as the luck of the draw would have it, the film did not earn back its cost. It was and is a very funny movie, but it could have been much better. Cassandra had wanted Penelope Spheeris, whose future credits would include the 1992 smash movie *Wayne's World* to direct. But Brandon preferred James Signorelli, who had directed most of the many TV commercial parodies for *Saturday Night Live*. Cassandra anxious not to pass up this opportunity and since we all liked his SNL parodies, she said OK. Unfortunately, once shooting began Signorelli did not show Cassandra and her ideas the respect he should have, and the film suffered for it. This was yet another great example of an entitled white man not listening to a woman, even though this particular woman created the very core of the project he was working on. Another reason for the movie's quick demise was, oddly enough, Brandon's loyalty to a former employee, Steve White. Steve was head of the movie department at NBC for many years. He was now in charge of movies at the studio, New World Entertainment and Brandon brought him this film to be partially financed and distributed through them. So far so good. Unfortunately, between the time the deal was made and its release, New World was financially in free fall with no money for any sort of meaningful advertising and promotion. They released the movie in theaters over a Labor Day weekend, the traditional dumping ground for expected flops. If they had just waited a couple of months until Halloween, Elvira's prime season, the movie might have had a chance. You can see the movie through Roku as well as on Amazon Prime.

But every producer has his share of flops, right? Undaunted, I pitched NBC on a TV version of the composer Jerry Herman's (*Hello, Dolly!*) other Broadway smash musical, *Mame*, which ran on Broadway for four years. The musical had long history; first came a novel written by Patrick Dennis. Next came "Auntie Mame" a Broadway play written by Jerome Lawrence and Robert E. Lee, which starred Rosalind Russel, then a movie of the play also starring Russel, then a Broadway musical staring Angela Lansbury (*Murder She Wrote)* and finally a movie musical starring Lucille Ball. This would have been the first live musical on any network in forever. Now they are commonplace. The character "Mame" is an heiress and free spirit who adopts and grooms her sweet 7 yr. old nephew while constantly battling the nephews' very conservative bank trust manager. *Mame* made it to the big screen in 1974 with the star everyone had thought would guarantee its success: Lucille Ball. For reasons detailed richly in many books, *Mame* turned into a legendary bomb. Lawrence and Lee who wrote the original stage play, the musical, the movie and who had also written *Inherit the Wind*, desperately wanted *Mame* to have another shot at the piece being done "correctly" for posterity. They felt, and I agreed, that the title character could not be played by a clown, even the best clown ever, which Lucy was. The role needs a sophisticated actress (think today's Christine Baranski (*The Good Fight* and Sybil Shepard's best friend on *Cybil)* with a talent for words more than broad physical comedy. Because of my close and successful working relationship with Lawrence and Lee during *Inherit the Wind,* they gave me an option for virtually nothing; I think the amount was five dollars. But I, the great casting director, could not find a single star willing to play the part. Offers went to Angela Lansbury (she passed because she felt she was too old and also needed a new hip), Mary Tyler Moore, Michelle Pfeiffer, Glenn Close, Sigourney Weaver, and even Diana Ross. Frantic, knowing it was not a good choice, we even met with Carol Burnett, another great clown. But she was wise enough to turn it down, too. When the former Broadway actress and singer Michele Lee, then starring on the hit TV night-time soap opera *Knots Landing,* passed on the project, I gave up.

But I couldn't allow another disappointment to stand in the way of my dreams. I made the decision to leave NBC. I had an assistant then, Lori Openden, whom everyone at NBC liked and whom I was grooming to move upward. I went to Brandon and told him I just had to take the plunge into fulltime producing. He was disappointed, but he'd seen it coming, and wished me well and wisely per my recommendation, chose Lori to succeed me. She continued at NBC until a management change ousted her. Undaunted she continued casting and was, until her recent retirement, the head of casting for the CW Network. I had left a job that no one leaves voluntarily, kind of like a U.S. Supreme Court Justice. But I knew I had to take a chance; if I didn't, I'd be haunted forever by thoughts of what might have been.

I was brave, but naïve. Even after having worked with TV and movie producers since the '70s, I had no clue as to what the main job of a producer was; and that was selling the project. I forgot that my two most recent producing efforts had been handed to me by Brandon. Stupidly I turned down a production deal from Les Moonves, who at the time was president and CEO of Warner Bros. Television. He and I had worked together successfully on many pilots and TV movies over the years. I found him a man of great taste who was very realistic in terms of what was needed in a project for network TV. He was the most like Brandon of any network executive I have known. Unfortunately, he was eventually fired by CBS because of sexual misconduct charges by more than a few women. I declined Moonves' offer because the money was terrible – even if I'd sold a pilot, I would have made less than I earned at NBC, unless it sold and was successful I then made a deal with much better financial numbers with Imagine Television, Ron Howard's production company, but it led nowhere. When it came to casting, I could be relentless in pursuing who I thought was right for a part. Unfortunately, I was a horrible salesman for myself and my own ideas. For most of the projects I pitched, I took no for an answer way too soon; after the third or fourth rejection, I would give up.   I just assumed that being as "smart and tasteful" as I was, things would fall in place. But like a spoiled rich kid who'd been thrown out of his cocoon, I was unprepared for what lay outside. TV life under the safe auspices of Brandon had been paradise, but my new reality was more like hell. Brandon left NBC in 1991 to become chairman of Paramount Pictures. His work sphere included running the film division, but he'd had almost no experience in producing theatrical features, and the now ever-present entertainment news vultures criticized his "television approach" to the job, since none of the films he green-lighted in his early days at Paramount worked. What the media didn't consider is that whenever a new regime comes in, there is always a pile of leftover projects from the former administration that must be dealt with. And those Paramount movies, most of them not very good ones, had to be released to fill agreements between the studio and the theaters in which their movies would be shown. Also, unlike television, theatrical movies can take years and years and even more years to come out of development and onto the screen. On TV, projects rarely linger around more than a year or two before being made or dumped. Many of the projects that Brandon put into development eventually became some of Paramount's big hits, including his buying the book of *Forrest Gump* and attaching Tom Hanks to the project. Another of Brandon's gifts to Paramount that keeps on giving was *Wayne's World,* produced by Brandon's long time buddy *Saturday Night Live*'s Lorne Michaels. The movie cost $15 million to make and grossed over $100 million. It also was the engine that started a new genre of *SNL* alumnae movies produced by Michaels that continues to this day.

The next time Brandon and I worked together was when he became Chairman of New World Entertainment. This company was founded by Roger Corman, who produced and directed many profitable exploitation flicks and once in a while released a good movie like *Little Shop of Horrors.* Two very smart and savvy lawyers, Harry Sloan and Larry Kuppin, had recently bought New World from Corman and taken the company public. I had known Sloan & Kuppin when they were managing NBC's biggest star at that time, twelve-year-old Gary Coleman (*Diffr'nt Strokes*). They ran Coleman's production company, which produced the TV movies we were contractually obliged to give to the young actor. Brandon called and asked if I wanted to join him at New World to do both casting and producing. What I didn't know is that Harry & Larry didn't give a shit about releasing movies or making television series, even though they had Marvel Comics founder, Stan Lee under contract. Stan was a delight to work with and for some reason called me Jolly Joel or sometimes JJ. We worked desperately hard trying to get a TV series based on *The Punisher* off the ground with no success. Harry & Larry had already acquired various cable stations and systems, which then became part of New World. The equally shrewd Rupert Murdoch, owner of 20th Century Fox, needed those stations in order to make Fox Broadcasting competitive with CBS, NBC, and ABC. He bought New World, got his cable stations, and I was out of a job. I was told that in addition to his salary, Brandon had a lot of New World stock options. They became very valuable because of the sale of the company. I'm guessing that this helped him to hang out his own shingle as producer. But Brandon never got to exploit his new-found independence; for during the prior twenty-five years, Brandon had battled Hodgkin's lymphoma cancer three times. In 1997, he finally lost the war. He was forty-eight. It wasn't until a few years later that Lilly Tartikoff took up his mantle and got a pilot he co-wrote, *Beggars & Choosers,* produced and on the air at Showtime. I cast the series.

There was nothing for me to do at that point but freelance casting. I must say the thought was comforting. Casting is what I did best. One day my phone rang. It was Scott Stone and David Stanley, partners in Stone-Stanley Entertainment, a company that specialized in a new trend that was starting to overtake television: reality TV, the Cinema Verité of the boob tube. Scott and David produced three very successful on-air programs: *The Man Show, Love Line,* and *Shop 'til You Drop.* They asked if I'd be interested in working with them to find performers and hosts for new projects. With nothing else anywhere near my plate except concern over how I would survive until Social Security and Medicare kicked in, I figured I'd give it a try. The first show they gave me was *The Mole,* an adaptation of a current hit in Europe. *Survivor* was then a U.S. smash, and *The Mole* (which ran sporadically from 2001-2008) stole from it shamelessly. It featured a group of contestants who traipsed about foreign locations and doing various tasks, like a scavenger hunt; among the group was a secret "mole" who was always sabotaging their efforts. Each week one of the contestants was "thrown off the island," so to speak, until only three remained for the big finale, one of them being "The Mole". It was my job to cast the host. ABC's recently appointed head of Reality Programming, Andrea Wong, asked me what I thought of thirty-three-year-old Anderson Cooper, former ABC news co-anchor. I knew what he looked and sounded like, and I thought he'd make an ideal host. I called his agents and was surprised when they told me that Anderson would be happy to meet me and be put on tape. We met for lunch. He was even cuter in person than he looked on TV, and I fell immediately in lust. He had those blue eyes, the premature silver hair and most importantly, his smarts and almost awkward, innocent manner. He also had and still has the sexiest giggle. Anderson explained that while he liked being a reporter, he had never done anything considered "pop" and wanted to try. What he didn't mention to me, but had told to a friend of mine, David Neuman (who had given Anderson his first job as a reporter for Chanel 1) is that Cooper's mother, Gloria Vanderbilt, was forever running short of money, and he felt it was his duty to help her financially; a very noble thing to do and *The Mole* host job paid well. When I suggested to him that this sort of show was beneath him and that he should really be hosting *The Today Show* or *Good Morning, America*, he demurred. Scott and David, whose default position was to always be wary about network suggestions, saw his tape, and soon agreed with me and signed Anderson as host of *The Mole*. He stayed two seasons; then decided after 9/11, that his heart lay in news reporting. Anderson accepted an invitation to return to CNN. You know the rest of his story.

I now turned my attentions to *Popstars*. Scott and David had licensed a show that began in New Zealand and spread to many European countries. *Popstars* was a forerunner of *American Idol*; the main difference is that its object was to put together a singing group rather than an individual performer. For the first season we held mass auditions in L.A, New York, Atlanta, and Dallas. There were three judges who, while not celebrities, were well-known and respected in the music business: Choreographer Travis Payne, Warner Music Group head and sister of music superstar David Foster, Jaymes Foster Levy, and Stephanie Diaz-Mata from London/Sire Records. Jaymes was the Simon Cowell of the group, but ABC's notes were to clamp down on her honesty which was perceived as being too negative. She was right, the network was dead wrong as proved by Mr. Cowell on *American Idol.*

Five contestants auditioned at a time, each with a thirty-second a cappella version of some pop song. In the first season, the group was all-girl. I helped to organize the mass casting calls and pre-screening those in the blocks long lines. During the tapings, I had much more fun sitting off to the side at a small desk with a TV camera pointed down at the top of it. There, I wrote notes that only the judges could see on their monitors. I was telling them who they *had* to bring back for a second audition. (call-back). The judges could of course bring back any others they liked. My judgment was based not only on the contestant's singing talent, but also and equally important on whose backstories and real-life histories would make for good TV. The five winners would live together for a month a la *Big Brother,* while working with their new record company, London/Sire, learning the music and choreography for an album and a video. Out of all these auditions came the 5 women who decided to call themselves Eden's Crush. Their album made the top ten and yielded a hit single "Get Over Yourself." Unfortunately, the group soon imploded because of internal dissention, and because London/Sire, their record company went out of business. But the most beautiful and talented member of Eden's Crush, Nicole Scherzinger, went on to sell fifty-four million records as the lead singer of another group, The Pussycat Dolls, and sixteen million as a solo artist. *Popstars*, alas, struggled for ratings and its second season was not a good one and show was gone.

My assignments at Stone-Stanley dwindled, but a few interesting freelance casting opportunities came along. I took what I could get. The miniseries *Too Rich: The Secret Life of Doris Duke* gave me the opportunity to meet and spend a few unpleasant moments with Lauren Bacall, who played America's famous and troubled heiress. In 2000 I also cast a new series that lasted two seasons for "the other" pay cable network, Showtime. Showtime was then and still is now the much poorer cousin of enormously successful HBO and HBO MAX. The series was *Beggars and Choosers*, the creation of Brandon Tartikoff and *Cagney & Lacey* writer and novelist Peter Lefcourt. Lilly Tartikoff had moved into Brandon's chair at the office and began trying to get his unfulfilled ideas and projects off the ground. This offbeat, satirical show was centered around the head of a TV network, much like Brandon himself. There was even a gay male head of talent, based loosely on me. I made sure he was played by the very handsome and talented actor, Tuc Watkins. Come on, wouldn't you do the same in my place? How many times does one get to cast a role based on him or herself? The other wonderful actors included Brian Kerwin in the "Brandon" role, Carol Kane, Beatrice Arthur, Charlotte Ross, Beau Bridges, Alexis Arqueete and even a guest appearance by Ivana Trump, who cost the show about $25,000 for wardrobe. There was also a discovery of mine in her first TV role, Christina Hendricks, later of *Mad Men*. If you've never watched *Mad Men* or NBC's series *Girlfriends*, Christina is bodacious and beautiful with gorgeous red hair, and she is a terrific actress. In the second season, we were adding a new female character, who according to Jerry Ofsay, then the head of Showtime, must appear topless from time to time. This had nothing to do with her character but rather his mistaken thought was this was the only way to compete with arch-rival HBO. Christina would not agree to this. I appealed to show runner, Peter Lefcourt, a practicing and presumed expert heterosexual, that Christina in a negligee would be even more provocative than nude, and he agreed. But Jerry Ofsay would not relent. I urged Christina to sign the nudity waiver, which was required by Screen Actors Guild rules because there was a work around. Each time nudity would be required, the actor or actress must sign an additional waiver for that specific scene; thereby being able to not sign and skirt the issue. Christina, being very honorable would not do that. Eventually Showtime gave in, and Christina appeared regularly and spectacularly but covered up. Hindsight is 20/20 and looking back at my notes, we turned down Bryan Cranston, the future Emmy-winning star of AMC's *Breaking Bad,* for the central character of the head of the network. *Beggars and Choosers* never got great ratings, but the show got good reviews, and I was nominated for a Casting Society of America award for my efforts. I had my acceptance speech all prepared, but alas I lost. Even though the show was getting better and better the series never got a third season due to among other things difficulties between Ofsay and Lefcourt . You can watch episodes of the show on You Tube.

In late 1996, I produced my last movie, *It's My Party.* Randal Kleiser, my colleague on *Grease* and *The Boy in the Plastic Bubble,* had suffered a painful breakup with his long-term partner Harry Stein about ten years before. Harry had lived with AIDS for quite a while without any overt symptoms but began to have memory problems. After a brain scan, his doctor told him he had developed an incurable and fast-moving brain infection called PML and that in less than two months he would most likely become a vegetable. Harry had planned well in advance for this type of situation, i.e., a suicide. He had written his will so that his mother, to whom he was devoted, would not have to worry financially. Nor would she and his family have to deal with him in being a permanent vegetative state. Wanting to say goodbye to his friends, he put together a going-away party. Randal, though viewed as the wicked ex by most of Harry's friends, was told about the situation and invited by Harry. He called me and we both went together. At the party, which was held at Harry's house, I had no idea what to say or do; neither did the other guests. Small groups of us would talk quietly among ourselves, but should Harry enter the group, we all vied for who could say the funniest things and act the silliest. Then, when Harry left the group to move on to another one, we all got very quiet. Harry thought it would be a great idea if I'd go get my camera, which I'd left in my car, to make a photo record. I snapped off three rolls of film. At several points in the party Randal and Harry had some intense conversations, obviously dealing with extraordinary emotions. Eventually all the guests left; only Harry, his family, a couple of his closest friends, including Randal, stayed for the finale, which was accomplished with a handful of Seconals washed down with a glass of scotch. After he'd passed out, a plastic bag would be placed over his head to make sure he did not accidentally survive. A few days later, I showed the photographs to Randal. They inspired him to write a screenplay about Harry and the party. After getting a green light from United Artists,

Randal asked if I would like to produce the movie with him. To do so, I turned down an offer from my old NBC colleague, Garth Ancier, to become head of talent for a new enterprise that was to become the WB Television Network, now morphed into the CW. Randal and I went to United Artists with Viggo Mortensen (*Lord of the Rings*) and Christopher Meloni (*Law & Order SVU*) before they'd made it big, as our leads. UA said no to them, while asking me to cram as many "star names" into the project as possible. I objected saying that it would resemble all the TV movies I worked on at Spelling Goldberg, but they were adamant. I came up with Eric Roberts, whom I first cast in the feature film *King of the Gypsies* as the Harry character and Gregory Harrison, best known for the TV series, *Trapper John*, standing in as the Randal character, plus Olivia Newton-John, Roddy McDowall, Margaret Cho, Oscar winners Lee Grant and Marlee Matlin, George Segal, and *The Blue Lagoon's* Christopher Atkins. I did my best, but for a film like this to succeed, it would need unanimous great reviews, which we did not get. The script had nice comedic moments, but it needed many more of them to lighten a dark and somber issue. Many critics dismissed *It's My Party* as "another AIDS movie" about rich white people and complained that it was not as good as some of its predecessors, like *Longtime Companion*. Almost every reviewer missed the point. The movie was not about AIDS, but about making a personal choice on how to end one's life, no matter what the reason. Since its release, however, Randal and I have had the satisfaction of seeing *It's My Party* become a mini-cult classic. Every now and then some organization decides to honor it with a screening and a Q&A. I am proud of my work on this project and only wish more people had gotten to see it.

And so, once again, it was back to my bread and butter, casting. But it was becoming increasingly difficult to keep bread and butter on my table. Either I intimidated some producers with my experience or reputation, or I was being aged out in a town where almost every kind of skill is preceded by the word young, i.e. "I just met great new young: actor, writer, director, editor, designer, casting director, etc. I was not young or new. But in 2005 I was approved to cast a half-hour comedy pilot for a new cable network, UPN. One big problem with job was its timing. It was now the end of pilot season and many actors I would have wanted for this project were already taken. *The Bad Girl's Guide* was based on a tongue-in-cheek self-help book by Cameron Tuttle, aimed at young women intent on living their dreams with the freedom to be "bad girls." The script was not funny – seriously not funny. Did I mention that it was not funny? What's more, I saw that the casting process had changed radically since I'd left NBC ten years before. Most studios were now parts of multinational corporations, and the process had become one of covering your ass more than getting good work done. That's what happened with *The Bad Girl's Guide*. The initial meeting went fine. A few days later, at the first casting session, which was supposed to be only for myself and new actors, a roomful of people showed up: two representatives from Paramount (which owned half of UPN), two from the production company, the four writers, a line producer, and others. All had their own opinions and vested interests. There was no way for me to interact with any actors in a situation like that. Anything I might have said regarding his or her reading or the script was bound to offend someone's interest in the room. The leading role required a beautiful young woman in her twenties who needed to be a good actress with strong comedy chops, a category of performers of either sex rarer than unicorns. I began to see a slew of unknown new young actresses. One day a beautiful one walked in and began to read. While not perfect, she managed to make sense of the unfunny audition material. I gave her the full script and asked her to come back the next day, reading new material. She came back and was very good. Her learning curve was an upward one. I added her to the list of those who would come in for callback auditions two days later. What you need to know is that this pilot was to start shooting in two-and-a-half weeks, and no one had been cast. At this session, a newly engaged Tori Spelling, Aaron Spelling's daughter, read for two other roles. The writers, all women, started talking about her famous father; one of them rudely asked if her dad had bought the nice but not huge diamond ring on her left hand. After she read, I walked her outside and apologized. No problem, she said; she was used to stuff like that. Then the actress I liked had her turn. She began reading even better than before. At the end of the first scene, I beamed with pride. Then I heard a female voice behind me saying "thank you," which means goodbye in casting-speak. I asked the actress to wait outside while we discussed her. I turned to the four writer/producers and explained that while not perfect, I thought she was very good, and with each reading had improved. I suggested we could make a "test deal," which would tie her to us but not obligate us to use her – a win-win situation, or so I thought. I reminded them that we had no one cast and had to start shooting very soon. They replied that she read a particular paragraph that "they knew was funny" and she didn't get any laughs. I literally had to bite my tongue to not say, "who told you that paragraph was funny? Your mothers?" I reminded them of how beautiful she was, how a great-looking though not world-class actress could work very well in a sitcom, as Suzanne Somers had proven in *Three's Company*. They would not budge. I went outside and broke the news to the actress, while assuring her that she was terrific and would go places. She seemed okay with this, but I wasn't. I walked back into the room and told the writers that since they knew everything, it was obvious they didn't need me. "Here is my casting book with all my notes, and there is no need to send my second check." With that, I quit and walked out. Of course, I had four phone calls of the "you'll never work again in this town again" nature on my cell by the time I'd reached my car. But I felt relieved and not anxious for the first time in a long while.

A great ending for this little story might have been to tell you that young actress' name and that she became a big star. Unfortunately, all that information and her name were in my notes left behind. However, the actual ending was the just one. The four writers were fired, and a much more talented one, Robin Schiff, was hired. Jenny McCarthy, an actress at least ten years too old for the part, but who had a pay or play contract with Paramount and CBS, was shoe-horned into the role. It was cheaper to make the episodes and air them rather than cancel the entire project. *The Bad Girl's Guide* ran for six episodes. I had ended my career on a small sweet-and-sour note.

EPILOGUE

As I write this, it's been over a half-century since David Merrick made me his casting director and almost the same since my first television job with Pearl Bailey. To compare those days with today is like holding the Wright Brothers' flying machine up against a space shuttle. Back then, both Broadway and TV were dominated by unique impresarios whose egos and talents propelled both industries. Today, multinational corporations are in control. Mostly gone, with the possible exception of Ryan Murphy, Shonda Rhimes and Dick Wolf, are the Fred Silvermans and Brandon Tartikoffs of television and the David Merricks of Broadway.

Broadway is now largely tourist-driven, with much smaller New York City and suburban audiences. The simple drama or comedy play, unless headlined by a big star, has gone Off-Broadway or to nonprofit organizations like Manhattan Theater Club or Playwrights Horizons. Tourists have brought tremendous growth in audiences and profits for Broadway. However, broadcast television networks like NBC and Cable keep losing viewership to streaming services like Netflix, Amazon Prime, Hulu, Disney+, etc. When I worked for Merrick, $35 was the top ticket price for a hit musical. In 2019, the premium tickets for *Hamilton* topped $850. This explosion of ticket prices is in part due to the prevalence of over-the-top musical extravaganzas that can cost upwards of $20 million to produce. Merrick's most lavish productions topped out at a million and a half.

Yet there is still wonderful product in each medium, along with the dogs. While I consider myself lucky to have been part of a golden age of great free broadcast network programming, the terrific, scripted TV programming on streaming and pay cable networks are in my opinion, in a platinum age. Today, most movie stars *want* to do television; it is no longer viewed as a comedown. Quality television has equal or greater status than the movies. Of course, the Oscars are still the most important awards for creative folk. If only the Emmys had fewer than thousands of categories, perhaps those awards would bring more status. But they are much heavier than Oscars and make better door stops. Of course, *finding* these TV shows is a monumental task. It used to be so simple when there were fewer networks: CBS, NBC, and ABC, along with PBS and later Fox. With so few choices, it's no wonder many shows were seen by thirty million or more viewers each week. For special or final episodes of hit shows like *M.A.S.H* and *Dallas*, eighty to ninety percent of the country watched the same shows at the same time. From 1972-1974, when I worked at CBS, the Saturday-night lineup started at eight p.m., with *All in the Family*, followed by *M.A.S.H, The Mary Tyler Moore Show, The Bob Newhart Show,* and *The Carol Burnett Show*. In the early 1980s, ABC dominated Saturday nights with back-to-back airings of *The Love Boat* and *Fantasy Island*. An extraordinary thing happened in both decades: Rather than leaving their homes on Saturday nights, people stayed there to watch nationally popular, free entertainment. Such nights helped to bring us together as a country. Folks from all different social, political, and economic stripes talked to one another about what outrageous things Archie Bunker said, or about *Maude*'s abortion or *Rhoda*'s wedding or who had really shot J.R. on *Dallas*. The closest we have to this in recent times might be the massive popularity of HBO's *Game of Thrones* or *The Sopranos* and Netflix's *Squid Game*. But without a cable or streaming subscription, many are unable to watch these shows.

I wish I had do-over powers, because there are many, many things I would have done differently. I wish I'd known early on that I could "sometimes" be wrong and given more consideration to other people's views. I wish I'd thought more about how a decision of mine could influence the rest of someone's life. I wish I had spent more time with my family, and given more thought to Joel Thurm, the person, than to Joel Thurm, the Casting Director. It took me more than five years after I had stopped working in TV to figure out what to do with myself. I rediscovered my family, who welcomed me back with open arms. I sold my "big house on the hill" and bought an apartment building in Oceanside, California, which I have renovated mostly by myself. I was rare among television executives: I could use power tools and build things. I feel like Sally Field, because my tenants like me – they really like me – because I treat the place as if I were living there.

Another thing I would like to have been able to do during my career was to cast with more ethnic diversity. Hollywood agents, managers, and casting directors in the '70s and '80s were treated very separately and very unequally. The first black agent I knew was Wally Amos, and he left the business for a very good reason. When we traded recipes for chocolate chip cookies, his was a lot better. You probably know him as "Famous Amos". There were virtually no black agents who handled white actors. I only knew three: Sheila Robinson, Jenny Delaney, and Dolores Robinson who later became the first black woman manager in film and TV. Among Dolores' clients were her daughter Holly Robinson Peete (*21 Jump Street),* LeVar Burton (*Roots),* Martin Sheen (*The*

West Wing), Wesley Snipes (*To Wong Foo...*, *Blade*) and Oscar nominee Rosie Perez. Right after Spike Lee's feature film *Do the Right Thing* came out, Dolores asked me to meet Rosie who in that movie played Lee's girlfriend and in one scene was seriously topless. When Rosie and I sat down to talk in my office, I told her how much I loved her in the movie, and "It was not because of your tits". She immediately asked, "What's wrong with my tits"? I said "Nothing; it's your acting and specially your voice and your Brooklyn accent that I fell in love with". We both roared with laughter. Today I would have been accused of all sorts of improper conduct and fired immediately. Same thing would have happened to me as well because of the advice I gave to Cathereine Keener (go back to Chapter 11).

Women of color, Lil Cumber and Ernestine McClendon owned the only two agencies that would handle you if you were a new black actor with few credits. One of those "new" actors was Sidney Potier who stayed with one of those women all thru his early film career. They also handled older familiar black character actors as well. I was fascinated to meet and talk to "Stymie" Beard from *The Little Rascals,* one of my favorite TV shows as a kid. If you were Asian, you went to Guy Lee at the Bessie Loo Agency, where almost all Asian actors first got representation. Through Guy, I met B.D. Wong (*Law & Order: SVU*) and many others. The only place in town for untried Latinos was the Carlos Alvarado Agency. Those are only four out of hundreds of agencies. That's how segregated things were.

The other black manager I knew was Lee Daniels, who was funny and smart and had one client terrific client, actress Khandi Alexander. He was a so-so manager, but a natural born hustler and I mean that in a good way. Unlike many in my position, I would answer calls from any manager or agent no matter how small or "unimportant" they were at least one time. If I thought they were smart and knew their stuff, from then on, I would take their calls and listen to their casting suggestions and of course exchange gossip. Lee suggested we have lunch and that is how we started our friendship. After a not-so-great start managing in Hollywood, Lee moved to New York and redeemed himself in the business as an award-winning movie and television producer/director with *Precious, Empire, The Butler,* and *The United States vs. Billie Holliday.* However, my two favorite early movies he directed were *Shadowboxer,* which starred Helen Mirren and Cuba Gooding, Jr., as lovers. The other was *The Paperboy.* Only Lee would have Nicole Kidman peeing on her co-star Zac Efron! After being interviewed by Oprah and by Henry Louis Gates, Jr. on Public Televsion's *Finding Your Roots,* the only thing left for him is to become a *Jeopardy* question.

As for casting directors, again there was a very small group: Reuben Cannon, Eileen Knight, Monica Swann, Robi Reed, Victoria Thomas, and in New York, Pat Golden. These excellent casting directors were ghetto-ized in that most of their work was for black projects. Rarely were they given the opportunity to cast "crossover", i.e., non-ethnic projects. One exception to this is Victoria Thomas, who cast the feature film, *Once Upon a Time in Hollywood,* and on TV, *The Watchmen.* Reuben Cannon is another crossover Casting Director another who has had one of the great careers in Hollywood. He very successfully moved from casting into producing many feature films, television series and movies, including five *Madea* movies. His casting work includes *Who Framed Roger Rabbit* and on TV, *Hunter,* and *Amen.* If I were jealous of anyone's career, his would be at the top of my list.

I also have returned to my high school hobby of photography with a vengeance. I've developed my own unique style, in which I do everything possible to my original photos, turning them into surreal images filled with colors that do not exist in nature. As of this writing, I have had solo exhibitions of my work in Los Angles, Provincetown, and Palm Springs. Check out JoelThurm. com and see for yourself.

All in all, I've had a fabulous time during all phases of my work life. I've been enormously lucky to go to places and see and meet people I would never have encountered had I stayed in Brooklyn and lived out the course set out for me by my parents. Speaking of family, while I have no biological children, I do have lots of progeny. A year after I had left NBC, three of my former assistants whom I had mentored and trained were themselves heads of talent for two networks and one studio. And many who were assistants to those assistants are now successful casting directors as well. Having worked with many household names, I've found myself in demand as a "talking head" on all kinds of TV shows and documentaries. I'm asked about Madonna, *Grease*, Olivia Newton-John and John Travolta, *Airplane!*, *Rocky Horror*, Allan Carr, and, of course, the casting couch, in all its eternal fascination.

Brandon's widow, the amazing Lilly Tartikoff, went on to raise hundreds of millions of dollars for cancer research by herself and by partnering with others such as Revlon CEO Ron Perelman. They created the cancer research fundraiser Revlon Walk/Run events in Los Angeles and New York and the Revlon UCLA Cancer Research Program. After years of single life, Lilly is now Lilly Tartikoff Karatz, having married homebuilder and fellow philanthropist Bruce Karatz in 2009. One last word here about my mentor, Ethel Winant, who was directly responsible for my casting career in California. Late in her life, while she was still heavily active in production, she developed macular degeneration, an incurable eye disease that eventually leads to blindness, and lost all but slight peripheral vision. Amazingly she carried on, learning Braille and continuing to work as a producer. Her good friend, TV writer Alan Burns, who made his fortune thanks to her efforts casting *The Mary Tyler Moore Show,* saved her financially after she lost everything to a trusted financial advisor. He proved invaluable in getting Ethel into the wonderful Motion Picture Home in Woodland Hills, California. Ethel thrived there for the short time she had left; she passed away in 2003. Brian Avnet, my original boss back at Westbury Music Fair still is alive and well and living in Bel Air with his second wife, Marcia, a former Nashville music maker. He and the crazy Cuban Maria divorced but they remained good friends until she passed away. Brian, who gave me all those great theater casting assignments in Los Angeles, finally hit it big when he became Josh Groban's manager – a long-delayed financial award for him. I look back at the three iconic movies I cast – *Grease, Airplane!,* and *The Rocky Horror Picture Show,* I know that however they will be watched, be it in movie theaters or on television, tablets, smart phones or watches, they will be seen and enjoyed forever.

As for being gay I never had to come out of the closet because I was never in one. It certainly helped that I started working in gay-friendly theater in New York rather than on a Texas oil field. As for casting, the gay Casting Director is almost a cliché. At every job I had, I was out to all those with whom I worked closest. Glass ceilings have been blasted open throughout show business by gays and lesbians. It is amazing that we went from closets to wedding planners and adoption agencies in so short a time. Movements such as #BlackLivesMatter and #MeToo have brought much needed awareness to all of us. Judging by all the young people I meet; things have changed. But in today's political climate we all still must watch our collective backs.

Many in this country suffering greatly from the Covid 19 pandemic and inflation and must choose between buying food, drugs or paying rent or making car payments. When I stopped working, I did plan how to retire modestly. The best car I have ever had is my 2006 Toyota Highlander Hybrid; and with mileage under 150K, I'm sure it will outlast me. While hardly being able to escape to a Caribbean Island and wait out Covid, I am vaxed up the kazoo and thereby have avoided the devastation many are facing today. These days I have also become closer to my family and neighbors. In Laurel Canyon, where children used to be an invasive species, it used to be when a couple had a baby, they would be gone within two years max; today almost all the houses on the street where I live (in the house I bought by accident in 1971) are inhabited by families with kids. In an odd way I have become a surrogate uncle/grandfather to all of them. If I were to be reincarnated today, I would choose to return to earth as one of the boys flying down my street on a skateboard, bike or scooter or one of the four-year-old girls doing the same but wearing a Disney Princess dress.

GLOSSARY

Affiliate Person or corporation who owns local TV stations that air a particular network's series, news, or sports program.

Agent vs Manager Agents have agreements with the various acting unions stating how much they can commission. Managers however are not allowed to solicit work for clients, technically only agents can do that. But rarely is this "rule" enforced

Backdoor pilot TV movie that is actually a pilot, aired in hopes that it will spawn a series.

House seats Seats held back from sale in a theater for use of the producer, lead actors, director, etc. Typically these are used by friends or business associates of the above.

Dailies/rushes Fillm or tape shot the day before viewing in a screening room or now can be seen on a phone or tablet.

In-house Product that a network produces itself.

One or three/ four camera show	One-camera shows are shot like a movie, out of sequence then edited together. For a comedy, a laugh track is added. Three/four-camera shows are rehearsed for four days, then shot in front of a live studio audience on the fifth day using that audience's laughter. *The Big Bang* was shot like a movie; *Will and Grace* was a four-camera show.
Pick-up	Order from a studio or network for a project.
Pilot	Prototype for what a series will be; it can run any length, from a half-hour episode to two-hour feature-length.
Pitch	Writer's or producer's proposal for a series, movie, miniseries, or feature film to a studio or network.
Rough cut	Movie or series episode that has been loosely edited, usually with a temporary music score consisting of familiar songs and melodies.
Series regular	Actor having a contract to make frequent appearances on a series: all episodes produced, ten or seven out of thirteen, depending on the contract. This ties the actor to the series for x number of years. A semi-regular makes sporadic appearances without a series contract.

Sides	A few pages of a script given to actors for auditioning
Show runner	Person in charge of a series. Formerly called producer. Now there are so many variations of the term (executive, supervising, artistic, etc.) that the expression "show runner" was introduced.
Spinoff	Series based on a character from an existing series or movie,
Stop date	The negotiated date by which an actor must be finished shooting and released from a project.
Story arc	When a story line in a series goes on for several episodes or even over a whole season.
Take	As in "Take 1, take 2, etc." It refers to each individual time a particular scene or portion of a scene is filmed or taped. Some directors do only a few, some do many.

NBC SERIES NOTES

The following is a list of every pilot that made it to series that aired on NBC during my time. It was my responsibility to see that all of these programs were cast "correctly." Being *correct* is very subjective. I chose to go with my own sense of what was right and blend it with what my boss, Brandon Tartikoff, wanted. Often, I had to convince him that his ideas were all wrong; many other times I adjusted my thinking to his. Overall, it was an excellent mix of ideas. The opinions herein are all mine, and each show is listed by year in alphabetical order. Feel free to agree, laugh, or disagree.

1981

B.J. AND THE BEAR (3 seasons)

Greg Evigan costarred with a chimp in this lightweight adventure series about a trucker who combs the American south with his pet chimp. The series was written by Glen A. Larson, who would later create two far more memorable shows, *Knight Rider* and *Magnum, P.I.*

BRET MAVERICK (1 season)

Almost twenty years after James Garner starred in *Maverick*, he was back in his old character, a poker-playing nomad. The revival was too little, too late, and honestly, Garner was too old.

BUCK ROGERS IN THE 25th CENTURY (2 seasons)

In 1978, Glen A. Larson launched one of the most lucrative franchises in showbiz history when he created the sci-fi series *Battlestar Galactica*. Glen recycled some of *Galactica*'s old sets, costumes, and props for *Buck Rogers in the 25th Century*. Universal gave the concept a test drive by giving the two-hour pilot a limited release in theaters. The response encouraged NBC to green-light a *Buck Rogers* series. Many felt the show was neither good sci-fi nor good camp. Ratings were weak, and the show was canceled after thirty-two episodes.

CHiPs (6 seasons)

One of NBC's hottest shows of the 1970s was still on the air when I arrived at NBC. Originally Erik Estrada and Larry Wilcox played equal leads on *CHiPs*, which depicted the California Highway Patrol's motorcycle cops. But Estrada's handsome face and blinding smile turned him into a teen heartthrob, and from then on he was the true star. Wilcox felt more and more diminished, and after five seasons of high earnings he decided to leave. It was my difficult task to replace him. The show was in a downward ratings spiral and offered little prestige to anyone connected with it, especially a rising young actor. The producers came up with a young, cute, blond motocross champion, Bruce Penhall, who auditioned in my office. Unfortunately Penhall could not act, a shortcoming I should have ignored. Instead I felt I could improve on the producers' choice with another new handsome blond actor, Tom Reilly. Reilly had given a great audition, and he got the part. We okayed the producers' request to use Penhall in the lesser role of a rookie cop. This was Reilly's first serious acting job, and unfortunately he made two big mistakes: He didn't get along with Estrada, and he was arrested by the real California Highway Patrol for speeding, driving under the influence, and possessing illegal substances. He couldn't overcome the bad publicity, and his role was severely reduced. The producers pushed up Penhall's part, but it wasn't enough to save *CHiPs*, whose ratings continued to crash until NBC pulled the plug.

THE DAVID LETTERMAN SHOW (1 season)

Fred Silverman deserves an "E" for effort for having given the green light this first incarnation of the Letterman show. It was a comedic morning-talk series with many of the bits that Letterman later made famous, such as stupid pet tricks. It also had a diverse group of regular and recurring guests, including Andy Kaufman, Steve Martin, Bill Murray, Jane Pauley, Nancy Reagan, Mary Tyler Moore, and Jimmy Breslin. But the morning TV audience at the time preferred game shows and soaps, so the show didn't make it. Thank God for the cancellation, because who knows if Letterman's late-night show would ever have happened otherwise.

DIFF'RENT STROKES (8 seasons)

When I arrived at NBC, this series was already there. *Diff'rent Strokes* starred Conrad Bain as a rich white widower who adopts the two children of his black housekeeper when she passes away. Gary Coleman and Todd Bridges played the boys. Coleman was the breakout star and generated most of the humor. Though a financial windfall for all concerned, money could not solve the actors' future problems. Three years after the series had ended, Gary Coleman sued his parents, who were also his managers, and won a $1.3 million settlement. But legal costs and unwise investments wiped out the money, and from then on he took any job he could find, including that of a mall security guard. Even before *Diff'rent Strokes* Coleman had suffered from kidney disease and was on dialysis a few times a week all during the series' run. He died in 2010 at the age of 42.

Just as sad was the story of Dana Plato, who played Bain's character's daughter who committed suicide at 34. In real life, Plato became pregnant in the middle of the sixth season and was written out of the show. She gave birth to a son, Tyler, and married his father. She had never been much of an actress, and could no longer find work. Having made $25,000 per episode, she was now living in Las Vegas and working at a dry cleaners. Plato was arrested for trying to hold up a video store with a pellet gun. Later she went to jail for forging a Valium prescription. She died of a drug overdose in 1999. Her son, who also had a drug problem, put a gun to his head at twenty-five.

Todd Bridges also had a hard time getting roles after *Strokes*; a crack cocaine addiction almost did him in. Bridges was accused of participating in the murder of a drug dealer; his lawyer was O.J.'s Johnnie Cochran, who argued that Bridges had been an abused minor, exploited by the entertainment industry and unfairly framed for murder. The jury agreed. Bridges managed to return to acting, notably with a recurring role on the Chris Rock series *Everybody Hates Chris*.

THE FACTS OF LIFE (8 seasons)

One of NBC's longest-running hits of the 1980s began as a spinoff of *Diff'rent Strokes*, the network's sole hit comedy at the time, in which Charlotte Rae played the housekeeper for a wealthy Park Avenue widower. On *The Facts of Life,* she took on a new job, that of housemother to a group of girls at a private boarding school. Also see Chapter 11.

FATHER MURPHY (2 seasons)

In this Western drama series, Merlin Olsen, an ex-NFL player and a former actor on *Little House on the Prairie*, played a 19th-century frontiersman disguised as a priest. He saves a group of orphans, then adopts them. Unfortunately, Olsen didn't have the charisma or acting ability of Michael Landon, who had created the show. The series is interesting historically, however, because it featured several young actresses who became well-known later on: Shannen Doherty, Kellie Martin, and Christina Applegate.

FLAMINGO ROAD (2 seasons)

Based on a 1949 Joan Crawford movie, *Flamingo Road* was intended as NBC's answer to *Dallas* and *Knots Landing*. Unfortunately, this very expensive show got lukewarm ratings, through no fault of the cast, which included Mark Harmon and Morgan Fairchild.

GIMME A BREAK (6 seasons)

See Chapter 15.

HARPER VALLEY PTA (2 seasons)

In 1978, Barbara Eden starred in the feature film *Harper Valley PTA*, based on the hit country song by Jeannie C. Reilly. A year later she reprised her role in a spinoff series. The show was nicely done, and Barbara Eden remained beautiful and warm, but the series didn't have enough juice to sustain it, even with a supporting cast that included Nanette Fabray, Ronny Cox, Louis Nye, and several fine "country" character actors.

HELLO, LARRY (2 seasons)

This was McLean Stevenson's third attempt at a new series following his unwise departure from *M*A*S*H**. A badly written, unfunny comedy, it survived for two seasons only because NBC was then at its lowest ebb and had nothing to replace it with. Kim Richards, an insufferable child actress, played Stevenson's daughter. She grew up to become an insufferable adult with a drinking problem on *The Real Housewives of Beverly Hills*. Also on *RHBH* is her sister Kyle, who was a less successful kid actor but who now outshines her sister Kim. I see a *Whatever Happened to Baby Jane* remake with them.

HERE'S BOOMER (2 seasons)

This action-adventure series starred Boomer, a super-cute mutt, played by the canine actor Johnny. *Here's Boomer* started out as a TV movie called *A Christmas for Boomer*, a ratings success. At the time NBC was short on new shows and we ordered a series based on the film. Someone had proposed calling the show *Here's Johnny*, but in order not to offend Johnny Carson – who already had it in for NBC's new head, Fred Silverman – Johnny became Boomer. *Here's Boomer* followed the exploits of a stray dog that roamed around, helping those in need. It was a sweet show, but never found an audience.

HILL STREET BLUES (7 seasons)

In my first season at NBC, this was the network's only new hit. It was a groundbreaking, semi-serialized police drama with comedic overtones and many overlapping story lines. The series was created by Steven Bochco and Mike Kozoll. Bochco went on to do several other first-rate shows, including *L.A. Law*, *Doogie Houser*, and *NYPD Blue*. In its first season, *Hill Street* won eight Emmys; throughout its run it scored 98 nominations. But I must put humility aside to say that things might not have gone so well if it weren't for me.

The casting process was long. While most of the supporting roles were filled effectively and easily by the show's casting director, Lori Openden, it was a lot more complicated to find an actor for the leading role of Frank Furillo, the superefficient, dignified captain of the Hill Street Station. Lori and I wanted Daniel J. Travanti, whom I had used with great success on *The Bob Newhart Show* as a member of a group-therapy ensemble. But Bochco wasn't sold on Travanti and had his own ideas, all of which Lori and I objected to strongly. Fred Silverman seriously questioned Travanti's "likeability" – a vague and subjective judgment that was frequently used to gauge the value of actors on TV. The likeability factor was considered more important than acting skills, because, it was believed, viewers would not welcome people into their homes who they didn't like. Dan, a very serious actor, is very guarded, and doesn't smile easily. But when he does, he's charming and leaves no doubt as to his "likeability."

A screen test was set up and during it I was worried; as always Dan acted well, but his "likeability" was not showing up. I wandered over to him during a short break trying very carefully not to let Bochco see me "interfering" and said, "I don't give a shit how you do it, but smile during the next take." He said he couldn't see where to smile in the scene. I said, "Just find a fucking place and do it. This is not about acting skills but your likeability." He understood what I was saying and smile he did, several times, and got the job.

LEWIS & CLARK (1 season)

This witless half-hour comedy was produced mainly out of contractual obligations to Johnny Carson's production company. It starred Gabriel Kaplan in his attempt at a follow up to *Welcome Back, Kotter*. According to the lame premise, New Yorker Gabe moves with his family to Luckenbach, Texas, where he buys a struggling country-western club. Nothing about *Lewis & Clark* worked.

ME & MAXX (10 episodes)

This was the very first pilot/series that I had to deal with only a few days after I arrived at NBC, about a father having his eleven-year-old daughter move in with him because her mother has had enough of motherhood. The show violated the first and most important rule of comedy – it wasn't funny. NBC was so desperate that it actually put this turkey on the air for almost a half season.

THE MISADVENTURES OF SHERIFF LOBO (2 seasons)

B.J. and the Bear yielded this equally terrible spinoff, also by Glen A. Larson. Both shows reeked of NBC's desperation for product. Nell Carter was added to the last fifteen episodes, to little avail.

NERO WOLFE (1 season)

NBC had hoped that Orson Welles would make his TV-series debut as Nero Wolfe, the portly, orchid-loving detective from a famous series of Rex Stout crime novels. But Welles never came through, and the part went to William Conrad, best known for his five-year run as a private investigator on the show *Cannon*. Although nicely done, with a strong performance by Lee Horsley as Wolfe's sidekick, *Nero Wolfe* didn't attract an audience.

PINK LADY (aka PINK LADY AND JEFF) (5 episodes)

See Chapter 11.

REAL PEOPLE (6 seasons)

Produced by George Schlatter, the man responsible for the revolutionary *Laugh-In*, *Real People* was the granddaddy of all talk-reality shows. In it, revolving hosts introduced and narrated pre-taped segments about average people with offbeat jobs or hobbies. ABC produced a knock-off version, *That's Incredible,* which was more successful. But it didn't have Richard Simmons, whom *Real People* thrust upon the viewing public as a campy fitness instructor.

1982

BARE ESSENCE (1 season)

A TV movie that starred *Dynasty*'s Linda Evans begat this nighttime soap. Alas, the cast did not include the much-beloved Linda. And even with *Knots Landing* star Donna Mills and *General Hospital*'s blond heroine Genie Francis, the show was a flop.

CHICAGO STORY (13 episodes)

This weak crime drama was built around a pair of doctors and a few prosecutors, defense lawyers, and cops. No one watched it, but like others, it came in a period when NBC was in the crapper big-time. Happily the cast included some talented actors, such as Dennis Franz and Craig T. Nelson, who went on to better things.

FAME (2 seasons on NBC; 4 more in first-run syndication)

The TV version of this classic high-school musical movie was written by William Blinn, whose writing credits ranged from *Starsky & Hutch* to Prince's *Purple Rain*. I met with Blinn when we first announced the series. Bill did not know who Debbie Allen was, and more importantly, that she played the role of dance teacher Lydia Grant, whose part was cut way down in the final edit to give more screen time to the students. So, I told him all about how terrific Debbie was as an actress, a person, and a choreographer and that she was the first person he should meet as he started work on the show. I told him that she should return to the TV series acting in her former character *and* I also suggested that he could make a good financial deal with her if she was also made the series choreographer as well. All that and more wound up happening; she began directing episodes, too, and eventually became executive producer. She later on took charge of *A Different World* as well.

After *Fame*'s first year on NBC, a new character was going to be added, and MGM, the studio that produced both the movie and the TV show, sent casting director Marcia Ross to New York for a series of auditions. No one from this search made it into the series. But years later, while going through my videotape library, I came across a copy of those auditions – and lo and behold, I discovered that the herd of actors included Madonna, age twenty-one. The rejection made complete sense, because she had auditioned for the role of the virginally pure girl-next-door – and as we all know, that is not in Madonna's bag of tricks. But the tape is fascinating, because in her interview she just sat and talked directly into the camera about what she was then doing: writing songs and choreographing videos around them. But when she tried to act two scenes, she was terrible. If you want to see for yourself, go to YouTube, where you will find me narrating what you just read.

The last interesting factoid about the series involves NBC's cancellation of it after two successful seasons. The network now had a wealth of popular and quality shows, and a "Sophie's Choice" arose between *Fame* and *St. Elsewhere*. Both shows were in healthy shape, with the latter having a bit more critical acclaim and the former an edge in the ratings. The problem was that that there was only room for one of those shows on the schedule. The choice came down to which show could make the most money for NBC – after all, the shows are only there to provide something to watch between commercials, and it's always about the Benjamins. While having a smaller audience, *St. Elsewhere* had an audience with deeper pockets, and the ad rates on *St. Elsewhere* were much higher than those on *Fame*. This was the beginning of targeting audiences for advertisers. It is the way TV broadcast networks have survived today, by delivering very specific audiences to specific sponsors.

It also didn't hurt that Grant Tinker, NBC's new chairman of the board, had two sons who were writers on *St. Elsewhere,* and the show had come from his former studio, MTM Productions… just sayin'. But *Fame* became even more popular in first-run syndication; it was a huge international hit, and it inspired a popular stage musical.

FAMILY TIES (7 seasons)

One day in 1982, writer Gary David Goldberg and his superb casting director, Judith Weiner, came into my office to present their "dream cast" – as Goldberg called it – for *Family Ties*, a series about the cultural and political shifts and the generation gap that had arisen between the '60s and the '80s. Unfortunately, his selections became his nightmare cast; his words, not mine. The choices were Matthew Broderick in the role of Alex, the conservative son of two ex-hippie parents, to be played (the creators hoped) by Christopher Sarandon (*Dog Day Afternoon*) and Donna McKechnie (*A Chorus Line*). Sarandon read very well, but my fellow executives hated him, deeming him unlikeable. Donna McKechnie fared even worse. Though a wonderful dancer, Donna was never a good actress – she has said so herself – and her reading was neither good nor funny.

We did like the rest of Goldberg and Weiner's choices, including Justine Bateman and Tina Yothers as the daughters of the two ex-hippies. When Gary asked if I had any ideas for the parents, out of nowhere I remembered Michael Gross, an actor I had seen on Broadway as a villainous German drag queen in *Bent*, which starred Richard Gere. "If you close your eyes," I said, "he sounds exactly like Alan Alda. He's a very good actor, and he's warm and likable." They brought him in, and he got the part. One problem solved; now onto the mother. I said, "I know this is not gonna sound original and new, and she hasn't done anything in a long while, but what about Meredith Baxter?" Meredith was TV's go-to ingénue of the early 1970s. "She's now the right age to play mothers," I said. "Why don't you take a look at her?" She got the part and then starred in just about every TV movie for the next decade.

Broderick ultimately decided to go to Broadway to take a career-making role in Neil Simon's *Brighton Beach Memoirs*. The second choice, Zach Galligan, became unavailable when he decided to take the lead in the comedy horror film *Gremlins*. Judith kept pushing this unknown Canadian kid named Michael J. Fox. He came in to read, and everyone liked him except Brandon Tartikoff, who said that Fox had neither comedy chops nor likeability nor looks. "His face is never going to be on a lunch-box," Brandon declared. "Brandon," I argued, "he's funny, he's cute. If everybody else thinks he's cute and funny and you're the only one who doesn't, you've got to give in." After much persuasion, Brandon relented. Upon getting the role that made him a star for life, Fox – who knew of Brandon's remark, had a lunch-box made with his face on it and sent it to Brandon, who placed it in a prominent place in his office. Michael went on to win three Emmys in a row as Outstanding Lead Actor in a Comedy Series. He became an A-list movie star as well because of Gary Goldberg's smarts. When Fox was asked to star in Steven Spielberg's *Back to the Future*, Goldberg shifted *Family Ties* production sideways and inside out, which allowed Fox to shoot the feature film and the series at the same time. This was the first crack in the wall separating film from TV.

GAVILAN (1 season)

This spy drama starred Robert Urich as a former CIA operative. No one cared about the show, and it is almost impossible to find anyone who remembers it, including me.

KNIGHT RIDER (4 seasons)

See Prologue.

LOVE, SIDNEY (2 seasons)

In 1980, NBC produced a TV movie called *Sidney Shorr: A Girl's Best Friend*. It told the story of Sidney, a lonely middle-aged man (played by Tony Randall) who meets a young single mother and aspiring actress (Lorna Patterson) at the Thalia, an actual revival movie-theater on New York's Upper West Side. They bond over their shared love of old films, and Sidney starts to feel he has a family. Sidney is gay, but the word is never used; the only acknowledgment is a picture on the mantelpiece of a handsome man. A hint is dropped that this is his late boyfriend. Tony, of course, was the ideal choice to play Sidney. Many viewers assumed he was gay because he had always played effete and somewhat prissy characters, such as neatnik Felix Unger on *The Odd Couple*. Much later, however, at age seventy he married twenty-five-year-old

Heather Harlan and had two children. Lorna, meanwhile, was terrific in her part: warm, sisterly, and sort of needy. The chemistry between Tony and Lorna was so strong that, even before the film had aired, we decided to turn *Love, Sidney* into a series. The airing of the film was delayed and delayed. The sales department hated the show because of the implication that the character was gay and said they could not sell the show to advertisers. As soon as NBC announced it, the Moral Majority and other watchdog groups mounted protests. Happily, NBC didn't bow, and the sales department did what they should do and sold ads.

By that time, however, almost a year had passed and Brandon Tartikoff had very kindly let Lorna out of her contract so she could star in a TV version of *Private Benjamin* for CBS. I begged him not to do this because I knew that *Love, Sidney* would get on the air. Although we replaced Lorna with a very good actress, Swoosie Kurtz, that special chemistry with Tony was gone. The series premiered in 1981, and in its two struggling seasons, what little evidence there was of Sidney's gayness evaporated until his character was virtually a eunuch. *Love, Sidney* did okay in the big cities but died everywhere else. TV was still not ready for a positive gay character, I guess. Sadly, Tony passed away in 2004 and Lorna converted to Judiasm and is now a cantor living happily in Malibu with director Michael Lembeck.

ONE OF THE BOYS (1 season)

This flop starred Dana Carvey and Nathan Lane as college students who live with Carvey's grandfather, played by Mickey Rooney. I had put the up-and-coming Carvey and Lane under contract to NBC, and both deserved better than this. The show was taped in New York, where Rooney was costarring on Broadway with Ann Miller in *Sugar Babies*. Even when he deigned to rehearse, which hardly ever happened, the series barely had his attention. *One of the Boys* had no chance with Rooney's behavior, and it died a fast death. Carvey and Lane have deservedly gone on to much, much, much better things.

THE POWERS OF MATTHEW STAR (2 seasons)

See Chapter 11.

REMINGTON STEELE (5 seasons)

The writing and producing team of Bob Butler and Michael Gleason created this series as a showcase for Stephanie Zimbalist, then a very in-demand leading lady. She played a private detective who, no matter how good she is, cannot attract clients because she is a woman. To solve the problem, she invents a fictitious boss named Remington Steele. A former con man becomes her partner. During the casting of that role, Bob showed us a clip from a miniseries called *The Manions of America*, a historical romance. It starred a then-unknown Pierce Brosnan, who was excellent. Not wanting to commit until we'd seen him in person, we agreed to fly him in from Ireland to meet with us in my office. A few days later there he was, charming everyone he met. However, he had one major flaw: Like many British and Irish citizens, Pierce had horrible teeth. We told MTM to have them fixed, then they could hire him. They did and sent NBC the dental bill.

The first season earned impressive kudos for its sophisticated writing and stylish production. Then when some of the supporting actors had dropped out, including the one who played the detective agency's secretary, I suggested adding Doris Roberts, who later became famous as the costar of *Everybody Loves Raymond*. Though initially resistant to the idea (Doris was close to sixty, and the character was supposed to be in her thirties) Bob Butler eventually agreed, and adjusted the role to fit the actress. The show gained in popularity each year, but never did that well in the ratings and was canceled after four seasons in order to make room for a new series, *Hunter*. Reacting to a groundswell of viewer support, NBC reinstated the show, but the damage had been done, and it never regained its former numbers. Furthermore, Pierce had received a very public offer to be the new James Bond, replacing Timothy Dalton in his brief run in the role. The invitation came with the condition that he had to be released from the series. He asked and we said no. I strongly suggested that we shut down production, pay the key people necessary, and when finished with *Goldeneye,* Pierce could come back, only this time as a much bigger star and stay with the series for his contractual two more seasons. No one liked the idea, so Pierce came unhappily back for one more not-great season. Then the dying series was put out of its misery and Pierce became Bond, which placed him on the A-list of movie stars.

ST. ELSEWHERE (6 seasons)

This serialized medical drama was produced by Bruce Paltrow, aka Gwyneth's father. The writing and cast were superior, but the series initially floundered for lack of a heartthrob young doctor as its central character, such as George Clooney later played on *ER*. Mark Harmon's character came close but if we all had looked more carefully there was one actor already in the cast who could do it. That was Denzel Washington in his first and only series. However, he asked to be let out of his contract, and Bruce agreed, saying that Washington was becoming a movie star after starring in the feature film *A Soldier's Story,* and that since he was a member of a large ensemble cast, it would not affect the show and he would not hold him back. The rest of the cast were hardly chopped liver either: Howie Mandel, Ed Begley, Jr., William Daniels, Norman Lloyd (who continued to act past the age of 100), Bruce Greenwood, Helen Hunt, Jane Wyatt, Laraine Newman, Tim Robbins, Betty White, Louise Lasser, and Kathy Bates.

SILVER SPOONS (4 seasons)

In this decently successful sitcom, Joel Higgins played a millionaire father whose ex-wife dies, leaving him with custody of his son Ricky (played by Ricky Schroder). The show wasn't great, but the chemistry between Ricky and his best friend (Jason Bateman) was excellent and led to healthy ratings for two seasons. Then Schroder's mother demanded that NBC fire Jason, wrongly thinking he was stealing the show from her son. She should have taken a tip from *Happy Days* where nominal star Ron Howard, when paired with Henry Winkler's "Fonzie," created magic for both actors and the series. We caved and replaced Jason with Alfonso Ribeiro, who later became the straight man opposite Will Smith on *Prince of Bel Air*. Unfortunately, two straight men with no comic foil – actually boys – do not make a good team and the show limped on. Jason was immediately snapped up for another NBC series, *It's Your Move*, which unfortunately was a dud. We then put him on Valerie Harper's series, *Valerie*, where he was the best thing on the show.

TAXI (2 seasons on NBC, 2 on ABC)

See Chapter 9.

VOYAGERS (1 season)

As he was just about the most handsome man I had ever met, I signed Jon-Erik Hexum to NBC for a year. We cast him and teenager Meeno Peluce in this not-so-good time-travel show, which was almost a kid show. Hexum was as good in it as one could have been. This was the first TV series in Hexum's very short career. A year and a half later, while shooting a series on ABC, he accidentally shot himself in the temple while fooling around with a prop gun. It seems that when one puts even a prop gun to one's head and presses the trigger, it can kill. Sadly, he was gorgeous and charismatic, but unfortunately not gun smart.

1983

THE A-TEAM (5 seasons)

One of NBC's biggest hits of the 1980s, *The A-Team,* was co-produced and written by Stephen J. Cannell, whose dozens of TV credits include *The Rockford Files, Baretta, 21 Jump Street*, and *The Commish.* The idea for this show started with Steve Cannell and Brandon Tartikoff watching the crowd at a basketball game watching another spectator, Mr. T. Having seen this and the movie *Rocky,* they wisely figured there was a series in the man. There was actually no real pilot for this show, just a few scenes with Mr. T thrown together. Now that Mr. T was set and the few cut scenes satisfied everyone, Can-

SEX, DRUGS, & PILOT SEASON • 355

nell came into my office and asked me whom I preferred for the lead, George Peppard or Robert Blake, and said he would be happy with either. I said Peppard, and when the rest of the NBC execs came in, that's who he said he wanted. That kind of thing never happened to me before or since. Oh, btw, the show told the story of a troupe of Green Beret-like soldiers of fortune. A lame 2010 feature film with Liam Neeson but without Mr. T barely made back its cost.

BAY CITY BLUES (1 season)

This show about a minor-league baseball team was the next show from Steven Bochco, who gave NBC a huge hit, *Hill Street Blues*. *Bay City Blues* was nicely written and had an excellent cast, including Michael Nouri, Kelly Harmon (Mark's beautiful sister, known for her Tic Tac commercials), Ken Olin (later of *Thirtysomething*), and Sharon Stone; but eventually even Bochco admitted that the setting of a minor league baseball team was hardly compelling TV.

BUFFALO BILL (2 seasons)

This terrific show was way ahead of its time. Today, when anti-heroes are sometimes at the center of sitcoms – like *Barry,* starring *SNL* alumni Bill Hader – *Buffalo Bill* might have had a chance. It was written by Tom Patchett and Jay Tarses, my producers from *The Bob Newhart Show.* In *Buffalo Bill*, Dabney Coleman played a wonderfully nasty talk-show host in Buffalo, New York. The series, which also featured Genna Davis and Joanna Cassidy, never fared well in the ratings, but it scored eleven Emmy nominations and earned a Golden Globe for Joanna.

JENNIFER SLEPT HERE (2 seasons)

Ann Jillian starred in this lame descendent of *Topper* and *The Ghost and Mrs. Muir*, in which a family moves into a house inhabited by the ghost of its former owner, a blond movie bombshell. Six years after I had cast Georgia Engel on *The Mary Tyler Moore Show*, she did thirteen forgettable episodes on this turkey.

MAMA'S FAMILY (2 seasons)

Joe Hamilton, Carol Burnett's husband and the producer of her variety series, masterminded this spinoff of a popular recurring segment on her show. Vicki Lawrence, Ken Berry, and Harvey Korman repeated their original roles, and Carol made a half-dozen appearances, but *Mama's Family* didn't survive on NBC for long. Undaunted, Joe sold the show into first-run syndication, where it was a hit and lasted for five more seasons.

MANIMAL (8 episodes)

Handsome, dashing Brit Simon MacCorkindale played a college professor who can transform himself into any animal he chooses to help the police fight crime. *Manimal* was the brainchild of Glen A. Larson, the creator of *Knight Rider*. Glen had a knack for conceiving high-concept shows; this one aimed a bit too high.

MR. SMITH (13 episodes)

The less said about this show, which concerned a talking orangutan, the better; because it is one of the lesser works by multi-award-winning writer-producer, Ed. Weinberger; his credits include *The Mary Tyler Moore Show, Taxi,* and *The Cosby Show.* A young Joaquin Phoenix made one guest appearance.

THE ROUSTERS (13 episodes)

Jim Varney and Chad Everett starred in this clinker, set in a traveling carnival. Jim was my choice. I had seen a few commercials in which he played his famous original character, Ernest P. Worrell, a pesky, rubber-faced redneck. When Jim and his agent came to L.A. to exploit Ernest, they came to NBC first. What they wanted was a TV movie starring Ernest, but since none was in the offing, Jim signed on to play a variation of Ernest as the comic sidekick to Chad Everett. But nothing could save *The Rousters,* and luckily for Jim, he went on to make several successful Ernest movies. Shortly after the series pick-up, Jim came into my office with a most unusual present for me, his squirrel knife. I can only imagine what it would do to the poor squirrel since I immediately cut myself.

WE GOT IT MADE (2 seasons)

NBC's knockoff of *Three's Company* just didn't work. It concerned two bachelor roommates who hire a sexy live-in housekeeper/maid. The only reason to watch *We Got It Made* was costar Tom Villard, a wonderful and immensely funny actor who died of AIDS in 1994.

THE YELLOW ROSE (1 season)

This *Dallas*-inspired nighttime soap starred David Soul and Cybill Shepherd. Neither critics nor viewers cared for it, but

I liked it a lot. At that time, to go from movie star to TV star marked a distinct comedown in stature. I was given the task to go to Cybill's condo in Studio City and convince her why this was actually a good move. Two glasses of red wine and my charm did the trick. Unfortunately, the show did not do well and was cancelled. But she then went on to star in two very successful shows: *Moonlighting*, which costarred a young Bruce Willis; and *Cybill*, in which Christine Baranski played her best friend and most say stole the show. In any event her switch to TV paid off.

1984

THE COSBY SHOW (8 seasons)

See Chapter 11.

DOUBLE TROUBLE (1 season)

This was NBC's attempt to do a "twins" show a la *The Patty Duke Show*. Jean and Liz Sagal, younger twin sisters of *Married....with Children*'s Katie Sagal, played a pair of mischievous teens with a widower father. They were not so great, and the writing didn't help. This show was produced by Norman Lear's production company, but he personally had nothing to do with it until he saw the finished product. He was so embarrassed by it that he became very hands-on trying to save it, but to no avail.

THE DUCK FACTORY (13 episodes)

NBC replaced *Buffalo Bill* with this MTM sitcom written by Allan Burns about a starry-eyed young man who goes to Hollywood and lands a job at a low-budget animation firm. *The Duck Factory* is memorable mainly because it gave Jim Carrey his first leading role. A good cast and clever writing weren't enough to sustain it.

HIGHWAY TO HEAVEN (6 seasons)

This wholesome family drama starred Michael Landon as an angel who has been stripped of his wings and lives on "probation" on Earth, where he and his human sidekick (played by Victor French) help various earthlings in need. The show was NBC's successful attempt to get the enormously popular Landon back on NBC after his nine seasons as Charles Ingalls on *Little House on the Prairie*. On *Highway to Heaven*, Landon had one hundred percent free reign; he owned the series outright and served as executive producer, writer, director, and star. *Highway to Heaven* was an interesting counterpoint to many of NBC's new shows at that time, which were hipper and, while popular in major cities, did not hold much appeal in the smaller and more rural towns in the U.S. However in some of those places, *Highway to Heaven* often hit No. 1 in the ratings.

HOT PURSUIT (12 episodes)

This short-lived drama concerned a young professional couple, played by Eric Pierpoint and Kerrie Keane, who are plunged into a whirlwind of murder and espionage, orchestrated by arch villainess Dina Merrill. Pierpoint fared much better in a series of roles in all four spinoffs of the original *Star Trek*.

HUNTER (7 seasons)

For years I tried to find the right vehicle for the former NFL star-turned-actor Fred Dryer. He was one of the finalists reading for

Cheers but thankfully did not get the part. Finally, I found him the perfect lead role: that of a hard-boiled detective on the crime drama *Hunter*. Stepfanie Kramer, who played his beautiful but tough partner, was an excellent actress as well as a trained mezzo-soprano; she sang a number of times on *Hunter*. A first on a cop show.

IT'S YOUR MOVE (1 season)

On their way to creating a blockbuster hit, *Married with Children*, Ron Leavitt and Michael G. Moye devised this minor effort. It starred Jason Bateman as a high school student who embarks on all kinds of scams to earn money. Leavitt and Moye were a unique writing team for the time in that Leavitt was white and Moye, black. Leavitt was also known for showing up at network meetings looking like the "bad" plumber, wearing pants that always showed severe hairy-butt crack.

LEGMEN (6 episodes)

This flimsy drama starred Bruce Greenwood and John Terlesky as a pair of college students who earn extra cash by working for a private eye. Bruce developed an enduring career as an actor on such shows as *Mad Men*, *American Crime Story*, and an interesting HBO flop, *John in Cincinnati*; John, too, went on to better things, including *The Blacklist*, *Castle*, and *Criminal Minds*.

MIAMI VICE (5 seasons)

This violent and sexy crime series was set in Miami, and populated by drug dealers, hookers, money-launderers, and cops. It started as a TV movie/backdoor pilot called *Gold Coast,* created by Anthony Yerkovich and Michael Mann. Brandon Tartikoff is said to have pitched the idea to Yerkovich with a simple phrase, "MTV cops"; Yerkovich claims he was already working on a Miami-based crime show. In any event, *Miami Vice* proved a taste changer in men's fashion, Miami colors (no earth tones allowed), and architecture. It showed ultramodern, midcentury and art deco side-by-side in Miami Beach. The show used current music in innovative ways and employed quick MTV-style editing.

The casting of undercover cop Rico Tubbs was easy. I had worked with Philip Michael Thomas on a musical a few years earlier, and when the producers brought him up, it was an easy yes from me. Both his and Johnson's character started out as equals; obviously that did not continue. It was more difficult to cast the role of Rico's partner, Sonny Crockett. Mann and Yerkovich wanted Don Johnson, but NBC's executives were divided. I was a huge fan of Johnson's and had put him in several pilots and TV movies, among them *Elvis and the Beauty Queen.* But Don had tested very badly in a couple of failed pilots, and against my better instincts I joined the naysayers. I much preferred Gary Cole, a handsome, intense young theater actor from Chicago. But Yerkovich and Mann did not agree. Other NBC executives wanted Larry Wilcox, who had played Officer Jon Baker from *CHiPs.* Finally, Brandon Tartikoff decided wisely to let the Michael Mann have his choice and he was right.

NIGHT COURT (9 seasons)

I first saw Harry Anderson in Los Angeles at the Magic Castle, where he was performing as a comedic magician. From there, his career zoomed. He made a string of appearances on *Saturday*

Night Live and played the recurring role of con man Harry "The Hat" Gittes on *Cheers*. In 1984 we cast him as the boyish, Barry Manilow-hating Judge Harry Stone on *Night Court*, one of NBC's blockbuster successes of the decade. The wonderful supporting cast included John Larroquette, who had previously worked mainly as a dramatic actor. The show had less luck in the casting one of its two bailiffs. Richard Moll was superb as the tall bald guy. Unfortunately, the women cast as the other bailiff kept dying – for real, not their characters. Older and cigarette-voiced Selma Diamond lasted two seasons, Florence Halop, a virtual twin for Diamond, did season three. Tall, imposing comedienne Marsha Warfield was completely opposite of those two wonderful women and stayed alive for the rest of the series' nine seasons. A reboot is rumored to be in development. A good idea if the writing and casting stays as good as the original.

PARTNERS IN CRIME (1 season)

Take Linda Carter (*Wonder Woman*), pair her with Loni Anderson (the smart, sexy blonde from *WKRP in Cincinnati*), put them together as private detectives in San Francisco, and what do you have? A huge flop. Bad writing and directing killed this show, which never found the *Charlie's Angels* secret sauce.

PUNKY BREWSTER

This silly but charming series involved an abandoned young girl who is raised by a foster father. The idea came from Brandon Tartikoff, who saw possibilities in the memory of a girl he had known as a child. Massive, televised talent searches were held in New York and Los Angeles, yet the title role went to an established

L.A. kid actress, Soleil Moon Frye. This one has been rebooted with the now 45-year-old, still beautiful Ms. Frye as the lead.

RIPTIDE (3 seasons)

Frank Lupo and Stephen J. Cannell returned to NBC with this macho detective series, which starred Perry King and Joe Penny. One innovative element of the show involved its third lead character, a computer-hacking genius (played by Thom Bray); I dare anyone to name recent detective or police show now without one.

SPENCER (1 season)

In this unfunny sitcom, a high school student, played by Chad Lowe (Rob's brother), gets in and out of typical teenage predicaments. Chad went on to marry Hilary Swank, who famously did not thank her husband when she won her Academy Award for *Boys Don't Cry*. She divorced him soon afterward. But Chad got his reward later in the form of an Emmy for his role as a young man with HIV on ABC's *Life Goes On*.

V (1 season)

The series *V* came from the hugely successful miniseries of the same name a year earlier. It was a sci-fi piece written and directed by Kenneth Johnson about space aliens who, disguised as humans, come to Earth to harvest its population for food. The best moment of the miniseries, which was repeated in the series, is when the lead alien villain, played deliciously evil by actress Jane Badler, picks up a nice-sized guinea pig by the tail and by means of a totally unexpected articulated jaw opens wide allowing the hapless rodent to disappear down her throat, snake-like bulge and all. The miniseries already had a very close airdate when it was picked up, which meant every aspect of the production had to be done at warp speed, including special effects and casting. Warner Brothers head of talent, the excellent Phyllis Huffman, and I sat down, and in just a few hours we agreed on several choices for just about every major role. I love casting when there is no time to diddle around, and you have to make fast decisions. There were readings for Ken Johnson, but since all the actors he saw were pre-approved by NBC, casting happened in no time.

There was one tragedy associated with this show. Its original ingénue was to be played by up-and-coming actress Dominique Dunne, daughter of author Dominick Dunne. She had shot a couple of scenes when on a day off her ex-boyfriend came to her house and murdered her. Her role was recast and the scenes she shot were redone. There was an attempt by NBC to revive the series in the 2009 but it didn't work, despite the presence of Ms. Badler and her articulated throat.

1985

AMAZING STORIES (2 seasons)

Steven Spielberg himself created this anthology series of fantasy, horror, and science fiction stories. Not surprisingly, it was an ambitious and well-done hour-long show. But even with Spielberg and Clint Eastwood directing and an incredible cast of stars – including Kevin Costner, Danny DeVito, Kiefer Sutherland, Jon Cryer, Christopher Lloyd, Patrick Swayze, Charlie Sheen,

Tim Robbins, Loni Anderson, and Rhea Pearlman – the ratings were never high enough to keep *Amazing Stories* on the air. This, too, has been rebooted.

BERRENGER'S (13 episodes)

This was one of NBC's several failed attempts to create a *Dallas*-style hit nighttime soap. *Berrenger's* was set in a luxury New York department store owned by a rich and glamorous family. The show wasn't bad, but never found an audience. The cast included Sam Wanamaker and Yvette Mimieux, but for me the standout was Anita Morris, a tall, strikingly beautiful redhead who had won a Tony for her role in the musical *Nine*. She played one of the Berrenger daughters, a dissolute heiress who is finally getting her life together. Anita combined enormous sex appeal with true vulnerability. She died of ovarian cancer in 1994, leaving behind her husband, dancer-choreographer Grover Dale, and their son, James Badge Dale, now a successful actor. You can see how wonderful she was by streaming the feature film *Ruthless People,* where she played Danny DeVito's girlfriend.

THE GOLDEN GIRLS (7 seasons)

See Chapter 12.

HELL TOWN (13 episodes)

Years after his hit detective series *Baretta*, Robert Blake re-emerged in this short-lived drama about a street-fighting Catholic priest in a skid-row parish. Blake was in charge of everything to do with the show, which was unfortunate. While the character was a good fit for Blake's skills, the writing was pretty awful. He had a reputation for being difficult and having drug problems, but he showed none of that in his interactions with me. I enjoyed all the casting sessions I had with him in my office; I found him very pragmatic, and we had good give-and-take. I think NBC would have kept the series on the air, but his ill behavior erupted in his dealings with most of the other executives, and it turned into a "you can't fire me – I quit" situation. He left, and the show was over. In 2004 he was acquitted of murdering his wife but later lost a civil suit.

MISFITS OF SCIENCE (16 episodes)

This tongue-in-cheek fantasy series, which concerned a scientific research team with superhuman powers, was *X-Men* without spandex. It was scheduled against *Dallas* – a good counter-programming move that failed, even with twenty-one-year-old Courteney Cox in the cast. I had seen Courteney in the Bruce Springsteen video for "Dancing in the Dark"; she's the girl he brings onstage from the audience to dance with him. Right after seeing the video, I put her under contract to NBC. *Misfits of Science* was her first series. Prior to this she starred in a very silly NBC comedy movie, *If It's Tuesday, It Still Must Be Belgium*, opposite the Tony-nominated New York actor Lou Liberatore and a host of other NBC supporting players, notably Doris Roberts. Courteney went on to play Michael J. Fox's girlfriend in *Family Ties*; then, of course, she became a huge star on *Friends*.

SARA (13 episodes)

Witten by *Family Ties'* Gary Goldberg and set in a law office, this sitcom was our attempt to build a show around Geena Davis, of whom I was big fan. Her early work on NBC included a regular role on *Buffalo Bill* and guest shots on *Knight Rider*, *Riptide*, and *Remington Steele*. Although the show got good reviews, it was scheduled against *Dynasty* and died a swift death. Among the other cast members who went on to bigger things were Bill Maher, Alfre Woodard, and Bronson Pinchot, who played one of the first gay characters on a U.S. series.

227 (5 seasons)

In the mid-1980s, Brandon Tartikoff went to a small L.A. theater to see *227*, a play about the residents of an inner-city apartment building; 227 was the street number. It was produced by actor-director Angela Gibbs as a vehicle for her mother, Marla Gibbs, who was then famous as Florence Johnston, George Jefferson's maid in *The Jeffersons*. Marla took the premise to Brandon and as soon as *The Jeffersons* went off the air, *227* began a long run. The centerpiece of the show was Marla, in the role of a gossipy but warmhearted housewife. Marla's character was more serious than the sassy and outlandish Florence; on *227* it was Jackée Harry, as Marla's neighbor, who got most of the laughs. Marla had initially resisted our casting of both Jackée and, in her acting debut, the recent Academy Award-winning and then fourteen-year-old Regina King, who played Marla's brilliant, boy-crazy daughter. My theory is that Marla was used to getting all the laughs and found it hard to sit back and play the less-funny lead. She kept trying to minimize Jackée's part, but NBC would not let this happen. It didn't help matters when Jackée won an Emmy for her role. She and Regina King totaled five nominations, and Marla got none. But with the show's success the rivalry became moot, and Marla cried all the way to the bank.

1986

ALF (4 seasons)

An extraterrestrial from the planet Melmac crash-lands into a suburban family's garage in this ultra-funny hit sitcom. The title character (an acronym for Alien Life Form) was a hand puppet manipulated by Paul Fusco, who created *ALF* with Tom Patchett. All the NBC executives gathered in my office for an "interview" with the puppet. I started interviewing ALF/Paul as I would any actor, and his answers were hysterical. ALF engaged with the other execs as if he was at a Hollywood roast, ripping us all apart and leaving us rolling on the floor in laughter. This was my favorite office moment in all the years I spent at NBC. Alf lived in a perfectly normal San Fernando Valley suburban home with the befuddled head of the household (Max Wright) and his wife (Ann Schedeen). As the busybody neighbor, *ALF* had the sensational Liz Sheridan, who held the distinction of having been James Dean's only known girlfriend. I still have the ALF plush toy on my bed.

ALL IS FORGIVEN (9 episodes)

Glen and Les Charles, who had given us *Cheers*, followed it less auspiciously with this sitcom about a female soap-opera writer who in one day becomes its producer as well as the wife of a donut executive with a teenage daughter. *All Is Forgiven* had a strong supporting cast – Carol Kane, David Allen Grier, Valerie Landsburg – but the lead, a good actress named Bess Armstrong, lacked the comedy skills to center the show and it failed rather quickly.

AMEN (5 seasons)

This show was a favorite of mine. Written by Ed. Weinberger, it starred Sherman Hemsley as the shady deacon of a church in Philadelphia, where he lives with his single daughter. There wasn't much difference between Deacon Ernest Frye and Hemsley's previous character, George Jefferson, which was kind of the point. Both were hilarious. As good as Sherman was, he was equally matched by Anna Maria Horsford, a force of nature, who played his daughter, Thelma. My contribution to the cast was Clifton Davis, in the role of the new pastor of the church and Thelma's eventual bridegroom. The casting directors had not come up with anyone suitable, when I remembered Clifton, whom I had met when he understudied one of the leads in the Pearl Bailey version of *Hello, Dolly!* Immediately after his *Dolly* contract was up, Davis went to Hollywood. His career was on the rise in the 1970s with a TV variety show with then-girlfriend Melba Moore, but drugs interfered. Davis cleaned up and became a minister in suburban L.A. *Amen* brought him back to acting. He now has a ministry in Philadelphia and makes appears frequently on Trinity Broadcasting.

BLACKE'S MAGIC (13 episodes)

This was a whodunit series starring Hal Linden (of *Barney Miller* fame) as a magician who solves real-life mysteries along with his con-man father, played by Harry Morgan of *M*A*S*H*. While well-received critically, the show did not catch on with viewers.

CRIME STORY (2 seasons)

Miami Vice's executive producer, Michael Mann, followed that towering success with *Crime Story*. It explored the conflict between a Chicago police lieutenant, real-life former Chicago detective, Dennis Farina, in his first series lead, and a Mafia big-shot, Anthony Denison. The pilot was a theatrical movie that did well when it aired on TV after an episode of *Miami Vice*, but the series couldn't stand up to its Tuesday night competition, which was *Moonlighting,* with Bruce Willis and Cybill Shepherd, and it lasted for only two seasons. Nevertheless, *Crime Story* inspired many of the serialized crime shows of today, in which one story line plays out over an entire season. The show attracted an amazing group of guest stars such as Pam Grier, Kevin Spacey, Debbie Harry, and Andrew Dice Clay.

FATHERS AND SONS (4 episodes)

Few, if any, NBC shows had ever flopped so fast as this painful sitcom, which starred Merlin Olsen as a father who coaches his son's baseball team. I honestly remember nothing about this show; nor do I know why we were so intent on finding vehicles for the very uncharismatic Mr. Olsen.

L.A. LAW (8 seasons)

This runaway commercial and critical hit earned fifteen Emmys and five Golden Globes, along with a mountain of prestige for NBC. The show was created by Steven Bochco and Terry Louise Fisher, who was fired after season two. David E. Kelly took over writing chores; later he moved on to such legal-themed successes as *Pickett Fences*, *Ally McBeal*, and *Boston Legal*. As if that were not enough, he also married Michelle Pfeiffer. He's a nice guy, too.

My casting contribution was Corbin Bernsen. I had signed him to NBC after meeting him at a neighbor's party. He was charming and even more handsome in person than he was on TV. I'd seen him in a few shows and thought he was an okay actor but had something special going on. I had thought he would wind up on NBC in what I called a "bullshit" (high concept) show that relied more on action than words. Bochco amazed me when he called and thanked me for sending him Corbin. At first I thought Bochco was joking. But Corbin held his own on *L.A. Law* amid one of the best ensemble casts on TV.

THE LAST PRECINCT (8 episodes)

This was a woeful attempt by Stephen J. Cannell and his frequent writing and producing partner, Frank Lupo, to do a TV version of the blockbuster series of *Police Academy* films. Comedy wasn't Cannell's forte, and after this flop he never again attempted a sitcom for us.

MATLOCK (9 seasons)

My ex-boss at NBC, Fred Silverman, scored his first major success as an independent producer with this courtroom drama, which starred Andy Griffith as a southern criminal defense attorney. Fred specialized in enlisting older TV stars to play new versions of their familiar personas. He cast Dick Van Dyke in *Diagnosis: Murder*, Carroll O'Connor in *In the Heat of the Night*, and William Conrad in *Jake and the Fatman*. He also made twenty-six Perry Mason TV movies with the show's original star, Raymond Burr, right up until Burr died in 1993.

OUR HOUSE (2 seasons)

NBC went up against *60 Minutes* in this slight, unsuccessful Sunday night dramatic series. *Our House* was an attempt to transform one of the network's biggest soap stars, Deidre Hall, into a primetime star. *Our House* was simple family fare about three generations who live together in the same house with curmudgeonly grandfather Wilford Brimley. The teenage daughter was a young Shannen Doherty in her pre-*90210* days.

EASY STREET (1 season)

This nice try of a sitcom starred Loni Anderson as a former showgirl who marries well, only to have her husband die on her, leaving her to deal with his snooty family. She reconnects with her down-and-out uncle and his friend, who are nearly homeless, and invites them to move into her mansion. Comedy should have ensued, but alas it did not, even with the wonderful Dana Ivey and James Cromwell as the disapproving in-laws.

STINGRAY (2 half-seasons)

This one-hour, high-concept drama from the ultra-prolific Stephen J. Cannell starred Nick Mancuso, Universal Television's original choice for David Hasselhoff's role in *Knight Rider*. Mancuso played Ray, a shadowy, detective-like figure with extraordinary crisis-solving abilities; he offers his services not for pay, but in exchange for one predetermined favor. Ray drives a black Corvette Stingray. Sting ... Ray ... get it? I did, but most viewers did not.

VALERIE retitled VALERIE'S FAMILY then THE HOGAN FAMILY (5 seasons on NBC, 1 on CBS)

The former star of TV's *Rhoda* returned to series TV in this troubled sitcom. In 1986, NBC made a deal with Valerie Harper to star in her own series as the wife of an airline pilot. Because he's away most of the time, she shoulders most of the responsibility for raising their three young sons. To play the oldest one, a girl-crazy, egotistical 16-year-old, we cast an NBC favorite, Jason Bateman, then a teen heartthrob. Josh Taylor, an NBC soap star (*One Life to Live*), played Valerie's minimally invasive husband.

The show earned modest ratings at first, then grew in popularity. The series was supposed to focus on Valerie, but it turned out that the audience liked the kids more than they liked the adults. Viewers also adored Jason's super-cute twin brothers, played by Danny Ponce and Jeremy Licht. NBC asked for more shows centered on the kids. Valerie did not love this request because after all it was *her* show.

After two seasons, Valerie's lawyers began the usual financial renegotiations to increase Valerie's financial take. When discussions stalled, Valerie and her husband, Tony Cacciotti, also one of the show's producers, used a time-honored ruse of not showing up for work for several days. The friction dragged on and on. Finally, both sides managed to come to an agreement. According to Valerie, consensus was even reached on the creative future of the series with more screen time for the kids. Valerie went back to work, and on a Friday the first show of the third season was filmed without incident.

But then Lorimar, the production company where executive producers Tom Miller and Bob Boyett had their production deal, changed their minds, and wanted to go back to an earlier agreement. Valerie and Tony objected to this, and then Lorimar, with NBC's okay, fired Valerie. Never before had the titled star of a successful series been sacked midstream. She was suddenly killed off in an automobile accident and replaced by the character of her sister-in-law, who steps in as surrogate mother.

In the few weeks leading up to her dismissal, Brandon had asked me if I had any ideas on who could replace Valerie. I suggested either Ann Jillian or Sandy Duncan. Brandon ran with Sandy's name, and Lorimar approved.

Almost immediately after the firing, Sandy joined the show (now called *The Hogan Family*) to come to her brother's aid after his wife's demise. The first few new episodes dealt with the family's grieving process and their eventual return to happiness; the emphasis was now on the boys. Shortly thereafter, Valerie held a well-attended press conference in which she laid out her side of the situation. Valerie emphasized that she had not quit but had been fired, and that she planned to sue Lorimar and NBC for breach of contract, and she did just that.

During the year or so run-up to the trial, Valerie became persona non grata at NBC. Her name was never brought up for any parts – that is, until 1988. We were doing a generic woman-in-danger mystery movie, *The People Across the Lake*, and we couldn't find a star leading lady. Valerie's agent called me and jokingly suggested her. A lightbulb moment went off over my head. I went to Brandon and told him that it was not great optics to virtually blacklist her. I added that it would be a good all-is-for-given, come-on-home public-relations move to have her back on NBC. He agreed okayed her casting in the movie. Valerie turned in a good performance, and the movie did all right in the ratings. Even better, Valerie dropped NBC from the lawsuit. Either she or her lawyers realized that her legal claim that NBC had blacklisted her and ruined her reputation was no longer appropriate. And so she proceeded to sue only Lorimar. Valerie won her case and received almost two million dollars in back pay and up to fifteen million in possible future profit participation. As Robert Blake's and O.J. Simpson's murder trials have shown, it is very difficult to convict a celebrity or win a lawsuit against one – especially a star as beloved as Valerie. Because I was called to testify about the timing of my suggestions of Jillian and Duncan as replacements, I was not allowed to attend the trial. Had I seen the type of arguments the defendants' lawyers were using against Harper, I could have told them they were going to lose big time. One of their main arguments was that Valerie had treated the kid actors abusively and could not be trusted alone with them. Where that strategy came from, I have no idea, but it failed miserably, with many strong character witnesses testifying that it was untrue. The show continued for another two seasons at NBC. When ratings dipped, the network canceled it. Lorimar moved it to CBS for one last unsuccessful season.

A YEAR IN THE LIFE (1 season)

The seed of this short-lived drama was a hit miniseries about the travails of a Seattle family. NBC fleshed the story out in a show that starred Richard Kiley as a company owner whose four grown children move back in with him after the death of their mother. One of the sons was played by David Oliver, a talented actor who later died of AIDS at thirty. Sarah Jessica Parker played his wife. Two Emmys and a Golden Globe could not sustain the series beyond a season.

YOU AGAIN? (2 half-seasons)

A hit British sitcom, *Home to Roost*, was the basis of this troubled series, which brought Jack Klugman back to TV after his long, celebrated runs in *The Odd Couple* and *Quincy, M.E.* Klugman played a depressed and irascible supermarket manager whose son Matt comes to live with him after a ten-year estrangement. Matt was supposed to be an ill-mannered and oddball lout who drives his father crazy. We had a hard time casting the role of the son; ultimately we made the wrong choice in John Stamos. He wasn't bad, just so good-looking and normal that he wasn't too believable in the part. *You Again?* did well enough in its first thirteen episodes, but with four time-slot changes and the lack of chemistry between the leads, it was a goner.

1987

THE BRONX ZOO (1 season)

Gary David Goldberg (*Family Ties*) created this dramatic vehicle for Ed Asner, who played the new principal of a tough Bronx high school. Despite a fine cast and one Emmy (okay, for Graphic and Title Design), *The Bronx Zoo* couldn't make a dent in the ratings.

THE DAYS AND NIGHTS OF MOLLY DODD (2 seasons on NBC; 3 on Lifetime)

This single-camera, half-hour comedy starred Blair Brown as a thirty-something, divorced Manhattan woman who is intelligent, funny, pretty, vivacious, yet unable to figure out what she wants to do with her life. Written and often directed by Jay Tarses (*Buffalo Bill, The Bob Newhart Show*) it earned eleven Emmy nominations, including five for Blair. It was ahead of its time in mixing comedy and drama and might have been a hit today. The regular and supporting cast included a wealth of fine New York actors, including Broadway veterans Allyn Ann McLerie as Molly's mother and George Gaynes as the mother's gentleman friend, Wesley Snipes, Victor Garber, David Straitharn, John Glover, Nathan Lane, Gina Gershon, and Dan Butler. Even the acclaimed Broadway director Joe Mantello acted on one episode. The show was part of a trend of network shows that moved successfully to cable after cancellation.

A DIFFERENT WORLD (6 seasons)

As almost every fan of 1980s TV knows, this was a spin-off of *The Cosby Show* and followed it at 8:30 on Thursday nights for most of its life. As the perfect companion piece, it held on to *Cosby*'s ratings and stayed in the top five for its first four seasons. In its first year, *A Different World* was built around *The Cosby Show*'s character's daughter Denise (Lisa Bonet), a college student at a fictitious historically black college in Virginia. Meg Ryan was originally cast as her White roommate, but when Meg had to pull out, the part went to Marisa Tomei. In the course of the season,

Bonet became pregnant by husband Lenny Kravitz. There was talk of having her stay on the show as a pregnant student, but Mr. Cosby would not have a single pregnant woman as his TV daughter. He was also very pissed off that Bonet had appeared nude in the Mickey Rourke/Robert DeNiro film *Angel Heart*, which was made before *Different World* but released during the show's first season.

By the second season, Lisa was gone, along with much else, including Marisa Tomei. A few actors stayed, notably the very funny Jasmine Guy as the spoiled rich girl and Kadeem Hardison, Darryl Bell, and Dawnn Lewis as fellow students. Debbie Allen came on board as the show's main creative force and remained there for the rest of its run. She did a superb job keeping the humor alive while incorporating controversial social issues, including date rape, the Persian Gulf War, the n-word, Anita Hill, and Rodney King. Meanwhile, a talented new cast member, Jada Pinkett, upped the game for everyone when she was added to the series. *A Different World* had a huge impact on attendance at historically Black universities and colleges like the one in *Different World*.

J.J. STARBUCK (16 episodes)

A clinker from Stephen J. Cannell. With as many pilots as he wrote, there had to be a few. *J.J. Starbuck* concerned a Texas billionaire (played by Dale Robertson) who drives around in a Lincoln convertible with steer horns as a hood ornament and acts as a Good Samaritan. When Robertson injured his hip and leg in a real-life horse-riding accident, his condition was written into the show, and Ben Vereen was cast as his driver and sidekick. The

Vereen character wasn't new; he had played it on an earlier, superior Cannell series, *Tenspeed and Brown Shoe*. But the show never caught on, and NBC wisely replaced it with an eight-season hit, *In the Heat of the Night,* starring Carol O'Connor.

MY TWO DADS (3 seasons)

Five years after Paul Reiser's heralded debut in the movie *Diner*, he made his series debut in this sitcom about two men who had dated a woman who had died. One of them – it was never revealed which – had fathered her adolescent daughter; when the mother passed on, she left the girl in the custody of both men who obviously decided not to do a DNA test. Suffice it to say that Paul went on to better things.

PRIVATE EYE (12 episodes)

Anthony Yerkovich, who wrote the pilot for *Miami Vice*, should have scored again with his later creation, *Private Eye*. Set in 1950s Hollywood, it told of a troubled ex-cop, virtuous and unfairly framed by his colleagues for trying to expose their corruption. The casting wasn't as strong as the writing, with the exception of a nineteen-year-old Josh Brolin in his first TV series.

RAGS TO RICHES (1½ seasons)

In this *Annie* rip-off, set in early-1960s England, a millionaire (played by Joseph Bologna) adopts five female orphans, who periodically burst into songs of the day. Weak scripts and horrible singing doomed this show, which was cancelled halfway through its second season.

ROOMIES (8 episodes)

Sy Rosen, the co-creator (with Mort Lachman) of *Gimme a Break!*, later whipped up *Roomies*, a clinker from concept through production. It concerned a retired Marine drill instructor, played by Burt Young, "Paulie" from all the *Rocky* movies. He uses the G.I. Bill to go back to college. Troubled Corey Haim, who died at thirty-eight after years of drug addiction, was his fourteen-year-old genius roommate. As hard as he tried, Young could not defeat the show's lame concept and bad execution.

SWEET SURRENDER (6 episodes)

A businesswoman trades her career for motherhood in this dud sitcom. Its only notable asset was its star, Dana Delany, in her series debut. She went on to win two Emmys for her role in *China Beach* and to work for three seasons on *Desperate Housewives*. Well, we all have to start somewhere.

THE TORTELLIS (13 episodes)

This first *Cheers* spinoff starred semi-regulars Dan Hedaya and Jean Kasem as a TV repairman and his bimbo wife. Kasem was never a great actress, and she couldn't transcend the initial sight gag of a tall, stacked blonde with a silly voice. The series folded quickly, and its two leads made a few return appearances on *Cheers*. Another *Cheers* spinoff, *Frasier*, did much better.

1988

AARON'S WAY (1 season)

William Blinn (*Starsky & Hutch, Fame*) wrote this snoozer about an Amish father who moves his family from Pennsylvania to a California winery. *Aaron's Way* was one more attempt to star ex-NFL star Merlin Olsen in a series. This one was pretentious as well as boring, and disappeared quickly.

BABY BOOM (8 episodes)

This was based on the Diane Keaton movie *Baby Boom,* written by Nancy Meyers and her writing partner and husband, director Charles Shyer. Casting the TV series version was the most disagreeable experience I had at NBC. Almost every exec involved with this project felt the same. We all had the feeling that both Shyer and Meyers felt they were slumming and doing everyone a favor by doing TV.

After many auditions the finalists for the leading role were Kate Jackson and Kate Capshaw, aka Mrs. Steven Spielberg. NBC favored Jackson and she was cast. Jackson had already proven herself a good at light comedy in the Diane Keaton vein; and after two successful shows, *The Rookies* and *Charlie's Angels*, she was a very popular and well-liked TV star.

Being a new mother, Jackson had negotiated specific contract terms. The most important of them was that she had to be released from the set no later than six p.m. every day. Within the first week of shooting, Shyer and Meyers were already asking Kate to stay later. Kate refused and went home. Immediately Shyer and Meyers wanted to replace Jackson with Capshaw. NBC said no, which created tensions on the set. Worse still, the finished product just fell flat. At Shyer and Meyers' insistence, there was no laugh track; and since the show was not very funny, viewers wondered if this a comedy or what? With a low-rated, bad product, NBC yanked the show and promised to return it to the schedule after making much-needed changes. But as so often happens, the show just disappeared. Shyer and Meyers went back to movies and divorced in 1999. Meyers' solo movie career zoomed into the stratosphere with the Meryl Streep, Steve Martin, and Alec Baldwin movie *It's Complicated*. Shyer continues working in movies, too, but much less successfully so than his ex.

DAY BY DAY (4 seasons)

Created by Andy Borowitz and Gary David Goldberg, this series is remembered mainly because of a great performance by Julia Louis-Dreyfus in a major supporting role. The series best episode somehow managed to include all the actors from *The Brady Bunch*. What a difference a year made for Ms. Louis-Dreyfus who went directly to *Seinfeld* for the next 9 years.

DEAR JOHN (4 seasons)

This series was set in a support group for divorced and widowed people. Judd Hirsch, who had centered the ensemble on *Taxi*, did the same for *Dear John*. His fellow players included the terribly British Jane Carr, Jere Burns, Isabella Hofmann, and Broadway star Harry Groener. This intelligent and funny sitcom was based on a British series of the same name. For the first two seasons, *Dear John* thrived as part of NBC's highly rated Thursday lineup. Then the show was bumped around the schedule in different time slots, and the ratings got lower and lower until it got canceled. Pity.

EMPTY NEST (4 seasons)

Richard Mulligan, a marvelous New York actor, had previously starred in *Soap*, the huge hit by *Golden Girls* creator Susan Harris. Both she and NBC were looking for a vehicle for him. They found it in this, a spinoff from a Mulligan appearance on *The Golden Girls*. *Empty Nest* starred him as a recently widowed doctor whose two grown and divorced daughters move back home to help. The daughters were played by Kristy McNichol and Dinah Manoff. Mulligan's office nurse was played by Park Overall, who managed to steal every scene she was in and went on to win two Emmys. Previously, I worked with Kristy on two of her first jobs, as a very young girl in *Apple's Way* and as the pre-teen daughter of Sada Thompson and James Broderick on the much-lauded series *Family*. I got Dinah her first big role on screen in the movie, *Grease*. She was the youngest of the Pink Ladies at 21 playing "Marty Maraschino", the character who flirts with Ed "Kooky" Byrnes at the dance. Everything went well both critically and ratings-wise, until Kristy began having "problems," which were later explained as bipolar disorder. She left the show and basically retired from show business, although she did come back for the final episode. Kristy also came out in 1992 as a lesbian. To those who knew her, this was no great surprise; she and Jodie Foster had been the best young tomboys working in Hollywood.

IN THE HEAT OF THE NIGHT (8 seasons)

Produced by Fred Silverman, this major NBC hit was based on the film of the same name, which starred Rod Steiger and Sidney Poitier. Carroll O'Connor and Howard E. Rollins, Jr., filled those very big shoes extremely well. O'Connor had many run-ins with the writers, directors, and NBC executives; eventually he took creative control of the show. During one intense rene-gotiation with O'Connor for both money and power, Steiger was approached to replace him. He said he would accept only after O'Connor had truly left, instead of just threatening to do so. Sur-prise! NBC caved and O'Connor got everything he wanted. It is highly unlikely for a star to lose in such cases. Removing just one element out of a hit show can upset the entire project, and net-works are loathe to take that chance.

Behind the scenes, a tragic story unfolded for Howard Rollins, Jr. A brilliant and handsome actor, Rollins had earned an Oscar nomination for his performance in *Ragtime*. He had also starred in *A Soldier's Story*. His impressive TV credits included NBC's *The Member of the Wedding* with Pearl Bailey. He was also a clos-eted gay man. It's hard to be famous and in the closet in New York or L.A., but it's a hell of a lot harder to be closeted, black, and gay in Covington, Georgia, where *In the Heat of the Night* was shot. Rollins sank into drug and alcohol addiction and had numerous run-ins with the police, including several driving-while-black stops and a DUI arrest. Carroll O'Connor felt a special kinship with Rollins and did everything possible to help him keep his job. I'm guessing that Rollins reminded him of his son, Hugh O'Connor, an actor who appeared on the series and who also had drug problems. Hugh committed suicide while the show was still running. Rollins returned to the show after several absences, but eventually he had to be let go. What very few people knew is that Rollins had AIDS. His life must have been a living hell.

He died in 1996. So, so sad. On a more upbeat note, Alan Autry, the actor who played Captain Bubba Skinner, a deputy to O'Con-nor, became mayor of Fresno, California, for two four-year terms.

MIDNIGHT CALLER (3 seasons)

In this well-reviewed dramatic series, Gary Cole (my choice for the Don Johnson role in *Miami Vice*) played an ex-cop who had accidentally shot and killed his partner; he goes on to host an overnight radio talk show in which he tries to solve callers' problems. Gary's work in both comedy and drama constantly amazes me and he has maintained a varied and successful career. He played Mike Brady in the two *The Brady Bunch* movies, plus key roles in *The West Wing, Desperate Housewives, Entourage, Veep,* and continues to appear on CBS's *The Good Fight*.

SONNY SPOON (2 half-seasons)

The incredibly prolific Stephen J. Cannell along with several other writers created this one-hour adventure series, a starring vehicle for Mario Van Peebles. I had seen Mario's excellent work as a guest star on *The Cosby Show, L.A. Law,* and *One Life to Live*. We met in my office and I was very impressed, not only with his athletic physicality but his smarts about using acting as a back door into directing. His father, Melvin Van Peebles, was a true renaissance man, having achieved success as the author of a Broadway hit, *Ain't Supposed to Die a Natural Death,* of Blaxploitation-era films, and even as an options trader on the American Stock Exchange.

We signed Mario to NBC and sent him around to meet many of our best writers. Stephen recognized what I saw in Mario and a marriage was made. *Sonny Spoon* told of an urban Robin Hood who, with the help of his con-man father (played by Melvin), a bar owner, goes around the neighborhood righting wrongs and settling scores. Unfortunately, the series didn't live up to its ambitious premise, and no one watched.

TATTINGERS (13 episodes)

Bruce Paltrow, Tom Fontana, and John Masius (three of the executive producers of *St. Elsewhere*), devised this comedy-drama series about a Manhattan restaurant owner (played by Steven Collins) and his ex-wife (Blythe Danner), the real-life Mrs. Paltrow. The Collins character was a fixer of people's problems. Danner, with whom he was still in love (and vice versa), was funny as well as irritating to him. The show had great elements that never quite fit together. In a desperate attempt to salvage *Tattingers*, the initial hour-long version was cancelled, and the show was revamped in a streamlined half-hour format. It died after two episodes.

1989

ANN JILLIAN (13 episodes)

Named after its pretty blond star, who played one of the leads in ABC's *It's a Living*, this half-hour sitcom concerned a widow who moves from New York to California with her teenage daughter to start a new life. I am falling asleep as I type these words. Why this show ever happened I have no idea; either someone slept with someone or it was some sort of contractual payoff.

FATHER DOWLING MYSTERIES (1 season on NBC, 2 on ABC)

This series followed the template of Fred Silverman's freelance years in that it starred a well-known and likable star, Tom Bosley of *Happy Days*, in a one-hour drama. Bosley played a Catholic priest whose sidekick is a streetwise young nun played by Tracy Nelson, the granddaughter of Ozzie and Harriet Nelson and daughter of singer, Rick Nelson. It didn't work.

MANCUSO, F.B.I. (1 season)

In the hit NBC miniseries *Favorite Son*, Robert Loggia had played an idealistic F.B.I. man who is frustrated by the coldness of his bureaucratic superiors. That character was spun off into *Mancuso, F.B.I.*, but despite Loggia's terrific acting, the show never took off.

NIGHTINGALES (1 season)

Suzanne Pleshette starred as the supervisor of a group of nursing students in this one-hour series, produced by Aaron Spelling, who was now free of a long-term exclusive contract at ABC and now able to work for NBC. Brandon Tartikoff was such a fan of Spelling's that he welcomed him into the

NBC offices in Burbank by hiring the USC marching band to play for his entrance into the building. While never having been fond of realism on his shows, Spelling veered dangerously close to camp with this one. A reviewer for the *Chicago Tribune* described the show as a story of nursing students who don't spend much time studying but hang out a lot in their underwear. The show was criticized as demeaning to the profession for portraying student nurses as lusty bimbos. Suzanne was her usual delightful and raunchy self, but the students and the writing were far from *Charlie's Angels* material. But what did the critics expect, Masterpiece Theater from Aaron Spelling? In this case, luck wasn't with Aaron or NBC. When advertisers began pulling ads in response to letter-writing campaigns from nurses' organizations, the show was cancelled.

QUANTUM LEAP (5 seasons)

Named one of "Top Cult Shows Ever" by *TV Guide*, *Quantum Leap*, created by *Magnum P.I.*'s Don Bellisario, was a science-fiction series about Dr. Sam Beckett, a physicist who finds himself in different bodies at different times in history due to a time-travel experiment gone wrong. Beckett's aim is to find a way to return to the present as himself. His advisor is a hologram that only he can see of his best friend, a Navy admiral, played by Dean Stockwell.

As Sam, we cast Scott Bakula, whom I had first seen in an Off-Broadway show, *Nite Club Confidential*. We had a meeting, and I was certain this guy would be a big star. I wanted to sign him to NBC on the spot. But his agent, Maggie Henderson, knew his potential worth, and thought it best to keep him free for any and all opportunities. Since he was working steadily and didn't need the money from NBC to keep him alive, she made the right choice.

After a few series failures on other networks, we got him. Scott earned four Best Actor Emmy nominations for his work on *Quantum Leap*, and has not stopped working since – check him out on *CSI: New Orleans*. While the show never got huge ratings, it fared well with eighteen- to forty-nine-year-olds, the most desirable demographic for advertisers. NBC kept confusing them: The timeslot was changed five times, which surely contributed to its ultimate demise.

SEINFELD (9 seasons)

Jerry Seinfeld and Larry David created one of the most innovative and important shows in TV history. The untold hero who made this show happen was Rick Ludwin, NBC's vice president of Late Night and Specials. My only participation was a short conversation in which Rick asked me if I knew and liked Seinfeld's proposed supporting actors, Julia Louis-Dreyfus, Jason Alexander, and Michael Richards. I said yes, yes, and yes. Rick had been a major fan of Jerry for many years, and Jerry and his camp liked, and more importantly, trusted Rick. Seinfeld, David, and two executive producers, George Shapiro and Howard West (Seinfeld's managers) took their idea for the show to Rick; subsequently it was developed by him, *not* by the comedy executives at NBC. Jerry's team knew Rick would not interfere with their creative vision.

The first viewing of the pilot by Brandon Tartikoff and the NBC comedy department screened quite well but the research on it came back truly awful. The comments included "too New York-Jewish," "loser characters," and "weak stories." In order not to lose all the money they'd invested, NBC aired the show, then called *The Seinfeld Chronicles*, during the summer doldrums. It finished second in its slot, and proved almost equally popular in the big cities and the Midwest. This made Brandon think it might not be too New York-Jewish after all. But those mildly encouraging results did not help the show land on NBC's fall schedule.

Warren Littlefield, NBC's head of comedy, wanted to order the show to series but dragged his feet, hoping to build more network support. He dragged those feet until the night before NBC's option on the series was to run out. But by this time the programming department's finance guys said there was no money left for buying the show. But Rick Ludwin saved the day. As sole manager of his Late Night and Specials budget, he could side-step the programming department's finance guys and cancel one Bob Hope special. He then used that money to pay for four more *Seinfeld* episodes. This was a bold and smart move. NBC for years had been contractually bound to produce a certain number of Bob Hope specials each year. By 1989, however, Hope was 86, and totally out of synch with both the programming department at NBC and the viewing audience. NBC could not have cared less if there was one less Hope special. The new *Seinfeld* episodes aired on Thursday nights during the summer, following reruns of *Cheers*. The show started gaining traction with viewers and the press. NBC ordered thirteen more and began airing them in January 1991 at 9:30 p.m. Wednesdays. The rest is history. Hundreds if not thousands of articles and several books have been written about *Seinfeld*. I hope they gave Rick Ludwin the credit he deserves posthumously. He passed away in November of 2019.

SISTER KATE (1 season)

In this ill-advised knockoff of *The Facts of Life*, Stephanie Beacham, a terrific British actress, played a nun who is assigned the job of running a Chicago orphanage filled with difficult, unwanted children. The show never found an audience, but it was probably doomed from the start: NBC aired it on Sundays at eight p.m., opposite *Murder She Wrote* (CBS), which dominated that time slot. Any kids who might have been watching TV at that hour would have tuned into *America's Funniest Home Videos* on ABC, not *Sister Kate*.

SAVED BY THE BELL (5 seasons)

Brandon Tartikoff could be like a dog with a bone. In this case, the bone was a failed young-adult series, *Good Morning, Miss Bliss*, that had aired on NBC a couple of years earlier. It starred Hayley Mills as Miss Carrie Bliss, a character based on Brandon's real-life sixth-grade teacher, whom he had loved. The show flopped. Brandon thought that *Miss Bliss* could be revamped to run on Saturday mornings, normally a low-rated wasteland of cartoons. This time, the show – renamed *Saved by the Bell* – clicked, in no small part due to its first casting director, Shana Lansburg, who fought the show's producer, Peter Engel, to get *her* choices for the teen actors into the show. They were: Marc-Paul Gosselar, Mario Lopez, Dustin Diamond, and Lark Voorhies. These kids made the show successful. Again, there is a current reboot.

ACKNOWLEDGMENTS

I must thank many people who helped this first-time writer. No. 1 would be Joaquin Phoenix, who started all this when he said to me, "Man, you've got to write this stuff down." Next, to my good friend, author James Gavin, who taught me how to edit myself and was always available for my dumb questions. To my agent, Julia Lord for getting me a publisher. To Lilly Tartikoff Karatz and Heart Phoenix, for their patience and understanding and help with their stories. To John Travolta and the late Dame Olivia Newton-John for reading and correcting my memory of events. To Peter Golden, who helped me get past writer's block. To: Jeff Sagansky, Warren Littlefield, David Neuman, Garth Ancier, Lois Planco and Lori Openden, all former NBC co-workers, who corrected my errors and were sources for stories I had forgotten. To Glen Hanson for his brilliant cover art images and Rex Bonomelli for his title fonts and pulling everything together for the book's cover. To my immediate family: Freddy, Fran, Roz, Jennifer, Leah and Eric, who have always supported me. To great nieces, Phoebe and Mia for merely existing and to the two loves of my life, Lou Liberatore and Yvans Jourdain, for putting up with me. The last spot must go to my mother, Florence Balsam Thurm for being the best classic Jewish mother possible.

INDEX

Numbers in **bold** indicate photographs